Frommer's®

Paris day BY day®

3rd Edition

by Anna E. Brooke

John Wiley & Sons, Inc.

Contents

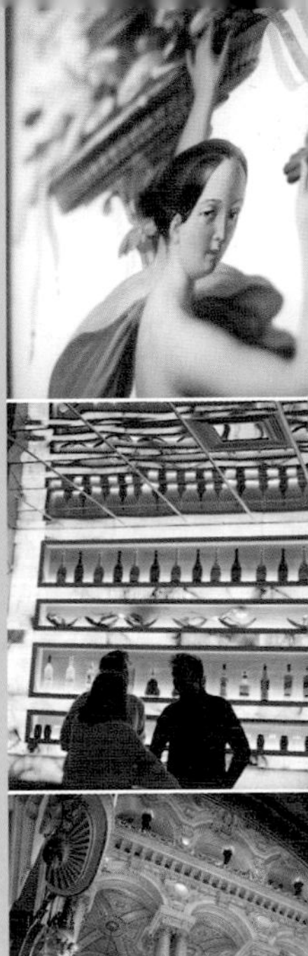

HOTEL CHOPIN
GALERIE
LIVRES

Published by:

John Wiley & Sons, Inc.

111 River St.
Hoboken, NJ 07030-5774

ISBN 978-1-118-02754-7 (paper); ISBN 978-1-118-16560-7 (ebk);
ISBN 978-1-118-16558-4 (ebk); ISBN 978-1-118-16559-1 (ebk)

Editors: Maureen Clarke and Jamie Ehrlich
Production Editor: Eric T. Schroeder
Photo Editor: Richard Fox
Cartographer: Elizabeth Puhl
Production by Wiley Indianapolis Composition Services

Cover Photo Credits

Front Left: ©Art Kowalsky / Alamy Images; Notre Dame Cathedral, Paris.
Front Middle: ©PhotoBliss / Alamy Images; French cheese.
Front Right: ©Roy Rainford / Robert Harding Picture Library Ltd / Alamy Images; Abbesses Metro station.
Back Cover: ©Art Kowalsky / Alamy Images; Louvre Pyramid, Paris.

For information on our other products and services or to obtain technical support, please contact our Customer Care Department within the U.S. at 877/762-2974, outside the U.S. at 317/572-3993 or fax 317/572-4002.

Wiley also publishes its books in a variety of electronic formats. Some content that appears in print may not be available in electronic formats.

Manufactured in China

5 4 3 2 1

A Note from the Publisher

Organizing your time. That's what this guide is all about.

Other guides give you long lists of things to see and do and then expect you to fit the pieces together. The Day by Day guides are different. These guides tell you the best of everything, and then they show you how to see it *in the smartest, most time-efficient way*. Our authors have designed detailed itineraries organized by time, neighborhood, or special interest. And each tour comes with a bulleted map that takes you from stop to stop.

Hoping to follow Hemingway's footsteps, or to tour the highlights of the Louvre? Planning a walk through Montmartre, or a whirlwind tour of the very best that Paris has to offer? Whatever your interest or schedule, the Day by Days give you the smartest routes to follow. Not only do we take you to the top attractions, hotels, and restaurants, but we also help you access those special moments that locals get to experience—those "finds" that turn tourists into travelers.

The Day by Days are also your top choice if you're looking for one complete guide for all your travel needs. The best hotels and restaurants for every budget, the greatest shopping values, the wildest nightlife—it's all here.

Why should you trust our judgment? Because our authors personally visit each place they write about. They're an independent lot who say what they think and would never include places they wouldn't recommend to their best friends. They're also open to suggestions from readers. If you'd like to contact them, please send your comments my way at mspring@wiley.com, and I'll pass them on.

Enjoy your Day by Day guide—the most helpful travel companion you can buy. And have the trip of a lifetime.

Warm regards,

Kelly Regan

Kelly Regan, Editorial Director
Frommer's Travel Guides

About the Author

Anna Brooke (annaebrooke@yahoo.fr) is the author of six Frommer's guides to Paris and France, and she regularly writes for *The Sunday Times Travel Magazine, Time Out,* and *Financial Times Magazine.* When she is not writing, she is acting in film and theater, and song-writing for her electro-pop group Monkey Anna (www.myspace.com/musicmonkeyanna).

Advisory & Disclaimer

Travel information can change quickly and unexpectedly, and we strongly advise you to confirm important details locally before traveling, including information on visas, health and safety, traffic and transport, accommodations, shopping, and eating out. We also encourage you to stay alert while traveling and to remain aware of your surroundings. Avoid civil disturbances, and keep a close eye on cameras, purses, wallets, and other valuables.

While we have endeavored to ensure that the information contained within this guide is accurate and up-to-date at the time of publication, we make no representations or warranties with respect to the accuracy or completeness of the contents of this work and specifically disclaim all warranties, including without limitation warranties of fitness for a particular purpose. We accept no responsibility or liability for any inaccuracy or errors or omissions, or for any inconvenience, loss, damage, costs, or expenses of any nature whatsoever incurred or suffered by anyone as a result of any advice or information contained in this guide.

The inclusion of a company, organization, or website in this guide as a service provider and/or potential source of further information does not mean that we endorse them or the information they provide. Be aware that information provided through some websites may be unreliable and can change without notice. Neither the publisher nor author shall be liable for any damages arising herefrom.

Star Ratings, Icons & Abbreviations

Every hotel, restaurant, and attraction listing in this guide has been ranked for quality, value, service, amenities, and special features using a **star-rating system.** Hotels, restaurants, attractions, shopping, and nightlife are rated on a scale of zero stars (recommended) to three stars (exceptional). In addition to the star-rating system, we also use a **kids icon** to point out the best bets for families. Within each tour, we recommend cafes, bars, or restaurants where you can take a break. Each of these stops appears in a shaded box marked with a coffee-cup-shaped bullet.

The following **abbreviations** are used for credit cards:

AE	American Express	DISC	Discover	V	Visa
DC	Diners Club	MC	MasterCard		

Frommers.com

Now that you have this guidebook to help you plan a great trip, visit our website at **www.frommers.com** for additional travel information on more than 4,000 destinations. We update features regularly to give you instant access to the most current trip-planning information available. At Frommers.com, you'll find scoops on the best airfares, lodging rates, and car rental bargains. You can even book your travel online through our reliable travel booking partners. Other popular features include:

- Online updates of our most popular guidebooks
- Vacation sweepstakes and contest giveaways
- Newsletters highlighting the hottest travel trends
- Podcasts, interactive maps, and up-to-the-minute events listings
- Opinionated blog entries by Arthur Frommer himself
- Online travel message boards with featured travel discussions

A Note on Prices

In the "Take a Break" and "Best Bets" sections of this book, we have used a system of dollar signs to show a range of costs for 1 night in a hotel (the price of a double-occupancy room) or the cost of an entree at a restaurant. Use the following table to decipher the dollar signs:

Cost	Hotels	Restaurants
$	under $100	under $10
$$	$100–$200	$10–$20
$$$	$200–$300	$20–$30
$$$$	$300–$400	$30–$40
$$$$$	over $400	over $40

An Invitation to the Reader

In researching this book, we discovered many wonderful places—hotels, restaurants, shops, and more. We're sure you'll find others. Please tell us about them, so we can share the information with your fellow travelers in upcoming editions. If you were disappointed with a recommendation, we'd love to know that, too. Please write to:

Frommer's Paris Day by Day, 3rd Edition
John Wiley & Sons, Inc. • 111 River St. • Hoboken, NJ 07030-5774

13 Favorite **Moments**

Favorite **Moments**

1. Riding a riverboat down the Seine
2. Standing at Trocadéro watching the Eiffel Tower sparkle
3. Attending a ballet at the Opéra Garnier
4. Sipping tea in the Musée de la Vie Romantique's summer rose garden
5. Climbing the streets of Montmartre
6. Strolling along the Canal St-Martin
7. Visiting the digital art installations at the Galté Lyrique, then staying on for a concert
8. Marveling at the inventions in the Musée des Arts et Métiers
9. Rubbing shoulders with Notre-Dame's gargoyles
10. Getting lost in the Château de Versailles gardens
11. Ambling along the Seine
12. Walking through the courtyard of the Musée du Louvre
13. Sitting in the Musée d'Orsay

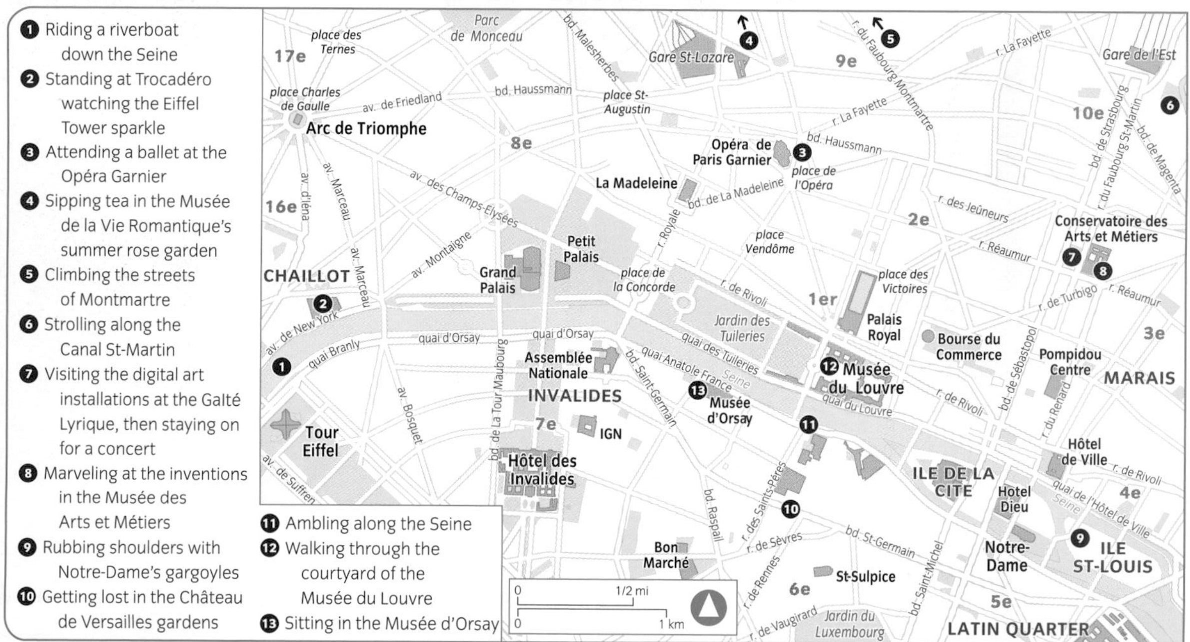

Previous page: Tour de France cyclists whiz past the Eiffel Tower.

Waiting for the Eiffel Tower to light up after dark, strolling along the Seine on a warm summer night—these could become your favorite moments in the world, not just in Paris. This city is electric—a "moveable feast," as Ernest Hemingway so aptly called it. The list of wonderful experiences to be had here is endless, but here is a start.

1 Riding a riverboat down the Seine, where all the buildings are artfully lighted so they seem to glow from within. On warm nights, take an open-top boat, and you feel as if you can reach up and touch the damp, stone bridges as you pass beneath them. *See p 11.*

2 Standing at Trocadéro watching the Eiffel Tower sparkle at nightfall. It's the best place in town to take in the tower's elegant, filigree proportions. That moment when somebody, somewhere, flicks the button, is matchless. *See p 25.*

3 Attending a ballet at the Opéra Garnier. Whether you're seeing a traditional rendition of Tchaikovsky's *The Nutcracker* or a contemporary version of Prokofiev's *Romeo & Juliette,* the Charles Garnier–designed grande dame of performance spaces provides a breathtaking backdrop for ballet. Climb the majestic central staircase, order champagne for the *entr'acte* (intermission), and then sink into your red velvet chair and admire Chagall's famous ceiling fresco before the lights go down. *See p 132.*

4 Sipping tea in the Musée de la Vie Romantique's summer rose garden. The pink, ivy-clad house once frequented by George Sand and Chopin feels like Paris's best-kept secret. Visit the museum, and then wind down in the garden over a Darjeeling tea and a *tarte du jour,* with just the buzzing of bees and the clinking of tea cups for company. *See p 38.*

5 Climbing the streets of Montmartre. This hilly, hopelessly romantic neighborhood is my favorite in all of Paris. A sweeping view of the city spreads out before you from every cross street. Every corner reveals another evocative stone staircase too steep to see all the way down, but at the bottom you know you'll find sweet old buildings painted pale colors, and streets of old paving stones. *See p 17.*

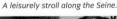

A leisurely stroll along the Seine.

❻ **Strolling along the Canal St-Martin,** passing delicate iron bridges, locks, and the occasional fisherman. You could spend the better part of a day losing yourself in the bohemian boutiques, stopping at a cafe, and then continuing along to the Parc de la Villette for a picnic in the park or a trip around the *Cité des Sciences*. *See p 29.*

❼ **Visiting the digital art installations at the Gaîté Lyrique, then staying on for a concert.** It's a great way to check out Paris's red hot electronic music scene and meet locals interested in the newest art on the block—digital art, which covers everything from computer graphics and animation to experimental video. *See p 125.*

❽ **Marveling at the inventions in the Musée des Arts et Métiers.** This museum is easy to miss, yet it contains some of the world's greatest inventions: Blaise Pascal's 17th-century calculator, the *Blériot 11* (the first plane to cross the English Channel), steam-powered carriages, and Henry Ford's Model T car and automated toys. It's a must-see for science fans big and small. *See p 39.*

❾ **Rubbing shoulders with Notre-Dame's gargoyles.** Climb the uneven stone steps to the top of Notre-Dame's towers, and you're in the precipitous realm of Quasimodo, where hideous stone sculptures stick out their tongues at the city below. The views from here are mesmerizing, especially on a cloudy day, when the sky looks moody. *See p 10.*

Don your finest attire for a night out at the Opera Garnier.

❿ **Getting lost in the Château de Versailles gardens.** This opulent château of the Sun King, Louis XIV, was the *bijou* (jewel) in the royal crown. Nowadays it is the glittering highlight of any visit to the Ile de France. Nothing can beat a day spent ambling through the terraced gardens, admiring the fountains and Marie Antoinette's hamlet. Classical music extravaganzas take place there during the warmer months. *See p 155.*

⓫ **Ambling along the Seine** toward the islands, watching the tour boats *(bateaux mouches)* cruise slowly by, the lights from their windows reflecting on the river. On summer nights, the riverside is packed, even after 10pm; sometimes it seems as if everybody in Paris is here. Bands play, lovers kiss, children frolic, everybody smiles—this is how life should be all the time. *See p 135.*

⓬ **Walking through the courtyard of the Musée du Louvre** early in the morning, hurrying to be one of the first in line, and catching the sun glinting off the glass pyramids in the courtyard—it only heightens the excitement of seeing the masterpieces inside. *See p 30.*

⓭ **Sitting in the Musée d'Orsay** in the center sculpture court, down below the entrance, looking up at the huge, ornate clock on the wall far above. Through the frosted glass around it you can see the shadows of people passing by on invisible walkways. The sheer scale is astounding; the look is pure drama. And all around you, the works of history's most talented sculptors lounge, leap, and laugh silently. *See p 8.* ●

1 The Best **Full-Day Tours**

The Best **in 1 Day**

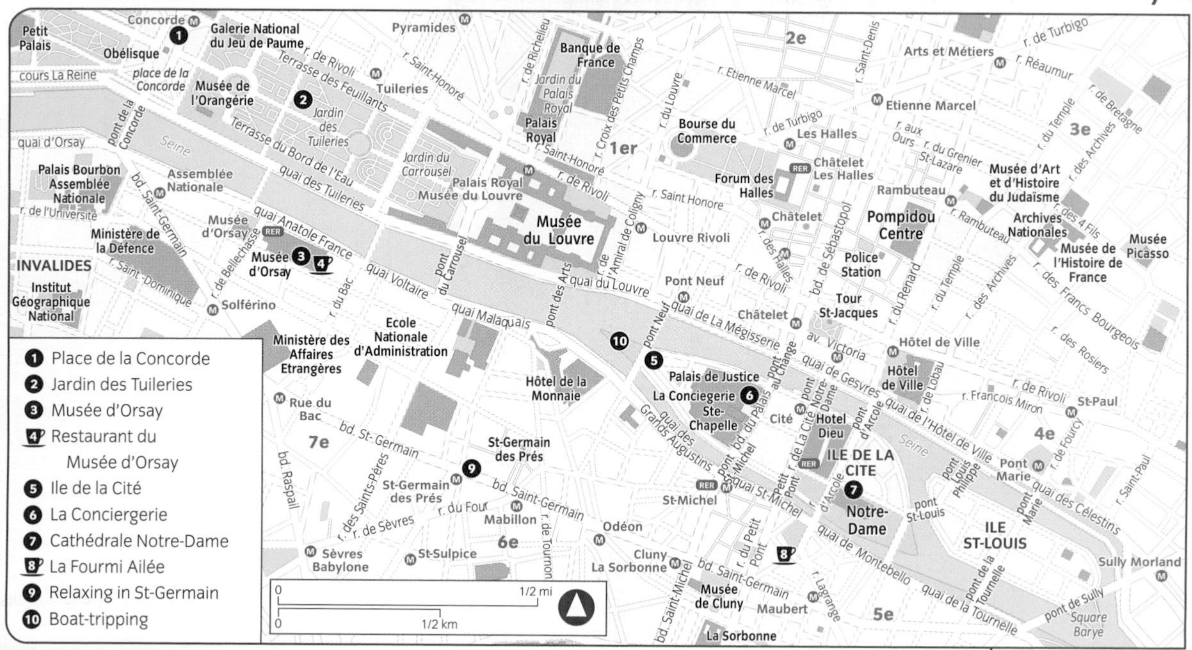

Previous page: The gargoyles of Notre-Dame watch over the city on the Seine.

From the fountain-strewn expanses of place de la Concorde, a mosaic of elegant squares, palaces, and parks unfurls. Once you've spent some time with the Musée d'Orsay's 19th-century masterpieces, the narrow cobblestone streets of Paris's islands beckon, before pointing you toward a cafe terrace in St-Germain for pre-dinner drinks. For this whirlwind, 1-day tour, we aim to show you everything we would want to see if we had only 24 hours in the City of Light. It's an ambitious itinerary, so start early and wear comfortable shoes. **START: Métro to Concorde.**

1 ★★ Place de la Concorde. From the city's largest square, you get immediate reward for your journey to the French capital. First admire the view of the Eiffel Tower, then position yourself to see down the iconic Champs Elysées to the formidable Arc de Triomphe. Now turn 180 degrees, and find the Tuileries gardens and the Palais du Louvre beyond. From here, you'll see the massive 19th-century, neoclassical Madeleine Church to your left—a mirror image of the Assemblée Nationale across the Seine (home to the lower house of the French Parliament). Amid the fountains, tourists, and traffic stands the sleek, 3,300-year-old Luxor Obelisk (a gift from Egypt in 1829), near the spot where, in 1792, thousands of revolutionary victims, including Louis XVI and Marie Antoinette, lost their heads on the guillotine. This perfect, lovely viewpoint is your own instant postcard. Welcome to Paris. ⏱ *10 min. Go early in the morning to avoid crowds, or just after sunset to see the edifices aglow. Free admission. Métro: Concorde.*

2 Jardin des Tuileries. Place de la Concorde ends where the Louvre's stately, sculpture-strewn gardens begin. On a space about the size of two football fields, lacy chestnut trees shade winding paths that stretch off the dusty main *alleé* leading down to the Musée du Louvre. It's a beautiful place in which to walk, read, or admire sculptures by greats like Rodin and Maillol. See p 90 for the "Jardin des Tuileries" tour. ⏱ *20 min. Summer daily 7am–9pm; winter daily 7am–nightfall. Métro: Tuileries or Concorde.*

An overview of the Musée d'Orsay, in a converted train station.

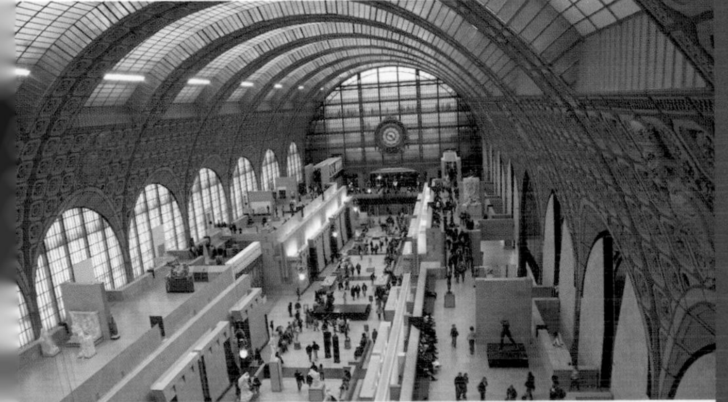

Gargoyles from the Renaissance-era pont Neuf, Paris's oldest bridge.

3 ★★★ **Musée d'Orsay.** Walk along the river until you reach the Gare d'Orsay, the old Belle Epoque train station built for the 1900 exposition and later turned into a museum devoted to works created from 1848 to 1914. Fans of Impressionism will be in paradise amid masterpieces such as Manet's *Le déjeuner sur l'herbe (The Picnic on the Grass)*, Renoir's joyous *Moulin de la Galette,* and Degas's ballerinas, who still twirl for the crowds alongside paintings by Cézanne, Sisley, and Monet. The post-Impressionist collection includes renowned pieces by van Gogh, Gauguin, and others from the School of Pont-Aven, Cross, Seurat, and the Douanier Rousseau. A huge, ornate clock dominates the light-filled central hall. Statues of robust maidens and eager men by Rude, Barye, and Carrier-Belleuse (all 19th-c. sculptors) stand where the train tracks once lay including Carpeaux's ***La Danse*** (once controversial for its frolicking nude figures). ***2–3 hr. 1 rue de la Légion d'Honneur, 7th. ☎ 01-40-49-48-14. www.musee-orsay.fr. Admission 8€ ages 26 and over, 5.50€ ages 18–25, free for children 17 and under and those 25 and under from E.U. countries. Tues–Wed & Fri–Sun 9:30am–6pm; Thurs 9:30 am–9:45pm. Métro: Solférino and Assemblée Nationale. RER: Musée d'Orsay.***

4 ★ **Restaurant du Musée d'Orsay.** Breakfast and lunch are served in the Musée d'Orsay's bustling first-floor restaurant—a historic, gilded, Belle Epoque dining room with stunning frescoed ceilings and large silvery mirrors. Between 2:45pm and 5:45pm, indulge your sweet tooth with a slice of rich chocolate cake and a cup of tea. $.

5 ★★★ **Ile de la Cité.** When the weather's fine, one of the most Parisian things you can do is stroll along the Seine to the Ile de la Cité, the birthplace of Paris. Take a right as you leave the museum. It's about a 15-minute stroll down to this island, home to **Notre-Dame Cathedral.** Cross onto the island at the **pont Neuf** (New Bridge), which, despite its name, is the oldest bridge in the city, characterized by the statue of Henri IV who commissioned the "pont" in 1578. On the island, tall, 19th-century buildings keep the narrow streets in perpetual shadow. The pretty Place Dauphine, recognizable by its pink brickwork, reflects Henri's taste for Italian classicism. ***30 min. Métro: Pont Neuf.***

6 ★★ **La Conciergerie.** The fairy-tale towers that soar above the north end of the island near the pont Neuf lead you to the fortress where Marie Antoinette was imprisoned before her execution. Its intimidating look is largely courtesy of an 1850s makeover, but most of the building is much older—several parts date to the 12th and 13th centuries when it was a royal palace. During the French Revolution, torture and execution were commonplace here, and it became a symbol of terror. You can visit cells in which prisoners were held (including a reconstruction of Marie Antoinette's), as well as the former banquet halls and guardrooms. Next door is the medieval **Ste-Chapelle** (buy a dual ticket upon arrival), one of the most beautiful chapels you'll ever see. It's famous for the breathtaking "light show" cast on the interior when the sun shines through the stained-glass windows. *1 hr. 2 bd. du Palais, 1st. ☎ 01-53-40-60-97. http://conciergerie.monuments-nationaux.fr. Admission 7€ ages 26 and over, 4.50€ ages 18–25, free for children 17 and under. Mar–Oct daily 9:30am–6pm, Nov–Feb daily 9am–5pm. Métro: Cité.*

❼ ★★★ **Cathédrale de Notre-Dame.** Wind your way to the eastern tip of the island to see the familiar silhouette of one of the world's most iconic cathedrals. Founded in 1160 by Maurice de Sully, bishop of Paris, Notre-Dame witnessed the passing of wars of religion and centuries of kings (Napoleon also crowned himself emperor here in 1804), before losing its riches to plunderers during the Revolution. By the 19th century, it had fallen into disrepair and was scheduled for demolition until author Victor Hugo, who wrote *The Hunchback of Notre-Dame,* led a successful campaign for its restoration.

8 ★ **La Fourmi Ailée.** Escape the crowds by crossing pont du Double to the Left Bank, where the "Flying Ant" tearoom serves sticky cakes and excellent hot dishes, such as veal blanquette (15€), in a lovely, shabby dining room reminiscent of a library. *8 rue du Fouarre, 5th. ☎ 01-43-29-40-99. $.*

For the price of a cafe au lait, you can squander time at Les Deux Magots cafe on bd. St-Germain.

Notre-Dame de Paris

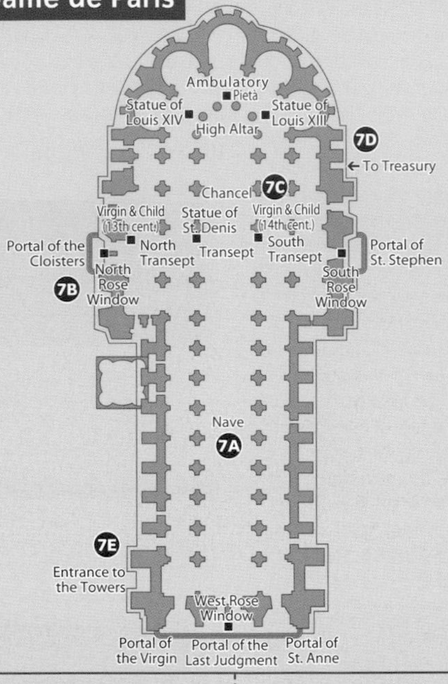

At the far end of the 7A **nave** are three elaborately sculpted 13th-century portals: on the left the Portal of the Virgin, in the center the Portal of the Last Judgment, and on the right the Portal of St. Anne. Above them all glow the ruby hues of the West Rose Window, its beauty surpassed only by the 7B **North Rose Window.** The colors are especially vivid in the late afternoon. Near the altar is the 14th-century 7C **Virgin and Child.** In the 7D **treasury,** you'll find a collection of crosses and ancient reliquaries, including the Crown of Thorns (brought from the Sainte-Chapelle). To get an up-close look at the cathedral's famous gargoyles you must climb 67m (220 ft.) up the 7E **tower** on old stone staircases—a strenuous workout, but the non-agoraphobic will love the views of the fanciful and detailed hobgoblins, devils, and birds of prey. *1 hr. Parvis Notre-Dame/ Place Jean Paul II, 4th. 01-42-34-56-10. www.cathedraledeparis.com. Free admission to cathedral, 8€ to towers, 3€ to treasury. Cathedral: daily 8am–6:45pm. Crypt: Apr–Sept daily 10am–6:30pm. Towers: Apr–Sept Mon–Fri 10am–6:30pm, Sat–Sun 10am–11pm; Jun–Aug daily 10am–11pm; Oct–Mar daily 10am–5:30pm. Treasury: Mon–Sat 9:30am–6pm, Sun 2–6pm. Métro: Cité.*

The 12th-century Cathédrale de Notre-Dame.

❾ ★★ **Relaxing in St-Germain.** Head right as you leave the cafe and go up rue Danté to join boulevard Saint-Germain (turning right), and after 5 minutes, the bustle of St-Germain-des-Prés. This area was the incubator for artistic creativity in the 1920s, for Nazi resistance in the 1940s, and for student revolution in the 1960s. These days, you can get a great cup of coffee, drop a wad of money on high-fashion clothes, or spend a night on the town. The best way to experience the neighborhood is to wander along glittering, tree-lined boulevard St-Germain, stopping at shops and bars that spark your fancy. The district is also the realm of Paris's historic literary cafes: the stylish **Café de Flore,** 172bd.St-Germain (☎ 01-45-48-55-26), a favorite of the philosopher Jean-Paul Sartre; and the more touristy **Les Deux Magots,** 6 place St-Germain-des-Prés (☎ 01-45-48-55-26), a regular haunt of both Sartre and Hemingway. Prices are high at either spot, but for the cost of your drink or meal, you can stay at your table and people-watch as long as you like.

❿ ★★ **Boat Tripping.** If you have any energy left after dinner, walk down to the riverside at the pont Neuf and catch one of Vedettes du Pont Neuf's long, low boats. By night, they glow with lights as they navigate the river, affording magical views of Paris. 🕘 ***1 hr. Square du Vert Galant, 4th.*** ☎ ***01-46-33-98-38. www.vedettesdupontneuf.com. Tickets 12€ adults, 6€ children 4–12, free children 3 and under. Mar–Oct daily 10:30am–10:30pm about every 30 min. Nov–Feb daily 10:30am–10pm about every 45 min.***

Budget Paris in 1 Day

Believe it or not, it is possible to spend a day in Paris with just 20€ in your pocket. Start your morning amid France's second-largest collection of Chinese art at the fabulous and free **Musée Cernuschi,** 7 av. Vélasquez, 8th (☎ 01-53-96-21-50; www.cernuschi.paris.fr; free admission; Tues–Sun 10am–6pm; Métro: Villiers or Monceau). The collection ranges from Neolithic terracottas and Wei dynasty funeral statues (A.D. 386–534) to Sung porcelain, and rare Liao dynasty gold objets d'art (A.D. 907–1125). Then, if the weather is fair, find a place in the sun for an early picnic lunch at the **Parc Monceau** next door. This elegant oasis was designed by Carmontelle in 1778 as a hideaway from the Duke of Orleans. If you haven't bought your food yet, consider the street market on rue de Lévis by the Villiers Métro stop (access on bd. de Courcelles, av. Velasquez, av. Van Dyck & av. Ruysdaël; Métro: Monceau or Villiers). If it's cold or rainy, opt for **Les Caves Populaires,** at 22 rue des Dames, 17th (☎ 01-53-04-08-32; Mon–Sat 8am–2am, Sun 11am–2am; Métro: Place de Clichy). This rustic local haunt is the perfect spot for a coffee or a glass of wine—a steal starting at just 2.50€. After your meal, while away the afternoon amid the arty streets of **Montmartre** (see p. 65). For dinner, you'll find some of the best no-frills French cuisine in town at **Chartier,** 7 rue du Faubourg Montmartre, 9th (see p 108).

The Best in **2 Days**

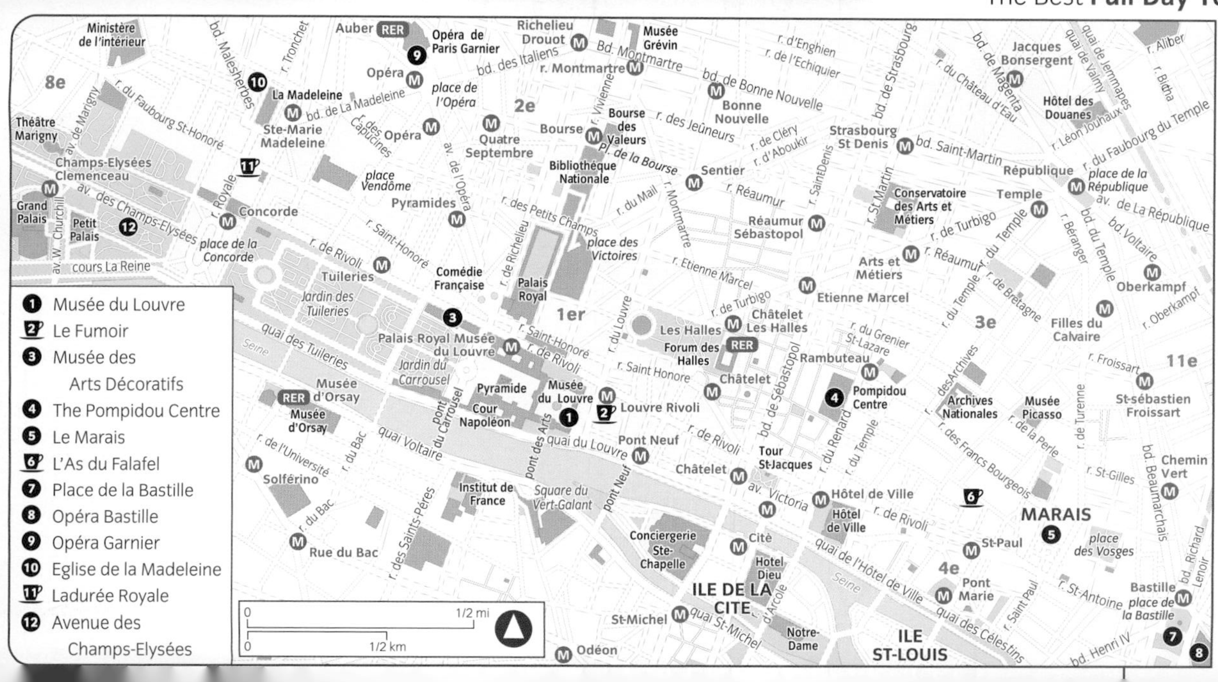

If you followed the 1-day tour of Paris you've already had a good introduction to the city, but there's obviously lots more to see. Start your day early with a coffee and a fresh croissant at Café Marly, 93 rue de Rivoli, 1st, nestled underneath the arches of the Louvre (☎ 01-49-26-06-60) is a good spot. **START: Métro to the Louvre.**

1 ★★★ Musée du Louvre. Arrive early, or after 6pm on Wednesday or Friday, to catch the shortest lines at what is arguably the world's greatest art museum. The Louvre is so enormous you could easily spend a day in each wing and fail to see everything. We highly recommend deciding what you want to see in advance. For help navigating the museum, opening times, and ticket prices see the **Louvre tour** on p 30. *2 hr.*

2 ★★ Le Fumoir. This handy spot near the Louvre and Arts Décoratifs museums has a faithful following among Paris's literary and media crowd. Sink into a Chesterfield armchair and order a refreshing fruit cocktail; or fill up on salads, steak, or vegetarian risotto. *6 rue de l'amiral Coligny, 1st. ☎ 01-42-92-00-24. Métro: Louvre-Rivoli. $$$.*

3 ★ Musée des Arts Décoratifs. This excellent museum (set inside the palace but separate from the Louvre museum) contains one of the world's primary collections of design and decorative art. Sharing its space with the Musée de la Mode and the Musée de la Publicité (fashion and advertising museums both open for temporary exhibitions only), the museum's collection covers a breathtaking anthology of pieces ranging from medieval liturgical items to Art Nouveau and Art Deco furniture; gothic paneling and Renaissance porcelain to 1970s psychedelic carpets; furniture by Philippe Starck to furnishings from France's high-speed TGV trains. Ten period rooms show how the museum's collections would have looked in a real house. The most memorable are couturier Jeanne Lanvin's early Art Deco purple boudoir and a grandiose Louis-Philippe bedchamber. *1–1½ hrs. 107 rue de Rivoli,*

The exoskeletal architecture of Richard Rogers' and Renzo Piano's Pompidou Centre.

1st. ☎ 01-44-55-57-50. www.lesartsdecoratifs.fr. Admission 9€ age 26 and over, 7.50€ age 18–25, free for children 17 and under and 25 and under from E.U. countries. Tues–Wed & Fri–Sun 11am–6pm, Thurs 11am–9pm. Métro: Palais-Royal Musée du Louvre.

4 ★★ The Pompidou Centre. If the Louvre's classic artworks leave you craving for modernity, walk eastward, past the shops and cafes surrounding Châtelet-les-Halles, to Paris's most avant-garde building, the Pompidou Centre—one of the world's leading modern and contemporary art museums. Even by today's standards the museum's bold, "exoskeletal" architecture—with brightly painted pipes, ducts, and escalator tubes crisscrossing on the outside—looks eccentric. *See p 42,* **1**.

5 ★★ Le Marais. After so much culture, I find nothing more relaxing than strolling around the winding medieval streets of the Marais district—traditionally the city's old Jewish quarter and home to magnificent 17th- and 18th-century mansions (called *hôtels*). You can spend hours perusing the district's charming boutiques, tiny Jewish bakeries, and absorbing museums if you take the **Marais tour** (p 61). One of its most picturesque squares is the **Place des Vosges**—Paris's oldest square, remarkable for its perfect symmetry, formed by 36 redbrick-and-stone arcades with sharply pitched roofs. In 1615, a 3-day party was held here celebrating Louis XIII's marriage to Anne of Austria. *2 hr. Jewish shops and restaurants close on Sat, the Jewish Sabbath. Many boutiques open on Sun. Métro: St-Paul.*

Falafel from Chez Hannah in Le Marais.

6 ★ L'As du Falafel. This tiny cafe, with a window for takeout orders, ties with Chez Hannah down the same street no. 54 for the best falafel sandwiches in the city (from 5€). Unless it's raining, eat it on a bench in nearby place des Vosges. (See previous stop.) *34 rue des Rosiers, 4th. ☎ 01-48-87-63-60. $.*

7 ★ Place de la Bastille. From Place des Vosges, it's a very short walk to Place de la Bastille, the site of one of the most famous moments in French revolutionary history. Here stood the Bastille prison, a massive building that loomed ominously over the city. On July 14, 1789, a mob attacked it, freeing all of France from the tyranny of its presence. Today, the site is home to the modern Bastille Opera House and a busy traffic circle. The central column, the Colonne de Juillet, honors the victims of the 1830 revolution, which ironically put Louis-Philippe on the throne after the upheaval of the Napoleonic wars. *15 min. Métro: Bastille.*

8 ★ Opéra Bastille. This behemoth, which opened in 1989, is the home of the Opéra National de Paris. It's clear that the designer of the building, Carlos Ott, paid a lot of attention to its appearance, but music lovers say it would have been nice if he had taken acoustics into consideration, too. Despite this, operas played here are of the highest standard. Tickets are sold online, at FNAC (p 88), or you can try your luck 40 minutes before the performance when remaining tickets are sold off at a discount. ⌚ *15 min. 2 place de la Bastille, 4th. ☎ 08-92-89-90-90 (0.34€/min) or 33-01-71-25-24-23 from abroad. www.operadeparis.fr. Tickets 20€–130€. Métro: Bastille.*

9 ★★ **Opéra Garnier.** On your second day (or third if you followed the 1-day tour), start by seeing what opera used to look like in Paris: Charles Garnier's architectural explosion goes beyond baroque and well into the splendors of rococo. This was the city's main opera house until Opéra Bastille came along, but now it also hosts dance performances beneath an elaborate false ceiling painted by Chagall in 1964. The facade is all marble and flowing sculpture, with gilded busts and multihued pillars. This is where the Phantom did his haunting (a man-made lake below the opera house inspired Gaston Leroux to create his tragic hero). Even if you don't want to see a ballet, buy a visitor's ticket (9€; 5€ ages 24 and under) to admire the flamboyant, gilded interior, including the grand staircase and the main theater (daily 10am–5pm; until 1pm on matinee performance days). ⌚ *20 min. Place de l'Opera, 9th. ☎ 08-92-89-90-90 (0.34€/min) or 33-01-71-25-24-23 from abroad. www.operadeparis.fr. Tickets 23€–130€. Métro: Opéra.*

10 ★★ **Eglise de la Madeleine.** Tear yourself away from the Art Nouveau–style department stores behind the opera house, on boulevard Haussmann (**Galeries Lafayette** and **Au Printemps,** p 84), and head west down bd. des Capucines to this neoclassical church, designed by Barthélémy Vignon in 1806 as a "temple of glory" for Napoleon Bonaparte. The exterior, which mirrors the **Assemblée Nationale** on the other side of place de la Concorde (p 7), is marked by fluted Corinthian columns, while inside highlights include a wonderful frieze of the Last Judgment and a painting of the history of Christianity by Jules-Claude Ziegler. The square around the church, **place de la Madeleine,** is a foodie paradise with top-end restaurants and luxury food shops such as **Fauchon** (p 87). ⌚ *30 min. Place de la Madeleine, 8th. ☎ 01-44-51-69-00. www.eglise-lamadeleine.com. Free admission. Open daily 9:30am –7pm. Métro: Madeleine.*

11 ★★★ **Ladurée Royale.** After a long day traversing the city, tea and cakes might be in order. The 19th-century dark wood, frescoed ceilings, and gilded mirrors make this one of the most atmospheric tearooms in Paris. The macaroons and pistachio pain-au-chocolats are a dream. *16 rue Royale, 8th. ☎ 01-42-60-21-79. www.laduree.fr. Open Mon–Thu 8:30am–7:30pm; Fri–Sat 8:30am –8pm; Sun 10am–7pm. Métro: Madeleine or Concorde.*

12 ★★ **Avenue des Champs-Elysées.** Although it's not as beautiful as most of us imagine, this 2km (1¼-mile) avenue is the symbolic gathering place for national parades and sports victory celebrations, thanks to Napoleon's early-19th-century **Arc de Triomphe** (p 24). It is also part of Paris's **Golden Triangle** (along with avenues Georges V and Montaigne), where Chanel, Louis Vuitton, and other designer boutiques stand alongside lavish palace hotels such as the Hôtel Georges V. You'll find plenty for tighter budgets, too: high-street shops such as Virgin Megastore, FNAC, and Zara line the sidewalk, along with cinemas, bars, the **Lido** cabaret (p 132), and the famous **Queen** nightclub (p 124).

The Best in **3 Days**

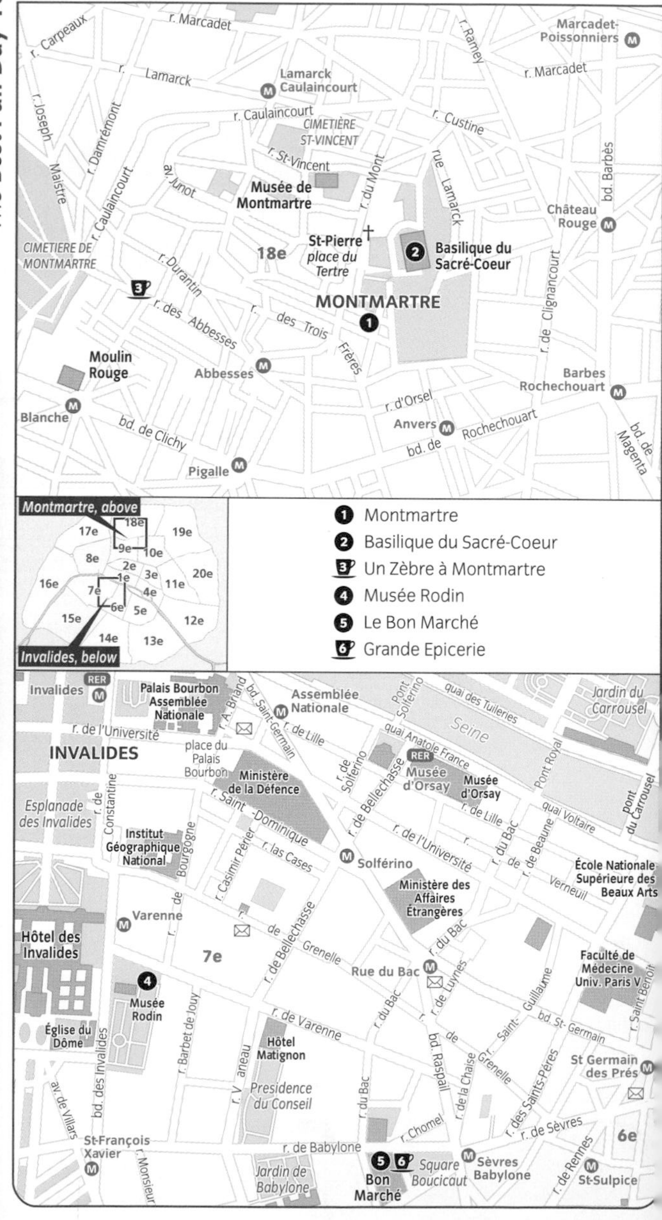

After a few days sightseeing, you may want to slow down a bit. A good way of getting a leisurely feel for two very different parts of the city is to spend the morning amid the cobbles and windmills of Montmartre, before heading to the throng of boutiques in the Saint-Germain district, south of the Seine, in the afternoon. If you fancy slackening the pace even more, choose one of these two areas and follow the full-day tours on p 4 or p 52. **START: Métro to Abesses or place Blanche.**

❶ ★★★ **Montmartre.** With its steep hills, staircase streets, quaint windmills, and sweeping views, this is the most romantic neighborhood in Paris—and many would say the most beautiful. Unfortunately, it's not exactly a secret—prepare yourself for some tacky souvenir shops and the ever-present tourist onslaught around the Sacré Coeur. Still, spending a morning wandering around the streets of Montmartre is enough to make the heart flutter (and not just from the exertion of climbing all those stairs). Take the Métro to Abbesses or Blanche, and head upward. Fall in love with streets like rue des Abbesses, rue des Trois Frères, or rue des Martyrs. Find the windmills on rue Lepic, or the racier one atop the still-titillating Moulin Rouge. For more guidance, try the Montmartre walking tour on p 64. 🕘 *2 hr. Métro: Abbesses or place Blanche.*

Sacré Coeur crowns the city's highest hill.

❷ ★★★ **Basilique du Sacré Coeur.** You can either take a funicular up from the end of rue Berthe or, better still, wander up via bustling place du Tertre; however you get here, this white, wedding-cake basilica will draw a gasp from you when it first hovers into view. Construction began in 1876, and didn't end until 1919—the whole thing was paid for by donations from the faithful to thank God for freeing Paris from the Prussian invaders. The mosaics inside—on the ceiling, walls, and floors—are almost dizzying, and the panoramic view from the steps out front is almost as splendid as the one from its dome, from where a panorama 50km (30 miles) into the distance unfolds. The Sacré Coeur's bell, called "La Savoyarde," is 3m wide and weighs 18,835 kg, making it the biggest bell in France. 🕘 *1 hr. Place St-Pierre, 18th.* ☎ *01-53-41-89-00. www.sacre-coeur-montmartre.com. Free admission to basilica; 6€ to dome & crypt. Daily 6am–10:45pm (9am–5:45pm dome). Métro: Abbesses.*

3 ★★ Un Zèbre à Montmartre. Back down on rue Lepic, tourist traps give way to pleasant, bohemian cafes like this one, not far from the Café des Deux Moulins where the title character worked in the film *Amélie*. Salads here are a meal in themselves and the atmosphere is wholly "Montmartrois." *38 rue Lepic, 18th. ☎ 01-42-23-97-80. $.*

4 ★★ Musée Rodin. A short Métro ride will bring you to this peaceful museum, where the sculptor Auguste Rodin once had his studio. Today his works are scattered inside and outside a somber 18th-century mansion of gray stone. *The Thinker* perches pensively in the courtyard, while the lovers in *Le Baiser* kiss in perpetuity inside. There's also a room devoted to the oft-overlooked works of Rodin's talented mistress, Camille Claudel. It's rarely crowded, so it's a good option when things are busy at the Louvre. *1 hr. Hôtel Biron, 79 rue de Varenne, 7th. ☎ 01-44-18-61-10. www.musee-rodin.fr. Admission 6€ ages 26 and over, 5€ ages 18–25, free for children 17 and under and 25 and under from E.U. countries. Apr–Sept Tues–Sun 9:30am–5:45pm; Oct–Mar Tues–Sun 9:30am–4:45pm. Métro: Varenne or Invalides. RER: Invalides.*

The Thinker *at the Musée Rodin.*

5 ★ Le Bon Marché. If you haven't found everything you hoped to yet, and you're tired of walking from boutique to boutique, do what the locals do and come to this swank department store. If you fancy an extra treat, book the personalized shopping service at the "Conciergerie." You can even have a manicure or be guided through the "Theater of Beauty." The shop is all very designer-label orientated, which may put some strains on the holiday budget. But this is Paris's oldest department store, and even the elevator is designer, so you should at least have a look. *2 hr. 24 rue de Sèvres, 7th. ☎ 01-44-39-80-00. www.lebonmarche.com. Mon–Sat 10am–8pm (until 9pm Thu–Fri). Métro: Sèvres-Babylone.*

6 ★ Grande Epicerie. In a building connected to the Bon Marché, this grand food hall peddles all the pâtés and cheeses your heart could desire. You can build yourself a gorgeous picnic, or take a seat in the excellent bar and restaurant and let someone else do all the work. *☎ 01-44-39-81-00. www.lagrandeepicerie.fr. Mon–Sat 8:30am–9pm. $$.* ●

2 The Best Special-Interest Tours

Monumental Paris

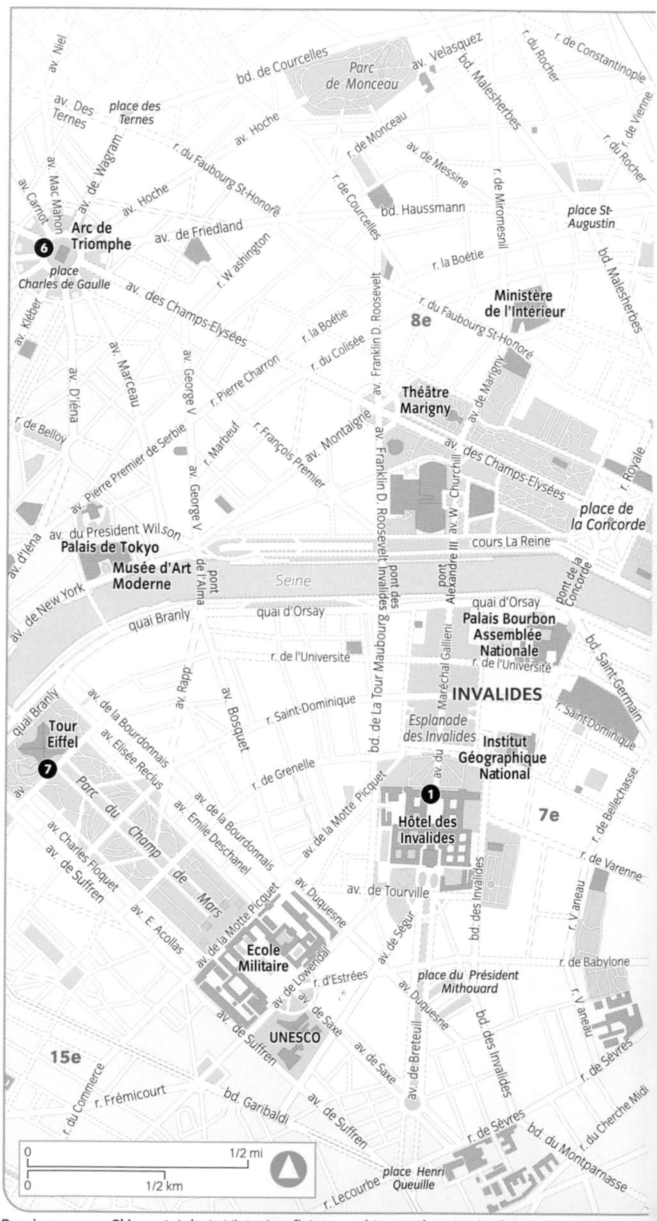

Previous page: Clément Ader's Victorian flying machine at the Musée des Arts et Métiers.

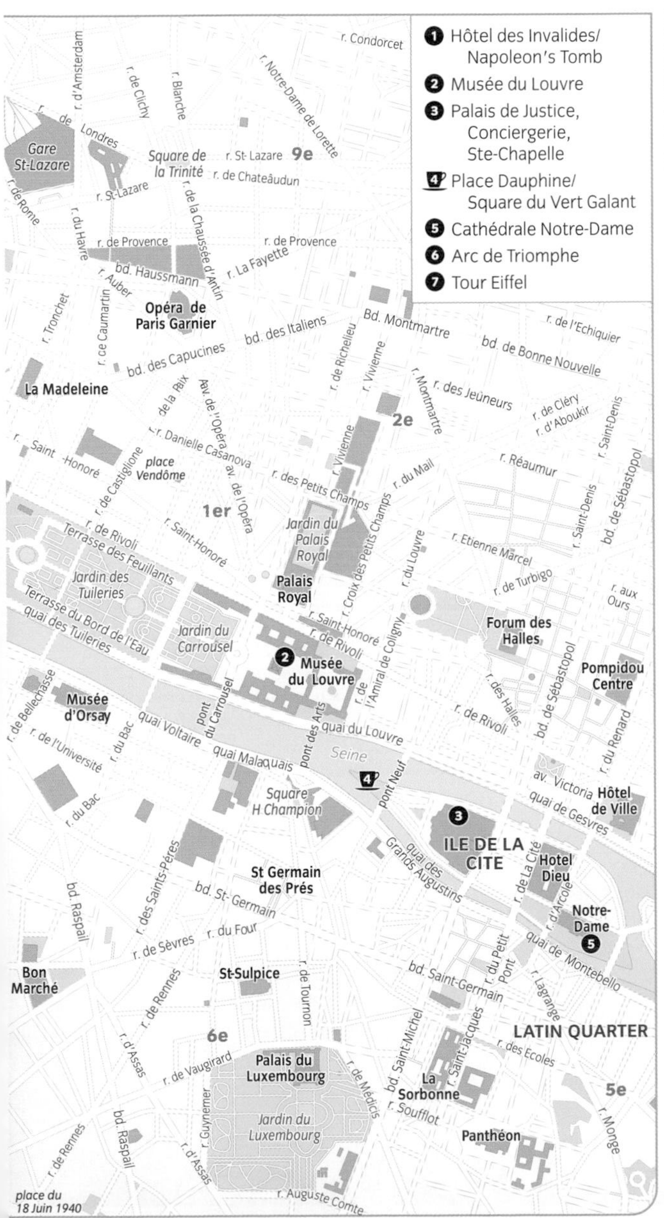

1 Hôtel des Invalides/ Napoleon's Tomb
2 Musée du Louvre
3 Palais de Justice, Conciergerie, Ste-Chapelle
4 Place Dauphine/ Square du Vert Galant
5 Cathédrale Notre-Dame
6 Arc de Triomphe
7 Tour Eiffel
Gare St-Lazare
Square de la Trinité
9e
Opéra de Paris Garnier
La Madeleine
place Vendôme
2e
1er
Jardin du Palais Royal
Palais Royal
Jardin des Tuileries
Jardin du Carrousel
Musée du Louvre
Forum des Halles
Pompidou Centre
Musée d'Orsay
Seine
Square H Champion
ILE DE LA CITE
Hotel Dieu
Hôtel de Ville
Notre-Dame
St Germain des Prés
Bon Marché
St-Sulpice
LATIN QUARTER
6e
Palais du Luxembourg
Jardin du Luxembourg
La Sorbonne
5e
Panthéon
place du 18 Juin 1940
r. Condorcet
r. Notre-Dame de Lorette
r. d'Amsterdam
r. de Clichy
r. Blanche
r. de Londres
r. St-Lazare
r. de Châteaudun
r. St-Lazare
r. de Rome
r. du Havre
r. de la Chaussée d'Antin
r. de Provence
r. de Provence
r. La Fayette
bd. Haussmann
r. Auber
r. Tronchet
r. ce Caumartin
bd. des Capucines
bd. des Italiens
Bd. Montmartre
r. de l'Echiquier
bd. de Bonne Nouvelle
r. de Richelieu
r. Vivienne
r. Montmartre
r. des Jeûneurs
r. de Cléry
r. d'Aboukir
r. Saint-Denis
r. de la Paix
Av. de l'Opéra
r. Danielle Casanova
r. Saint-Honoré
r. de Castiglione
av. de l'Opéra
r. Vivienne
r. des Petits Champs
r. du Mail
r. Réaumur
bd. de Sébastopol
r. Saint-Denis
r. de Rivoli
Terrasse des Feuillants
r. Saint-Honoré
r. Croix des Petits Champs
r. du Louvre
r. Etienne Marcel
r. de Turbigo
r. aux Ours
Terrasse du Bord de l'Eau
quai des Tuileries
r. Saint-Honoré
r. de Rivoli
r. de l'Amiral de Coligny
r. des Halles
bd. de Sébastopol
r. de Rivoli
r. de Bellechasse
r. de l'Université
r. du Bac
quai Voltaire
pont du Carrousel
pont des Arts
quai du Louvre
quai Malaquais
pont Neuf
r. du Renard
av. Victoria
quai de Gesvres
r. du Bac
quai des Grands Augustins
r. de La Cité
r. d'Arcole
r. des Saints-Pères
bd. St-Germain
bd. Raspail
r. de Sèvres
r. du Four
quai de Montebello
r. du Petit Pont
r. Lagrange
bd. Saint-Germain
r. de Rennes
r. de Tournon
bd. Saint-Michel
r. Saint-Jacques
r. des Ecoles
r. d'Assas
r. de Vaugirard
r. de Médicis
r. Soufflot
r. Monge
bd. Raspail
r. Guynemer
r. de Rennes
r. d'Assas
r. Auguste Comte

This tour covers a lot of ground, so be prepared for a busy day. For your efforts, you'll see the city's most glorious edifices all at one go. If you get an early start and keep moving, you should be able to make it to the Eiffel Tower (the last stop) by sunset.

START: Métro to Invalides.

1 ★★★ Hôtel des Invalides/ Napoleon's Tomb. The imposing Les Invalides complex, with its symmetrical corridors and beautiful Dôme church (Libéral Bruand and Jules Hardouin-Mansart's golden-domed masterpiece), was built in 1670 by Louis XIV as a military hospital and a showpiece of the Sun King's military power. Approach it from the Cherubin-clad Pont Alexandre III to see it as intended, from the end of its perfectly balanced gardens, lined with canons. Inside, along with accouterments of Napoleon's life and death, is the Musée de l'Armée, with enough historic weaponry (vicious battle-axes, clumsy blunderbusses) to mount another revolution. Among the collection's gems are suits of armor worn by the kings and dignitaries of France, including one worn by Louis XIV and François I's "armor suit of the lion." Henri II ordered his suit engraved with the monograms of both his mistress, Diane de Poitiers, and his wife, Catherine de Médicis. The complex also contains the Historical Charles de Gaulle, a high-tech audiovisual monument covering the whole of de Gaulle's life, particularly his role in World War II; the Musée des Plans Reliefs, the collection of scale model cities Vauban, Louis XIV's military engineer, used for planning military attacks; and of course, Napoleon's tomb. Set inside the Dôme church, his over-the-top tomb features giant statues that represent his victories surrounding his famously tiny body. You can also see his death mask and an oil painting by Delaroche, painted at the time of Napoleon's first banishment in 1814. *1 hr.129 rue de Grenelle, 7th. ☎ 01-42-44-38-77. www.invalides.org. Admission 9€ ages 26 and over, 7€ ages 18–25, free for children 17 and under and 25 and*

The Eiffel Tower and gold dome of the Hôtel des Invalides make it easier to navigate Paris.

The Musée du Louvre, viewed through I.M. Pei's glass pyramid in the courtyard.

under from E.U. countries. Oct–Mar daily 10am–5pm; Apr–May & Sept daily 10am–6pm. Closed 1st Mon of the month Oct–June. Métro: Invalides.

❷ ★★★ Musée du Louvre. The home of Da Vinci's *Mona Lisa* is one of the world's largest and best museums, set in Paris's former royal palace. It's worth spending a day here (see Exploring the Louvre, p 30), but for this tour, admire it from the outside. ⌚ *20 min.*

❸ ★★★ Palais de Justice, Conciergerie, Ste-Chapelle. Walk east along the river to pont Neuf—the bridge to Ile de la Cité. Turn left after you cross the bridge and you'll see the complex made up of the Palais de Justice (law courts), the Conciergerie (formerly a prison, now a museum), and the exquisite Sainte-Chapelle. The Palais is still the center of the French judicial system, and it's worth a peek inside at its grand lobby. Once a palace, the Conciergerie was converted to a prison during the Revolution and became a symbol of terror—Paris's answer to the Tower of London. Carts once frequently pulled up to the Conciergerie to haul off fresh victims for the guillotine. Among the few imprisoned here who lived to tell the tale was American political theorist and writer Thomas Paine. Inside, you can learn about the bloody history of the Conciergerie and visit some of the old prison cells, including a mock version of Marie Antoinette's. The Sainte-Chapelle—stunning in afternoon light—was built in the 13th century to hold a crown of thorns that King Louis IX believed Christ wore during his crucifixion (it's now in Notre-Dame). The chapel's 15 stained-glass windows comprise over 1,000 scenes depicting the Christian story from the Garden of Eden through to the Apocalypse, depicted on the great Rose Window. (Read them from bottom to top and from left to right.) The stained glass of Sainte-Chapelle is magnificent in daylight, glowing with reds that have inspired the saying "wine the color of Sainte-Chapelle's windows." ⌚ *1 hr. 2–6 bd. du Palais, 1st. ☎ 01-53-40-60-97. www.monuments-nationaux.fr. Free admission to Palais de Justice; Conciergerie 7€ ages 26 and over, 4.50€ ages 18–25; free ages 17 and under and 25 and under from E.U. countries. Sainte-Chapelle 8€ ages 26 and over, 5€ ages 18–25. Free for children 17 and under and 25 and under from E.U. countries. Combined ticket Conciergerie & Sainte-Chapelle 11€;*

concessions 7.50€ and free entry as above. Daily 9:30am–6pm. Métro: Cité.

4 ★ Place Dauphine/Square du Vert Galant. Place Dauphine, where the pont Neuf crosses the island, has several decent restaurants and cafes. If you've brought a picnic lunch, go to the Square du Vert Gallant opposite, at the tip of the island, and spread out on the grass or near the water's edge to eat with a view of the Louvre. *$–$$.*

5 ★★★ Cathédrale de Notre-Dame. For a good view of the buttresses, take the short bridge just behind the cathedral to Ile St-Louis. *1 hr.* *See p 9, bullet 7.*

6 ★★★ Arc de Triomphe. The world's largest triumphal arch was commissioned by Napoleon in 1806 to commemorate the victories of his Grand Armée. The monument is engraved with the names of hundreds of generals (those underlined died in battle) who commanded French troops in Napoleonic victories. The arch was finished in 1836, after Napoleon's death. His remains, brought from St. Helena in 1840, passed under it on the journey to his final resting place at the Hôtel des Invalides. These days the arch is the focal point of state funerals, and the site of the Tomb of the Unknown Soldier, in whose honor an eternal flame burns. It's also a huge traffic circle, representing certain death to pedestrians, so you reach the arch via an underground passage (well signposted). The constant roar of traffic can ruin the mood, but the view from the top (accessible via elevator or stairs) makes enduring the din worthwhile. The last leg of your tour is a 20-minute walk away. You can also hop back on the Métro to Trocadéro or flag down a taxi on the Champs Elysées. *45 min. The Arc de Triomphe is open late at night, so if you prefer a nighttime view, you can put this off until after dinner. Place Charles de Gaulle–Etoile, 8th. ☎ 01-55-37-73-77. www.monuments-nationaux.fr. Admission 9.50€ ages 26 and over, 6€ ages 18–25, free for children 17 and under and 25 and under from E.U. countries. Apr–Sept daily 10am–11pm; Oct–Mar daily 10am–10:30pm. Métro/RER: Charles de Gaulle–Etoile.*

A subterranean passage leads pedestrians safely to the Arc de Triomphe.

A view of the Eiffel Tower from the carousel in the Luxembourg Gardens.

7 ★★★ **Tour Eiffel.** At last. It's the Eiffel Tower to Americans and the *Tour Eiffel* to the rest of the world, but whatever you call it, it is synonymous with Paris. The tower was meant to be temporary, built by Gustave-Alexandre Eiffel (who also created the framework for the Statue of Liberty) in 1889 for the Universal Exhibition. It weighs 7,000 tons but exerts about the same pressure on the ground as an average-size person sitting in a chair. Praised by some and denounced by others, the tower created as much controversy in the 1880s as I. M. Pei's glass pyramid at the Louvre did in the 1980s. The tower, including its TV antenna, is 317m (1,040 ft.) high, and from the top you can see for 65km (40 miles). But the view *of* the tower is just as important as the view *from* it. If you go to Trocadéro on the Métro, then walk from the Palais de Chaillot gardens across the Seine, you'll get the best view (not to mention photo opportunities). I always come right at sunset or just after dark. Inside the tower's lacy ironwork are restaurants, bars, and historic memorabilia. Take your time, have a drink, or even book a table at Alain Ducasse's pricey restaurant **Le Jules Verne** (reserve 3 months in advance for an evening meal, ☎ 08-25-56-66-62), and enjoy sweeping views from the second level as you dine. If your pockets aren't that deep, his brasserie, Altitude 95, is an excellent compromise on the first floor. ⌚ *2 hr. Champ de Mars, 7th.* ☎ *01-44-11-23-23. www.tour-eiffel.fr. Admission lift to 1st floor 4.50€ adults, 2.30€ ages 3–11; lift to 2nd floor 7.80€ adults, 4.30€ ages 3–11; lift to top floor 12€ adults, 6.30€ ages 3–11; stairs to 1st and 2nd floors 4€ ages 26 and over, 3.10€ ages 3–25, free for children 2 and under. Open by lift Jan to mid-June & Sept 2–Dec daily 9:30am–11:45pm; mid-June to Sept 1 9am–12:45am. By stairs Jan to mid-June & Sept 2–Dec 9:30am–6:30pm; mid-June to Sept 1 9am–12:45am. Métro: Trocadéro, Ecole Militaire, or Bir-Hakeim. RER: Champs-de-Mars-Tour-Eiffel.*

Paris with Kids

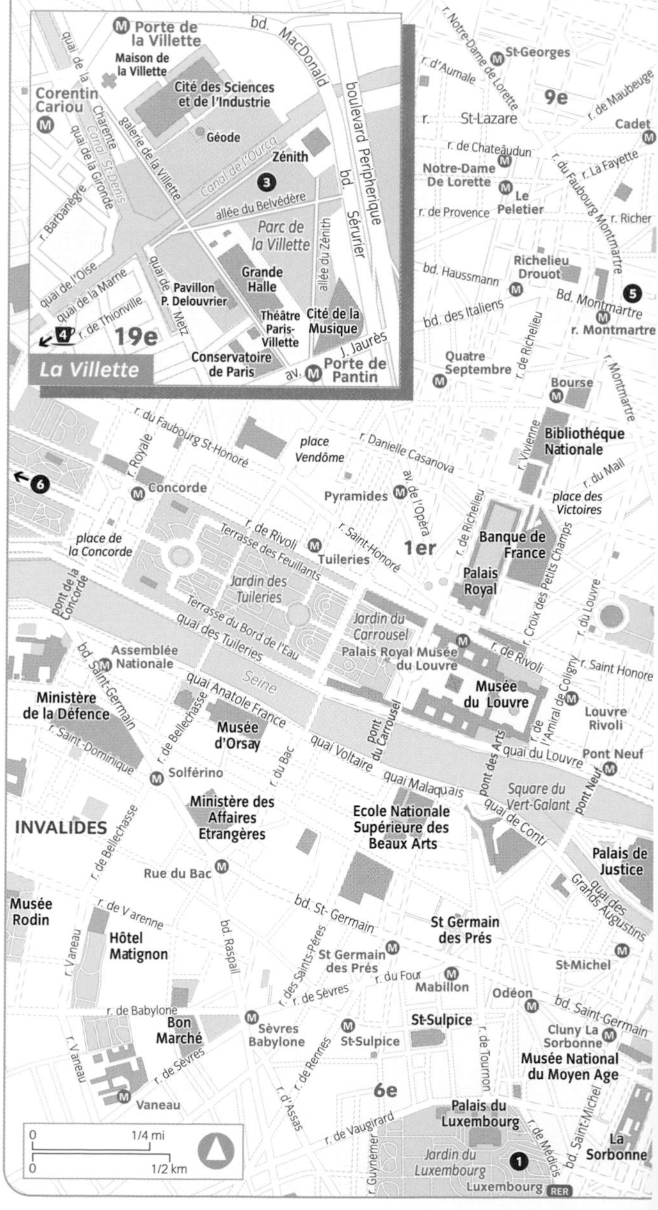

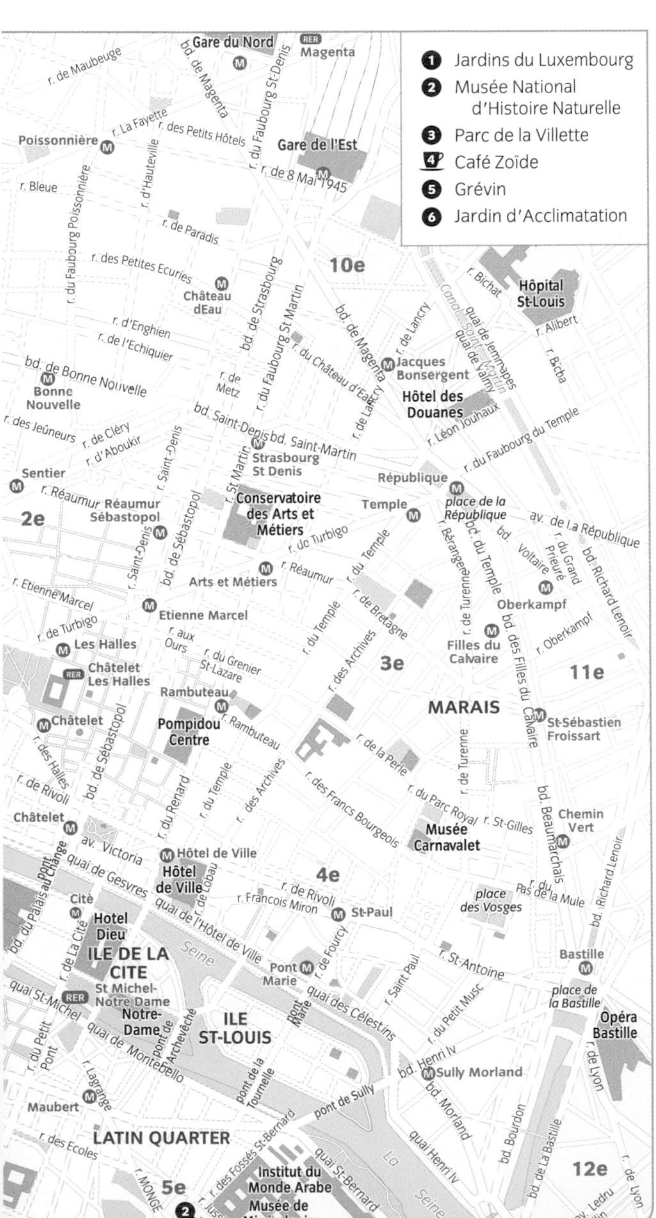
1 Jardins du Luxembourg
2 Musée National d'Histoire Naturelle
3 Parc de la Villette
4 Café Zoïde
5 Grévin
6 Jardin d'Acclimatation
Gare du Nord
Magenta
Gare de l'Est
Poissonnière
10e
Château dEau
Hôpital St-Louis
Jacques Bonsergent
Hôtel des Douanes
Bonne Nouvelle
Sentier
Strasbourg St Denis
République
Réaumur Sébastopol
2e
Conservatoire des Arts et Métiers
Temple
place de la République
Arts et Métiers
Oberkampf
Etienne Marcel
Les Halles
Filles du Calvaire
Châtelet Les Halles
3e
11e
Rambuteau
MARAIS
Châtelet
Pompidou Centre
St-Sébastien Froissart
Chemin Vert
Musée Carnavalet
Hôtel de Ville
4e
place des Vosges
St-Paul
Cité
Hotel Dieu
ILE DE LA CITE
Bastille
Pont Marie
place de la Bastille
St Michel-Notre Dame
Notre-Dame
ILE ST-LOUIS
Opéra Bastille
Sully Morland
Maubert
LATIN QUARTER
12e
Institut du Monde Arabe
5e
Musée de Minéralogie
Seine
La Seine

Let's face it: Most kid-approved attractions are outdoors, which means you're dangerously reliant on good weather. But this selection has been designed to keep them smiling come rain or shine. Yet even the best-laid plans fail—in which case you can rush them off for a day at Disneyland Paris (p 168). **START: Métro to Odéon.**

A merry-go-round in the Jardins du Luxembourg.

❶ Jardins du Luxembourg. Kids can run amok in these elegant gardens, which are done in classic French style, with urns and statuary and trees planted in patterns. Statues peek out everywhere as children sail toy boats on the ponds, ride the ponies, or catch a puppet show, if you get lucky with timing. Kids can also watch the locals play *boules* (lawn bowling), but are unlikely to be invited to join in. Don't miss the ornate, evocative Fountaines de Medicis, in the northeast corner of the park. ⏲ ***1 hr. Métro: Odéon. RER: Luxembourg.***

❷ Musée National d'Histoire Naturelle. The giant whale skeleton hanging just inside the front door of this natural history museum lets you know right off the bat that the kids are going to be fine here. Beyond those bones in the Galerie de l'Evolution are more skeletons of dinosaurs and mastodons, and galleries filled with sparkling minerals and rare plants. In the surrounding gardens (the Jardin des Plantes), there's also a wonderful menagerie with small animals in simulated natural habitats. A good place to linger if the weather turns gray. ⏲ ***1½ hr. 56 rue Cuvier, 5th. ☎ 01-40-79-54-79. www.mnhn.fr. Admission 7€ adults, 5€ ages 4–16, free for children 3 and under (one full-price ticket gives reduced price access to the Menagerie). Wed–Mon***

La Cité des Sciences children's museum in the Parc de la Villette.

Kids play king of the road in bumper cars in the Jardin d'Acclimatation.

10am–6pm. Métro: Jussieu or Gare d'Austerlitz.

3 ★★★ Parc de la Villette. Take the Métro to Jaurès or Stalingrad, then stroll or bike along the redeveloped Canal de l'Ourcq to Parc de la Villette, a retro-futurist succession of gardens for kids to run around in. There's an IMAX cinema at 26 av. Corentin-Cariou (☎ 08-92-68-45-40; www.lageode.fr; Métro: Porte de la Villette) and a fabulous children's science museum, **La Cité des Sciences,** at 30 av. Corentin-Cariou (☎ 01-40-05-70-00; www.cite-sciences.fr; Métro: Porte de la Villette). See p 70, bullet 5 for a fuller list of attractions. 🕘 *3 hr. 19th.*

4 ★ Café Zoide. If your family needs refreshments along the canal, try Café Zoide—a children-friendly cafe with dozens of games for babies to 16-year-olds. *92 bis Quai de la Loire, 19th; ☎ 01-42-38-26-37; www.cafezoide.asso.fr.* Or try **Okay café** just a bit further down for tasty crêpes. *49 bis quai de Loire, 19th. ☎ 01-42-01-56-04. $. Métro: Jaurès.*

5 Grévin. If the weather is bad, make this your last stop of the day. If it's fair, skip this stop and go on to the next one. At this waxworks museum, kids will enjoy wandering among stars—both American (Madonna) and international (soccer star Zinédine Zidane). Among the 300 wax figures you'll find heads of state, artists, writers, and historical figures—at times the museum even verges on educational. 🕘 *1 hr. 10 bd. Montmartre, 9th. ☎ 01-47-70-85-05. www.grevin.com. Admission 21€ adults, 13€ children 6–14, 9€ children 5 and under. Mon–Fri 10am–6:30pm; Sat–Sun 10am–7pm. Closed first week Oct. Métro: Grands-Boulevards.*

6 ★★ Jardin d'Acclimatation. Let the kids while away the rest of a sunny afternoon here. You can start with a ride on a green-and-yellow narrow-gauge train from porte Maillot to the entrance (every 30 min. Wed and Sat–Sun). Along the way there's a house of mirrors, an archery range, miniature golf, a small zoo, a bowling alley, a puppet theater, playgrounds, kid-size rides, shooting galleries, and food stalls. Kids can ride ponies and paddle about in boats—they can even drive little cars. Bear in mind that it's only for little ones; teenagers will hate it. 🕘 *2–3 hr. Bois de Boulogne, 16th. ☎ 01-40-67-90-82. www.jardindacclimatation.fr. Admission: 2.90€ to enter (then prices vary for each attraction), free for children 3 and under. June–Sept daily 10am–7pm; Oct–May daily 10am–6pm. Métro: Sablons or Porte Maillot.*

Exploring the Louvre

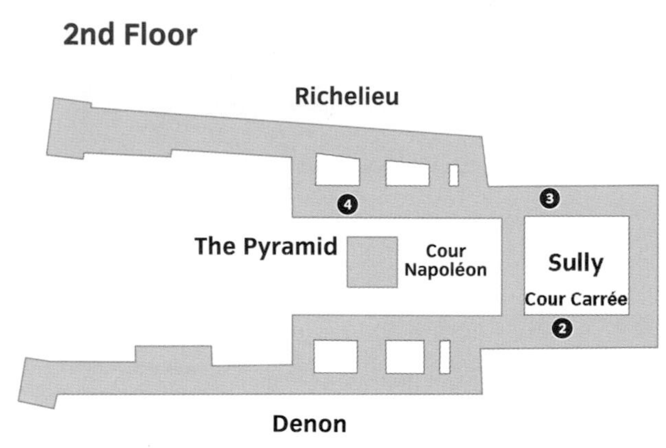

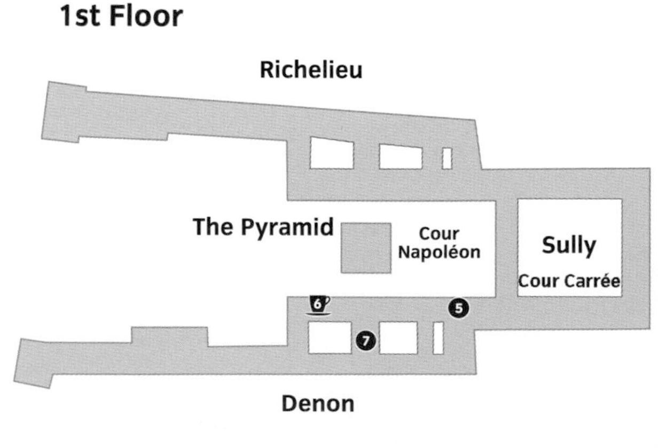

1 *Venus de Milo*
2 The *Turkish Bath*
3 *The Card Sharper*
4 *The Lacemaker*
5 *Winged Victory of Samothrace*
6 Café Mollien
7 *Mona Lisa*
8 Italian Sculpture

Ground Floor

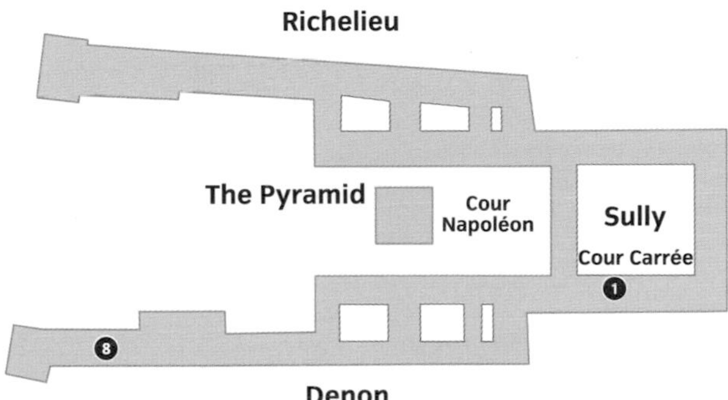

The Pyramid

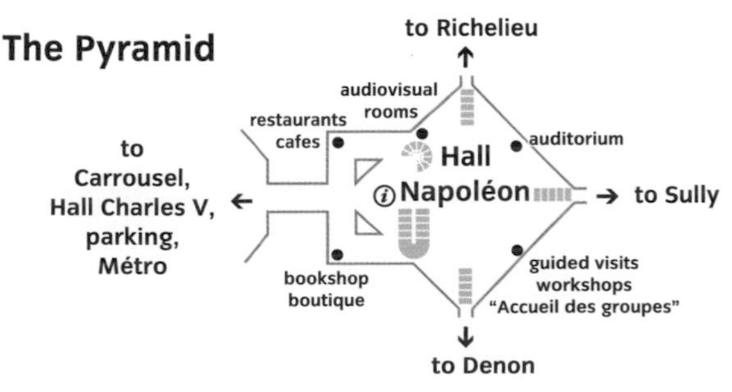

Before becoming a museum, the Musée du Louvre was France's main royal palace. In 1527, François I demolished most of the old castle to build a new one, which makes up part of the building you see today. (François also inadvertently founded part of the museum's collection—the *Mona Lisa* and *Virgin of the Rocks* once hung in his bathroom.) The rest of the building was completed over the centuries, particularly by Henri II and Napoleon. More recent additions include the glass pyramids designed by I. M. Pei (in 1989) and the brand new Cour Visconti extensions, which will house a world-class Islamic Art collection from 2012 onwards. **START: Métro to Palais Royal–Musée du Louvre.**

Travel Tip

Laid out end to end, the Louvre would be the size of several football fields, so put aside at least 3 to 4 hours to get a general feel for the place and browse a bit between stops. Pick up a map when you arrive at the museum and use it to find our suggested selection of works—the floor and rooms are marked for each entry.

1 ★★★ *Venus de Milo.* Begin your tour in Greek Antiquities, where Venus stands alluringly, her drapery about to fall to the floor. The statue dates to 100 B.C. Myths about her abound—one story maintains that her arms were knocked off when she was hustled onto a French ship. Another claims she was rescued from a pottery kiln. Both are untrue—she was found buried as you see her now, along with part of an arm, a hand holding an apple, and a pair of small columns, one of which fit neatly into her base and bore the inscription ALEXANDROS, SON OF MENIDES, CITIZEN OF ANTIOCH, MADE THIS STATUE. Sadly, those parts were all lost over time. ***Ground floor, Room 16.***

2 ★ *The Turkish Bath.* Take the stairs to the second floor (if you're from the U.S., remember that the French second floor is your third floor) where you'll see the lush nudity of A. D. Ingres's *The Turkish Bath.* Ingres was a popular French painter in the early 19th century, and this erotic idealized painting of overly friendly women lounging in a (very crowded) bath was the masterwork of his final years. ***Second floor, Room 60.***

I.M. Pei's glass pyramid and the Musée du Louvre, which stretches almost a kilometer.

After all these millennia, Venus de Milo still manages to please a crowd.

3 ★★ ***The Card Sharper.*** In Room 24 you'll find Georges de la Tour's sensational *Tricheur* (The Card Sharper), painted around 1630. In this gorgeous work complex relationships play out in shimmering colors. In the center, a courtesan holds her hand out for a glass of wine poured by a servant. Her cheating friend holds cards behind his back as she casts a colluding glance at him. The chubby-cheeked youth in the embroidered shirt is the victim of a plot. A cruel tale, playfully told. ***Second floor, Room 24.***

4 ★★★ **The *Lacemaker.*** *The Lacemaker* (around 1664) is one of Johannes Vermeer's most famous paintings. It shows a young woman bent over her work, her shape forming a subtle pyramid, and her face, hair, and rich yellow blouse aglow. The book in the foreground is probably the Bible, and sets the moral and religious tone of the painting. Vermeer's unique use of color and light are exemplified in this work, which is usually surrounded by a crowd of admirers. ***Second floor, Room 38.***

Cour Visconti: Islamic Arts

Opening in 2012, the new Arts de l'Islam section adds to the Louvre's already abundant offerings with over 2,000 pieces covering 1,300 years of Islamic artistic history. The fascinating collections (many of which we luxuriously made for the governing bodies of the time) highlight the development of Islamic art from its beginnings in the 7th-century, up until the early 19th-century, showing the difference in artistic styles according to culture, geography, and the era.

The Winged Victory of Samothrace presides over the Daru stairs.

5 ★ ***Winged Victory of Samothrace.*** Head toward the Denon Wing, where at the top of the Daru stairs stands Nike, the goddess of victory, her wings flung back in takeoff, and the fabric of her skirts swirling around her, as fine as silk. The statue's origins are uncertain. Most scholars date it to somewhere between 220 and 190 B.C. The statue was discovered on the Greek island of Samothrace in 1863, and its base was discovered in 1879. In 1950, one of the statue's hands was found; it's on display in a glass case near the statue. An inscription on the statue's base includes the word RHODHIOS (Rhodes) and this, along with the fact that the statue stands on the prow of a ship, has led some scholars to theorize that the statue was commissioned in celebration of a naval victory by Rhodes. Others believe the statue was an offering made by a Macedonian general after a victory in Cyprus. Regardless of its origins, this glorious work is considered one of the best surviving Greek sculptures from that period. ***Top of the Daru staircase.***

6 ★ **Café Mollien.** Ready for a break? Café Mollien is particularly enjoyable in the summertime when the outdoor terrace is open. The café au lait is good here, as is the fresh smoked-salmon sandwich. ***$.***

7 ★★★ ***Mona Lisa.*** It's a long way to the end of the Denon Wing and the hiding place of one of the world's most famous paintings, but everybody makes the trip. The enigmatic smile, the challenging eyes, the endless debates (Was she the wife of an Italian city official? Is she meant to be in mourning? Is "she" a man—perhaps even a self-portrait of da Vinci himself?) continue now as ever. The painting has been through a lot over the years. It was stolen in 1911 (by a Louvre employee who simply put the painting under his coat and walked out with it) and wasn't recovered until 1913. During World War II, it was housed in various parts of France for safekeeping. In 1956 the painting was severely damaged after someone threw acid on it. In 1962 and 1963 it toured the United States, and was shown in New York City and Washington, D.C. In 1974 it was shown in Tokyo and Moscow. All the hype and history aside, some find actually seeing Leonardo da Vinci's *Mona Lisa* (painted between 1503 and 1507) a disappointment. It's a very small painting to have caused such a fuss, and has been kept behind glass since it was slashed by a vandal in the 1990s. That, along with the crowds surrounding it, makes it difficult to connect with. Despite these shortcomings, few come to the Louvre

The Louvre: Practical Matters

The main entrances to the Musée du Louvre, 1st (☎ 01-40-20-50-50; www.louvre.fr) are at 99 rue de Rivoli, inside the Carousel du Louvre underground shopping mall, and the glass pyramid in the main courtyard. Tickets can be bought inside the museum, but expect a long line. To jump the queues, use the automatic ticket machines inside the Carousel du Louvre (just after the entrance at 99 rue de Rivoli) or buy them in advance at a FNAC (p 88) or online (www.ticketweb.com if you're from the United States or Canada, or http://louvre.fnacspectacles.com or www.ticketnet.fr if you're not), then go to the Passage Richelieu entrance, 93 rue de Rivoli.

To beat the crowds, arrive shortly after opening or after 6pm Wed or Fri. Admission is 10€, or free for children 17 and under and 25 and under from E.U. countries; and free for everyone first Sunday of each month. Hours are Wednesday and Friday 9am to 10pm, Thursday and Saturday to Monday 9am to 6pm. Métro: Palais Royal–Musée du Louvre and Louvre Rivoli.

without stopping by at least once. ***First floor, Room 6.***

❽ ★★★ ***Italian Sculpture.*** Make your way down to the ground floor of the Denon Wing and head to Room 4, which is filled with exquisite Italian sculptures. Michelangelo's two statues are among the most dramatic in the room—the muscular arms of his *Rebellious Slave* are tensed furiously against his bindings, while the *Dying Slave* seems resigned to his fate. Both were commissioned in 1505 by Pope Julius as funerary art. Look across the room for the delicate wings of Cupid, who clutches the breast of Psyche in a pas de deux in pure white marble in Antonio Canova's *Cupid Awakening Psyche* (1793). It is love carved in stone. ***Ground floor, Room 4.***

Leonardo da Vinci's The Mona Lisa *once hung over François I's bathtub.*

Paris for Museum Lovers

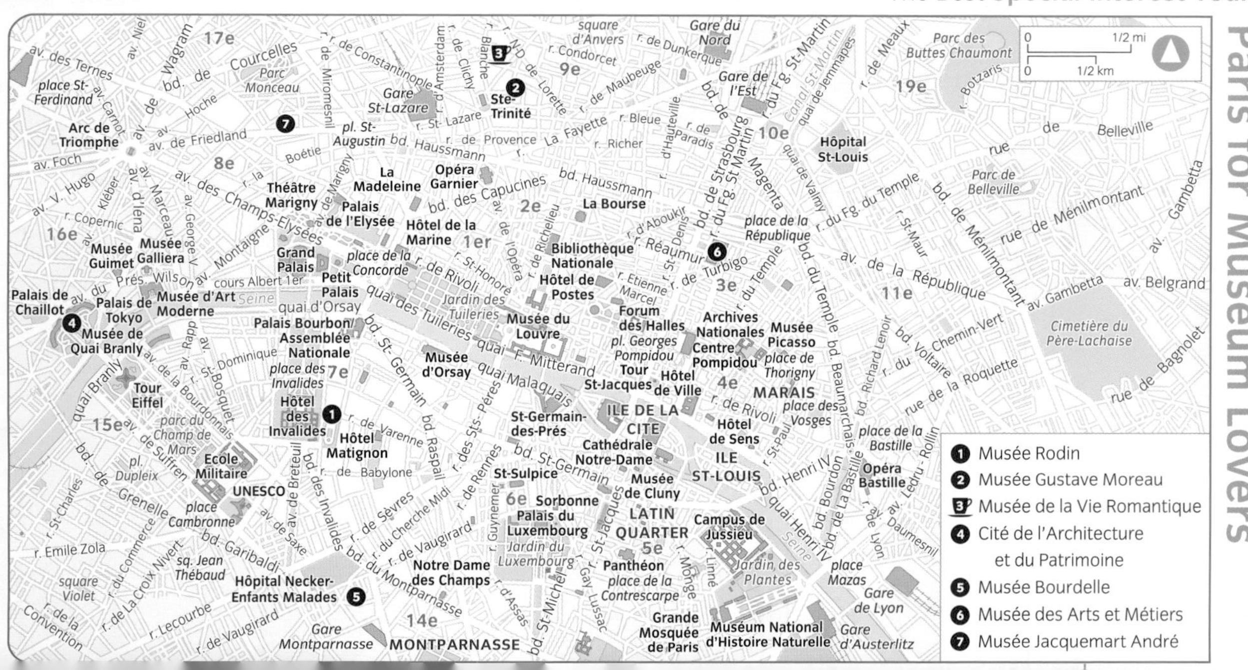

You'd need a lifetime to fully explore the hundreds of museums in Paris. Besides the world-renowned Louvre, Musée d'Orsay, and Centre Pompidou, there are dozens of beautiful, more intimate addresses dedicated to sculpture, inventions, and architecture. This section is not a tour per se, but a list to be dipped into at will. **START: Métro to Varennes.**

The Art Nouveau spiral staircase at the Musée Gustave Moreau.

Save on Admission Fees

All of Paris's municipal museums are free (see www.paris.fr for a full list). If you plan to visit several non-municipal museums over 2, 4, or 6 days, you'll save money with the **Paris Museum Pass** (www.parismuseumpass.com; 2 days 32€, 4 days 48€, 6 days 64€), available for purchase at more than 60 participating museums.

❶ ★★ **Musée Rodin.** This peaceful museum, housed in the building that was once Rodin's studio, can't help but inspire thoughts of romance. *The Thinker* ponders in the sublime gardens while the lovers in *Le Baiser* are locked in a permanent embrace inside. 🕘 *1 hr. Hôtel Biron, 79 rue de Varenne, 7th.* ☎ *01-44-18-61-10. www.musee-rodin.fr. Admission museum 6€ ages 26 and over, 4.50€ ages 18–25, free for children 17 and under; gardens only 1€. Apr–Sept Tues–Sun 9:30am–5:45pm; Oct–Mar Tues–Sun 9:30am–4:45pm. Métro: Varenne or Invaldies. RER: Invaldies.*

❷ ★★ **Musée Gustave Moreau.** Moreau was around at the same time as the Impressionists, but he worked against the prevailing mood, drawing inspiration from the Bible, Greek mythology, Leonardo da Vinci, and Indian miniatures. This atmospheric museum, where he lived and worked, reveals Moreau's obsession for knickknacks and furniture, which are displayed alongside his fabulous mythical beasts and fantasy worlds. 🕘 *1 hr. 14 rue de la*

Rochefoucauld, 9th. ☎ 01-48-74-38-50. www.musee-moreau.fr. Admission 5€ adults, 3€ ages 18–25, free ages 17 and under, free for everyone first Sun of the month. Wed–Mon 10am–12:45pm, 2–5:15pm. Métro: Trinité.

3 ★★★ Musée de la Vie Romantique. Hidden from the rest of the world is this charming, green-shuttered, 18th-century mansion that once housed Rossini, Chopin, George Sand, and Delacroix. It takes the *gâteau* (cake), quite literally, in the rose garden, which doubles as an outside tearoom. Decadence is yours for the price of your *cafe* and *tarte au citron* (lemon tart). *16 rue Chaptal, 9th. ☎ 01-55-31-95-67. www.paris.fr. Tues–Sun 10am–6pm. Free admission. Métro: Pigalle, St-Georges, or Blanche.*

4 kids ★★ Cité de l'Architecture et du Patrimoine. Comprising 8 sq. km (3 sq. miles) of space in the east wing of the Palais de Chaillot, the City of Architecture and Heritage contains more than 850 breathtaking copies of French architectural treasures including molded portions of churches, châteaux, and great French cathedrals such as Chartres. There are also reconstructions of modern architecture, the centerpiece of which is an apartment by Le Corbusier. *2 hr. Palais de Chaillot, 1 place du Trocadéro, 16th. ☎ 01-58-51-52-00. www.citechaillot.org. Admission 8€ adults, 5€ ages 19–25, free ages 18 and under, free for everyone first Sun of month. Wed, Fri–Mon 11am–7pm; Thurs 11am–9pm. Métro: Trocadéro.*

5 ★★ Musée Bourdelle. Hidden away from the hustle and bustle of Montparnasse is the workshop where Rodin's star pupil, Antoine Bourdelle (1861–1929), lived and worked. The sumptuous array of statues, many inspired by Greek mythology, includes *Centaure Mourant* (The Dying Centaur) writhing in agony; *Penelope,* Ulysses' wife, who waited 20 years for her

A frescoed ceiling at the Cité de l'Architecture et du Patrimoine in the Palais de Chaillot.

The Musée Bourdelle in Montparnasse.

husband to return; and, in the gorgeous walled garden, the colossal General Alvear horse statue (part of an allegorical monument that was never finished). *1½ hr. 16–18 rue Antoine-Bourdelle, 15th. ☎ 01-49-54-73-73. www.bourdelle.paris.fr. Free admission. Tues–Sun 10am–6pm. Closed public holidays. Métro: Montparnasse-Bienvenue.*

6 kids ★★★ **Musée des Arts et Métiers.** This museum, founded in the 18th century by Abbot Grégoire as "a store for useful, new inventions," is a gem. Housed in the former Benedictine church and priory of St-Martin-des-Champs, it exhibits some of the world's greatest inventions, from Pascal's calculating devices and celestial spheres to the first computers, steam-powered vehicles, and even airplanes (including the monoplane Louis Blériot flew across the English Channel in 1909). *2 hr. 60 rue Réamur, 3rd. ☎ 01-53-01-82-00. www.arts-et-metiers.net. Admission 6.50€ adults, 4.50€ ages 18–25, free ages 17 and under. Tues, Wed, Fri–Sun 10am–6pm; Thurs 10am–9:30pm. Métro: Arts et Métiers.*

7 kids ★★ **Musée Jacquemart André.** More of a stately home than a museum, this collection of rare 18th-century French paintings and furnishings, 17th-century Dutch and Flemish paintings, and Italian Renaissance works is fit for a king. The salons drip with gilt and the ultimate in fin de siècle style. Works by Bellini, Carpaccio, Uccelo, Van Dyck, Rembrandt, Tiepolo, Rubens, Watteau, Boucher, Fragonard, and Mantegna hang on almost every wall. If you fancy a decadent snack, Mme. Jacquemart's high-ceilinged tearoom complies, with delicious sticky cakes and piping hot tea (served 11:45am–5:30pm). *1 hr. 158 bd. Haussmann, 8th. ☎ 01-45-62-11-59. www.musee-jacquemart-andre.com. Admission 10€ adults, 7.50€ ages 7–17, free children 6 and under. Daily 10am–6pm. Métro: Miromesnil or St-Philippe du Roule.*

A sumptuous salon in the Musée Jacquemart André.

Paris's Best Modern Art

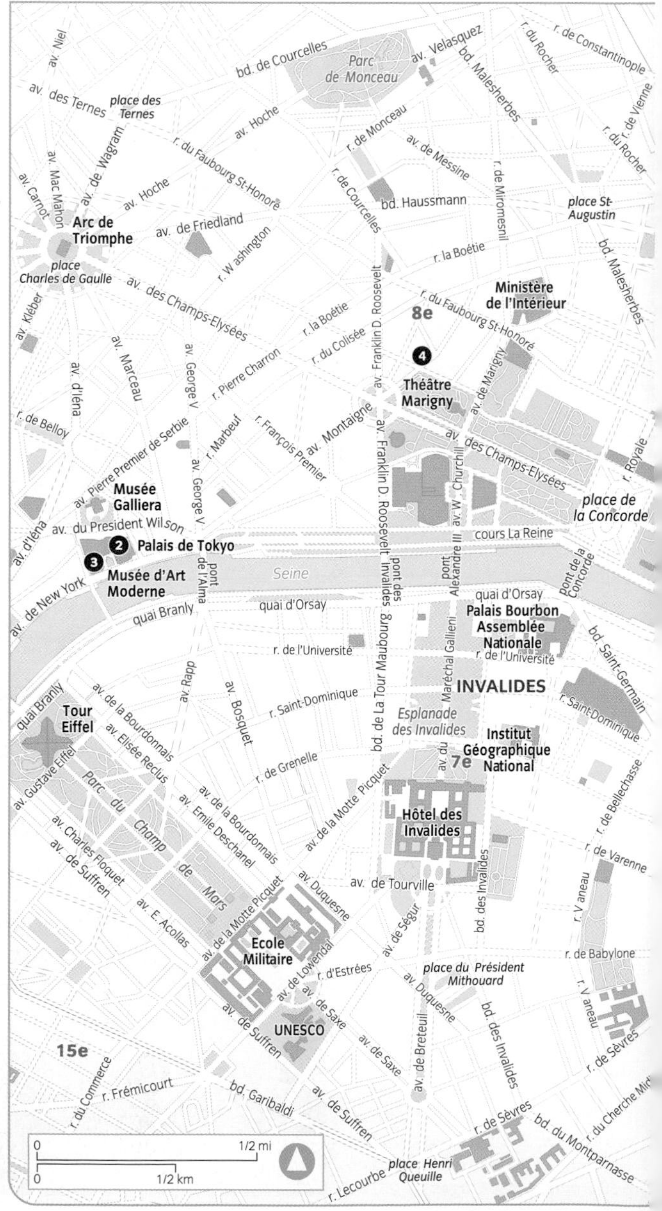
Parc de Monceau
place des Ternes
Arc de Triomphe
place Charles de Gaulle
place St-Augustin
Ministère de l'Intérieur
8e
4
Théâtre Marigny
Musée Galliera
2 Palais de Tokyo
3 Musée d'Art Moderne
Seine
place de la Concorde
Palais Bourbon Assemblée Nationale
INVALIDES
Esplanade des Invalides
Institut Géographique National
7e
Hôtel des Invalides
Tour Eiffel
Parc du Champ de Mars
Ecole Militaire
UNESCO
place du Président Mithouard
15e
place Henri Queuille
0 1/2 mi
0 1/2 km

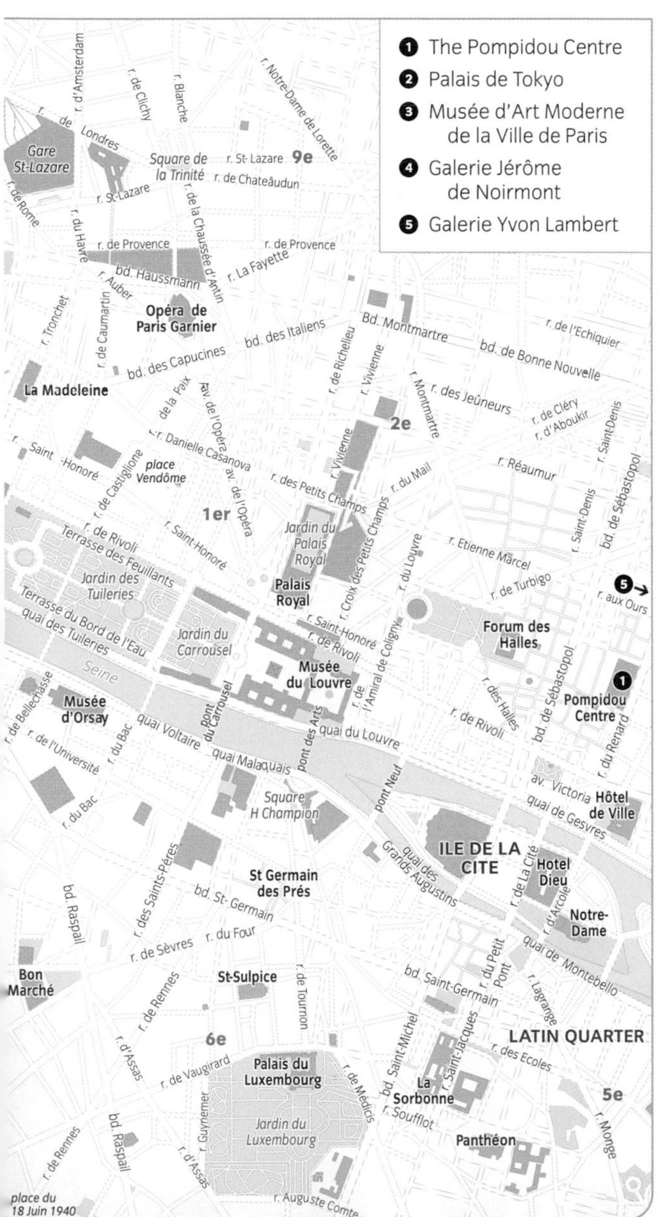
1 The Pompidou Centre
2 Palais de Tokyo
3 Musée d'Art Moderne de la Ville de Paris
4 Galerie Jérôme de Noirmont
5 Galerie Yvon Lambert
Gare St-Lazare
Square de la Trinité
9e
Opéra de Paris Garnier
La Madeleine
place Vendôme
2e
1er
Jardin du Palais Royal
Palais Royal
Jardin des Tuileries
Jardin du Carrousel
Musée du Louvre
Forum des Halles
Pompidou Centre
Musée d'Orsay
Seine
Square H Champion
Hôtel de Ville
ILE DE LA CITE
Hotel Dieu
Notre-Dame
St Germain des Prés
Bon Marché
St-Sulpice
LATIN QUARTER
6e
Palais du Luxembourg
Jardin du Luxembourg
La Sorbonne
5e
Panthéon
place du 18 Juin 1940
bd. Haussmann
bd. des Capucines
bd. des Italiens
Bd. Montmartre
bd. de Bonne Nouvelle
r. de Rivoli
quai du Louvre
quai Voltaire
quai Malaquais
bd. St-Germain
bd. Saint-Germain
bd. Raspail
bd. Saint-Michel
bd. de Sébastopol
r. Saint-Honoré
r. de Rennes
r. de Vaugirard

You only have to look at the Louvre's glass pyramid or the Pompidou Centre's madcap building to realize that Parisians can be unconventional when they put their minds to it—something that's also reflected in the city's art scene. This tour guides you through Paris's biggest contemporary art venues, plus a selection of its interesting smaller galleries. If you're looking for something more alternative, check out www.paris-art.com or www.art-process.com, which runs an "art bus" that ships you between Paris's hottest venues. **START: Métro to Rambuteau.**

The Pompidou Centre houses Europe's biggest collection of modern art.

1 kids ★★★ **The Pompidou Centre.** This benchmark art venue, designed by Richard Rogers and Renzo Piano, is one the best-known sites in Paris, holding the largest collection of modern art in Europe. The permanent collections cover 20th- and 21st-century art, with some 40,000 rotating works. The fifth floor is dedicated to modern art from 1905 to 1960 (fauvism, cubism, interwar art, surrealism, abstraction, and neorealism). Floor 4 covers 1960 to the modern day, providing themed rooms that focus on movements such as antiform art (*arte povera*) and video installations. Go it alone, or opt for the audio-guided visit in English. There's a special children's guide too for 6 to 12 year-olds. Whatever you do, don't miss the masterpiece on the top floor—a stunning view of Paris. *2 hr. Place Georges Pompidou, 4th. ☎ 01-44-78-12-33. www.centre-pompidou.fr. Admission 10€–12€ ages 26 and over, 8€–9€ students and ages 18–25, free for children 17 and under and 25 and under from E.U. countries. Wed–Mon 11am–9pm (until midnight for some exhibitions). Métro: Rambuteau or Hôtel de Ville. RER: Châtelet-les-Halles.*

2 ★ **Palais de Tokyo.** This "Site de Création Contemporaine" is a showcase for experimental art on a

The Palais de Tokyo is the place in Paris for contemporary art installations.

A visitor takes in a Modigliani at the Musée d'Art Modern.

big scale. Inside its stripped-back interior, selected artists (such as Pierre Joseph and Wang Du) fill the space with temporary exhibitions of whatever weird eccentricities they can muster. Visit this cutting-edge gallery if you enjoy having your perception of art challenged. ⌚ ***2 hr. 13 av. du President Wilson, 16th.*** ☎ ***01-47-23-54-01. www.palaisdetokyo.com. Admission 3€ ages 27 and over, 1€ ages 19–26, free for children 18 and under. Open Tues–Sun noon–9pm. Métro:Alma-Marceau or Iéna. RER: Pont d'Alma.***

❸ ★★ Musée d'Art Moderne de la Ville de Paris. Take yourself on a journey through 20th-century "isms": fauvism, cubism, surrealism, realism, expressionism, and neorealism to be exact, with works by artists such as Braque, Dufy, Picasso, Leger, and Matisse, all presented in chronological order. In addition to the permanent collection, expect more fascinating retrospectives on major 20th-century artistic movements, plus thematic exhibitions on the best of today's artistic pickings. ***11 av. du Président Wilson, 16th.*** ☎ ***01-53-67-40-00. www.mam.paris.fr. Free admission for permanent collections; temporary collections 5€–11€ adults, free for children 17 and under. Open Tues–Sun 10am–6pm (until 10pm Thurs for temporary exhibitions). Métro: Alma-Marceau or Iéna. RER: Pont d'Alma.***

❹ Galerie Jérôme de Noirmont. Whether you can afford to buy any art or not, pass by this excellent gallery to see French and international artists of worldwide recognition, plus a few newcomers the husband and wife owners have taken under their wing. Displays here are consistently eye-catching, featuring artists such as Jeff Koons, Fabrice Hyber, the kitsch cool double-act Pierre et Gilles, and hard-core eccentrics Eva and Adèle. ***36–38 av. Matignon, 8th.*** ☎ ***01-42-89-89-00. www.denoirmont.com. Mon–Sat 11am–7pm. Métro: Miromesnil.***

❺ ★ Galerie Yvon Lambert. Collections at this New York offshoot were so huge that a museum was dedicated to them in Avignon (Provence). This multidisciplinary Paris branch includes a gallery where art by leading international names like Sol LeWitt and Jenny Holzer is hung, a brand-new video space, and an art bookshop cum basement gallery where younger artists are given precious exhibition space. ***108 rue Vieille du Temple, 3rd.*** ☎ ***01-42-71-09-33. www.yvon-lambert.com. Tues–Sat 10am–7pm.***

Outside the Musée d'Art Modern de la Ville de Paris.

Hemingway's Paris

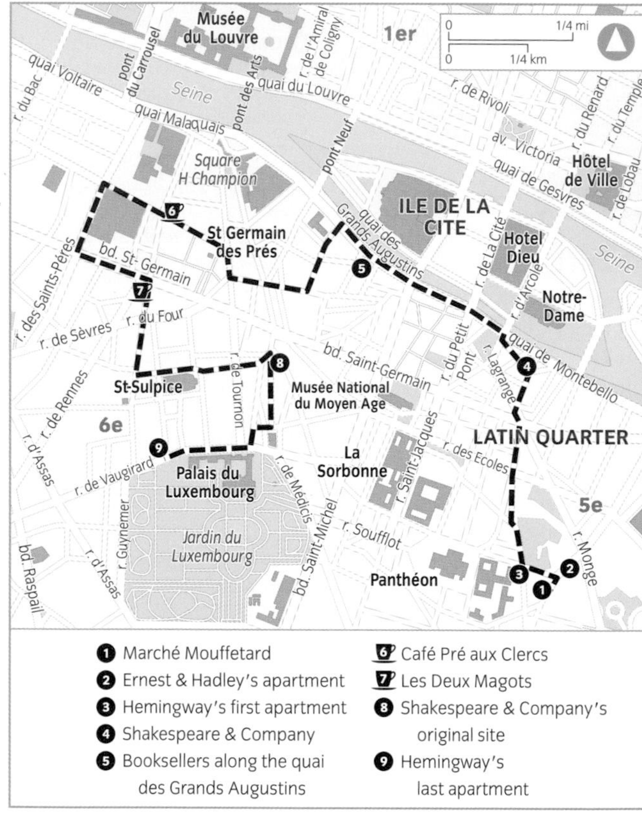

For fans of Papa Hemingway, a trip to Paris is a pilgrimage. This is where Hemingway honed his craft, bullied F. Scott Fitzgerald, and charmed Gertrude Stein. Here he married more than once and had countless mistresses, not the least of which was Paris herself. Oh sure, he cheated on her with Cuba and Spain, but we all know he really loved her. This tour follows his spectacular rise and charts the beginning of his fall. **START: Métro to Censier Daubenton.**

---

1 ★ Marché Mouffetard. At the beginning of his memoir, *A Moveable Feast,* Hemingway describes spending time on rue Mouffetard's "wonderful narrow crowded market street." That description still fits—it's narrow, crowded, and wonderfully Parisian.

2 Ernest & Hadley's apartment. Several blocks up rue Mouffetard, rue du Cardinal-Lemoine branches off to the right. A few houses down, on the fourth floor of no. 74, a 22-year-old Hemingway and his wife Hadley rented their first Parisian apartment together. This was not Hem's first home in Paris, though—that was around the corner on rue Descartes. (See the next stop.) *74 rue du Cardinal-Lemoine, 5th.*

❸ **Hemingway's first apartment.** When he first moved to Paris as a writer for the *Toronto Star* newspaper, Hemingway took a grimy, cheap room on the top floor of a hotel on rue Descartes. The small wall plaque wrongly states that he lived here for 4 years—he was actually here for 1. *39 rue Descartes, 5th.*

❹ ★ **Shakespeare & Company.** Walk toward the river for about 15 minutes, first on rue Descartes (which joins rue Montagne St-Geneviève) through place Maubert, then down rue F. Sauton, and then take a sharp left onto rue de la Bucherie to reach Paris's best expat bookstore. In the 1920s it was at 11 rue de l'Odéon, where Hemingway broke a vase when he read a bad review, Henry Miller used to "borrow" books and never bring them back, and *Ulysses* was first published. The current location is still a favorite of writers for its eccentric attitude and wonderful selection of books. 🕘 *½–1 hr. 37 rue de la Bucherie, 5th.* ☎ *01-43-25-40-93. www.shakespeareandcompany.com. Mon–Fri 10am–11pm; Sat–Sun 11am–11pm. Métro: St-Michel.*

❺ **Booksellers along the Quai des Grands Augustins.** Hemingway frequently shopped here among the secondhand book peddlers (called *bouquinistes*) along the edge of the Seine. Now, as then, their collections are bewilderingly eclectic—like a flea market for books. I once saw the complete Harry Potter collection, in English, next to a book of French erotica. 🕘 *½–1 hr. Quai des Grands Augustins, 6th.*

6 **Café Pré aux Clercs.** Next you'll come to a series of cafes where you can take a well-deserved rest, as Hem surely would, over a whiskey or a glass of the house red. The first cafe is this charming one reached by walking down rue des Grands Augustins. (No. 7 was once Pablo Picasso's studio.) Turn onto rue St-Andre des Arts, and then right along rue de Seine and left on to antiques shop–lined rue Jacob, which brings you to rue Bonaparte and this cafe. It was one of Hem's early haunts, a short walk from the Hotel d'Angleterre, where he slept (in room no.14) on his first night in Paris. *30 rue Bonaparte, 6th.* ☎ *01-43-29-74-34. $$–$$$.*

7 ★★ **Les Deux Magots.** Loop down noisy rue des Saints Peres to the more sophisticated hustle of boulevard St-Germain, and soon

Shakespeare & Company is still in business on the Left Bank after nearly 100 years.

The 1920s—Americans in Paris

The so-called Lost Generation, led by American expatriates Gertrude Stein and Alice B. Toklas, topped the list of celebrities who "occupied" Paris after World War I. Paris attracted the *littérateur, bon viveur,* and drifter, including writers Henry Miller, Ernest Hemingway, and F. Scott Fitzgerald and composer Cole Porter.

After the collapse of Wall Street, many Americans returned home. Even such die-hards as Miller eventually realized that 1930s Paris was collapsing as war clouds loomed. But not hard-core artists like Henry Miller, who wandered around smoking Gauloises when not writing *Tropic of Cancer,* or Gertrude Stein and Alice B. Toklas, who remained in France and are buried together in the Cimetière du Père-Lachaise (p 95, bullet ⓭).

you'll see the glass front of this cafe, which has gotten more mileage out of the gay '20s than any flapper ever could have. This was the preeminent hangout of the arty expat crowd, where Hemingway charmed the girls, picked fights with the critics, and hassled tourists. The feel today is admittedly touristy, and the food okay (but pricey), but it's still a good place to have a coffee and wonder what he'd think of it all now. ***6 place St-Germain-des Prés, 6th.*** ☎ ***01-45-48-55-25. www.lesdeuxmagots.fr. $$–$$$.***

❽ Shakespeare & Company's original site. You can get in a bit of shopping at the many posh boutiques and little jewelry stores on rue St-Sulpice before turning right onto rue de l'Odéon and passing a plaque marking the site of the original Shakespeare & Company bookstore. ***11 rue de L'Odéon, 6th.***

❾ Hemingway's last apartment. After turning down rue de Vaugirard and walking past the French Senate, look for this narrow lane near the Jardins du Luxembourg. The impressive building at no. 6 was Ernest Hemingway's last Paris apartment. My, how the fallen became mighty. From the look of its medallions, sphinxes, and heavy gates, you might get the idea that he'd written a successful novel *(The Sun Also Rises)* and left poor Hadley for somebody richer (Pauline Pfeiffer). And so he had. Here he reached the summit of his success, and his descent into alcoholism began. ***6 rue Férou, 6th.***

Un serveur at Les Deux Magots in St-Germain-des Prés.

3 The Best Neighborhood Walks

The Latin Quarter

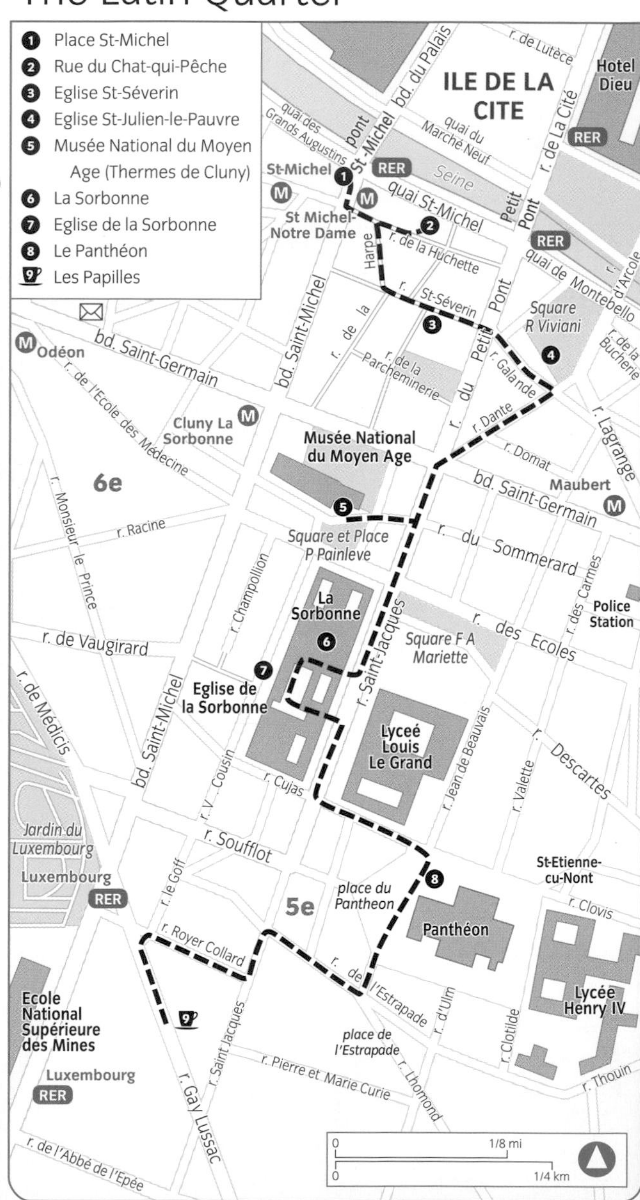

Previous page: Under the vaulted arcades of the Marais district.

In the 1920s this Left Bank neighborhood was the heart of Parisian cafe society. You'll still find plenty of cafes, plus universities and shops, all constantly buzzing with activity. Traditionally arty, intellectual, and bohemian, the area also has a history of political unrest. Today it is still one of Paris's most interesting, not to mention picturesque, quarters to explore. **START: Métro to St-Michel.**

1 Place St-Michel. An elaborate 1860 fountain of Saint Michael slaying a dragon presides over this bustling cafe- and shop-lined square, where skirmishes between occupying Germans and French Resistance fighters once took place. This is the beginning of busy boulevard St-Michel, which was trendy long ago, but is now a disappointing line of fast-food chains and down-market stores. It is, however, the main student quarters, and a young, lively atmosphere pervades.

2 Rue du Chat-qui-Pêche. Turn down rue de la Huchette, bypassing its endless kabob and pizza joints to reach this street, which is one of the narrowest in Paris at just 1.8m wide. Plenty of local tales exist about the history of the name ("Street of the Cat Who Fishes") but nobody knows for sure.

3 Eglise St-Séverin. Head back toward place St-Michel and turn left on rue de la Harpe, which leads to rue St-Séverin and this charming medieval church, built in the early 13th century and reconstructed in the 15th. Don't miss the whimsical gargoyles and monsters projecting from the roof. Inside, linger over the rare Georges Rouault etchings from the 1920s. *30 min. 1 rue des Pretres St Séverin, 5th. ☎ 01-42-34-93-50. www.saint-severin.com. Mon–Sat 11am–7:30pm; Sun 9am–8:30pm.*

4 Eglise St-Julien-le-Pauvre. Take rue St-Séverin to rue Galande, and after snapping a picture of its quaint old houses, find this medieval church, which dates, at least in part, to 1170. Note the unusual capitals covered in carved vines and leaves. The garden contains one of the oldest trees in Paris and affords a prime view of Notre-Dame. *20 min. Rue St-Julien-le-Pauvre, 5th. ☎ 01-43-54-52-16. Mon–Sat*

A lively cafe on Place St-Michel, a hangout for students from the nearby Sorbonne.

The Lady and the Unicorn tapestries at the Musée National du Moyen Age.

9:30am–noon, 3–6:30pm. Métro: Cluny–La Sorbonne.

5 ★★ Musée National du Moyen Age (Thermes de Cluny). With one of the world's strongest collections of medieval art, this small, manageable museum is a gem. Most visitors come to see the *Lady and the Unicorn* tapestries, but there's much more here than longhaired maidens and mythical creatures: This 15th-century Gothic building sits atop 2nd-century baths. The Gallo-Roman pools are in excellent shape—the *frigidarium* (cold bath) and *tepidarium* (warm bath) can still be clearly seen, though you can no longer take a dip. *1 hr. 6 place Paul-Painlevé, 5th. ☎ 01-53-73-78-00. www.musee-moyenage.fr. At press time admission was free, but that may change. Wed–Mon 9:15am–5:45pm. Métro: Cluny–La Sorbonne.*

6 ★ La Sorbonne. France's most famous university, dating back some 700 years, has all the venerable buildings and confident, scraggly-haired students you might imagine. Teachers here have included Thomas Aquinas, and the alumni association counts Dante, Calvin, and Longfellow among its past members. This is a sprawling

A bulwark of higher education in the French capital: La Sorbonne.

This 18th-century memorial hall honors France's greatest intellectuals.

place, and only the courtyard and galleries are open to the public (9am–5pm) when school is in session—follow the crowds and the scarce signs to get a peek. ◷ ***30 min. 12 rue de la Sorbonne, 5th.*** ☎ ***01-40-46-22-11. www.sorbonne.fr. Métro: Cluny–La Sorbonne.***

7 ★ Eglise de la Sorbonne. On the grounds of the Sorbonne, this 17th-century church holds the elaborate tomb of Cardinal Richelieu (1585–1642). Richelieu was a staunch defender of the monarchy's power and did much to unify the French state. The extraordinary statue at its feet is poignantly named *Learning in Tears;* the figure mourning at the cardinal's feet represents science, and the one supporting him represents religion. ◷ ***30 min. Rue de la Sorbonne, 5th.***

8 ★★ Le Panthéon. This magnificent building was built by Louis XV as a tribute to Saint Geneviève. Construction began in 1758. Since the Revolution, however, it's been used to honor more earthly heroes. Here are France's great dead, including Voltaire, Rousseau, Emile Zola, and Victor Hugo. Recent additions include Marie Curie, whose remains were moved here in 1995, and Alexandre Dumas, who arrived in 2002. Appropriately, Foucault's pendulum is here. The famous device, which proved that the earth rotates on an axis, was said to hang from "the eye of God." Although the pendulum appears to swing, it's not moving—the earth is. ◷ ***1 hr. Place du Panthéon, 5th.*** ☎ ***01-44-32-18-00. http://pantheon.monuments-nationaux.fr. Admission 8€ ages 26 and over, 5€ ages 18–26 from outside E.U., free 25 and under from E.U. countries and 17 and under from outside E.U. Daily 10am–6pm (until 6:30pm Apr–Sep). Métro: Cardinal Lemoine. RER: Luxembourg.***

9 Les Papilles. Dying for a break? This is just the place. The owners of this sweet, Provençal-style cafe are dedicated to Southern French food and adventurous wine. The small menu changes with the seasons, and the wines change with the owners' moods. If they're available, try the excellent stewed chicken or the hearty cassoulet. ***30 rue Gay-Lussac, 5th.*** ☎ ***01-43-25-20-79. www.lespapillesparis.fr. RER: Luxembourg. $$.***

St-Germain-des-Prés

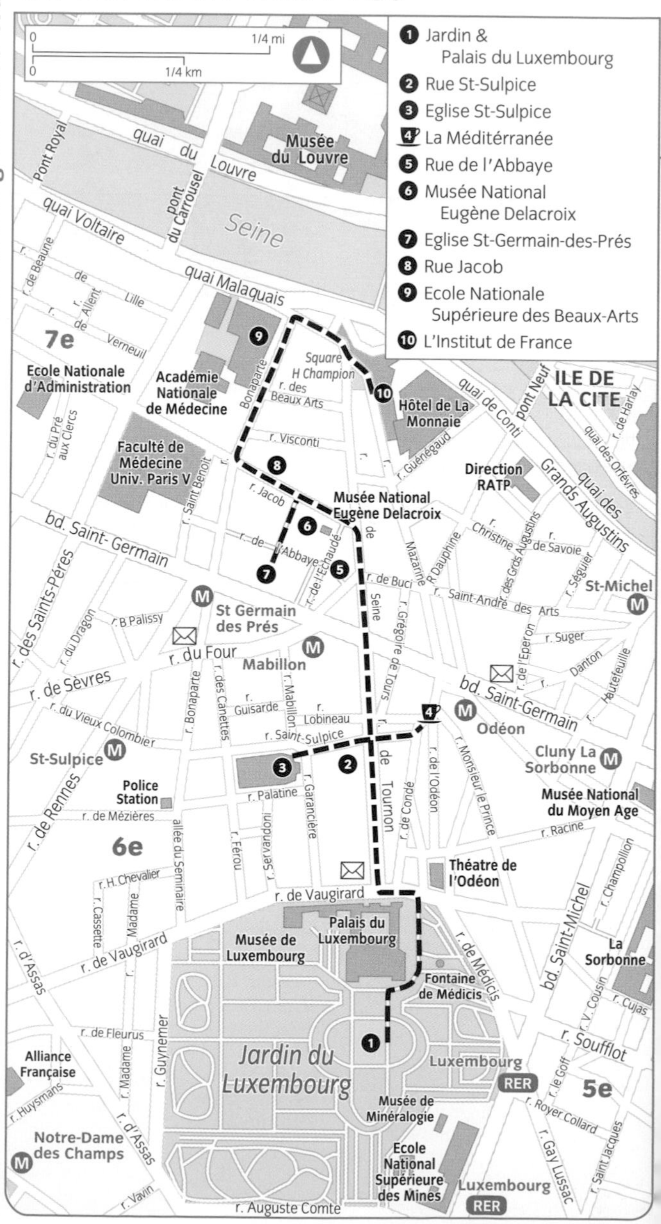

This neighborhood was the place to be in the 1920s. Here the literati met the glitterati, and *tout* Paris marveled at the ensuing explosion of creativity and alcoholism. On these streets Sartre fumed, while Hemingway and Fitzgerald drank and quarreled. Today the bookshops have been replaced by designer boutiques, but it's still the place to go for a night on the town. **START: Métro to Luxembourg.**

1 ★★★ kids Jardins & Palais du Luxembourg. There's a certain justice in the fact that this former palace, built between 1615 and 1627 for the widow of Henry IV, is now home to the democratically elected French Senate. The lovely Italianate building also houses the Musée du Luxembourg, famed for its world-class temporary art exhibitions (19 rue de Vaugirard, 6th; ☎ 01-40-13-62-00; www.museeduluxembourg.fr). Most people, however, come for the gardens. The picturesque paths of the Jardins du Luxembourg have always been a favorite of artists, although children, students from the nearby Sorbonne, and tourists are more common than painters nowadays. Hemingway claimed to have survived a winter by catching pigeons here for his supper, and Gertrude Stein used to cross the gardens on her way to sit for Picasso. The classic formal gardens are well-groomed and symmetrically designed. And there are statues everywhere. More than 80 of them vie for your attention—a longhaired French queen, a nymph playing a flute, a stern effigy of writer Claude Baudelaire. It's fanciful and delightful; you could spend hours here and not discover all of its secrets. Particularly popular with families are the pond in which children float wooden boats, the games area, and *pétanque* (French Boules) pitches. ⌚ ***1 hr. Métro: Odéon. RER Luxembourg.***

2 Rue St-Sulpice. Turn down any street on the river side of the gardens and walk a few blocks to place St-Sulpice and its surrounding streets. Welcome to shopping heaven (or window-shopping purgatory). This is where you'll find all the usual designer suspects for your inspection—agnès b., YSL, perfumer Annick Goutal, and more. If you want to stock up for a picnic, pop

Like Les Deux Magots, Café Flore has been a neighborhood institution for decades.

This merry-go-round is one of the many kids' rides in the Luxembourg Gardens.

down to 8 rue du Cherche-Midi to Poilâne bakery for some of the city's best breads and sandwiches to go. Or turn onto rue Bonaparte where Pierre Hermé (at no. 72) makes the city's most delicious macaroons.

3 ★★ **Eglise St-Sulpice.** Filled with paintings by Delacroix, including *Jacob's Fight with the Angel*, this is a wonderful church in which to meditate and take in some gorgeous frescoes. The church has one of the world's largest organs, comprising 6,700 pipes—a national treasure, especially when it's played. ⌚ ***30 min. Rue St Sulpice, 6th. ☎ 01-42-34-59-98. Daily 7:30am–7:30pm.***

4 **La Méditérranée.** A short walk away lies this restaurant filled with murals by 20th-century stage designers Christian Bérard and Marcel Vertés, and paintings by Picasso and Chagall. It was once a haunt of Jackie Kennedy, Picasso, and Cocteau (whose work enlivens the plates and menus). The chef delivers creative interpretations of traditional dishes, including delicious fried fish with fresh spinach salad, and an incredible bouillabaisse, thick with seafood. The prix fixe menu ranges from 28€ to 35€. ***2 place de l'Odéon, 6th. ☎ 01-43-26-02-30. www.la-mediterranee.com. Métro: Odéon. $$$.***

5 **Rue de l'Abbaye.** St-Germain was built around an old abbey that once towered over this street, although there's virtually nothing left of it today. With houses and churches built from brick, the street is charming, particularly rue de Furstenberg—once the abbot's stables, it's now filled with upscale interior design shops.

6 ★ **Musée National Eugène Delacroix.** The Romantic painter Eugène Delacroix lived and worked in this lovely house on rue de Furstenberg from 1857 until his death in 1863. The museum sits on a charming square, and has a romantic garden. Most of his major works are in the Louvre, but the collection here is unusually personal, including an early self-portrait and letters and

A Delacroix fresco at Eglise St-Sulpice.

notes to friends like Baudelaire and George Sand. You can also see his work in the Chapelle des Anges in Eglise St-Sulpice (see bullet 3 on this tour). *1 hr. 6 rue de Furstenberg, 6th. 01-44-41-86-50. www.musee-delacroix.fr. Admission 5€ adults, free children 17 and under and 25 and under from E.U. countries. Wed–Mon 9:30am–5pm. Métro: St-Germain-des-Prés.*

7 ★ Eglise St-Germain-des-Prés. This exquisite little church is the oldest in Paris, and a rarity in France—only a few buildings this old exist in such complete form. It dates to the 6th century, when a Benedictine abbey was founded here, though little remains from that time. Its aged columns still bear their medieval paint in breathtaking detail. You can visit the tomb of the French philosopher René Descartes (1596–1650) in the second chapel. At one time, the abbey was a pantheon for Merovingian kings. During the restoration of the site of their tombs, Chapelle de St-Symphorien, previously unknown Romanesque paintings were discovered. *30 min. 3 place St-Germain-des-Prés, 6th. 01-43-25-41-71. www.eglise-sgp.org. Mon–Sat 8am–7:45pm; Sun 9am–8pm. Métro: St-Germain-des-Prés.*

8 Rue Jacob. This elegant street, with clean lines and classic 19th-century architecture, was once home to such illustrious residents as the author Colette and the composer Richard Wagner. Today it is very posh-bohemian, with charming bookstores and antique shops.

9 Ecole Nationale Supérieure des Beaux-Arts. Turn onto rue Bonaparte and walk toward the river to reach this fine-arts school, where the main attraction is the architecture. The school occupies a 17th-century convent and the 18th-century Hôtel de Chimay. Attending an exhibition (held frequently) will grant you a peek inside. If none are on, just wander down rue Bonaparte, which is lined with lovely small art galleries. *30 min. 14 rue Bonaparte, 6th. 01-47-03-50-00. www.ensba.fr. Courtyard Mon–Fri 9am–5pm; during exhibitions only Tues–Sun 1–7pm. Métro: St-Germain-des-Prés.*

10 L'Institut de France. Turn right along the river and you'll see an elegant domed baroque building, home to five subgovernmental agencies all lumped together as the rather ominously named L'Institut. Here the Académie Française jealously (some would say too zealously) guards the purity of the French language from "Franglais" encroachment (Jacques Cousteau was once a member). Other lesser-known agencies (Sciences, Inscriptions et Belles Lettres, Beaux Arts, and Sciences Morales et Politiques) do . . . whatever it is they do. The brave can arrange for a guided tour (available in English) as most buildings are closed to the public—perhaps not surprisingly, considering that academy members are known as "the Immortals." *15 min. 23 quai de Conti, 6th. 01-44-41-44-41. www.institut-de-france.fr. Admission 4€. Guided tours Sat–Sun (usually 10:30am and 3pm but call ahead to check). Métro: St-Germain-des-Prés.*

One of the holdings at the Musée National Eugène Delacroix.

The Islands

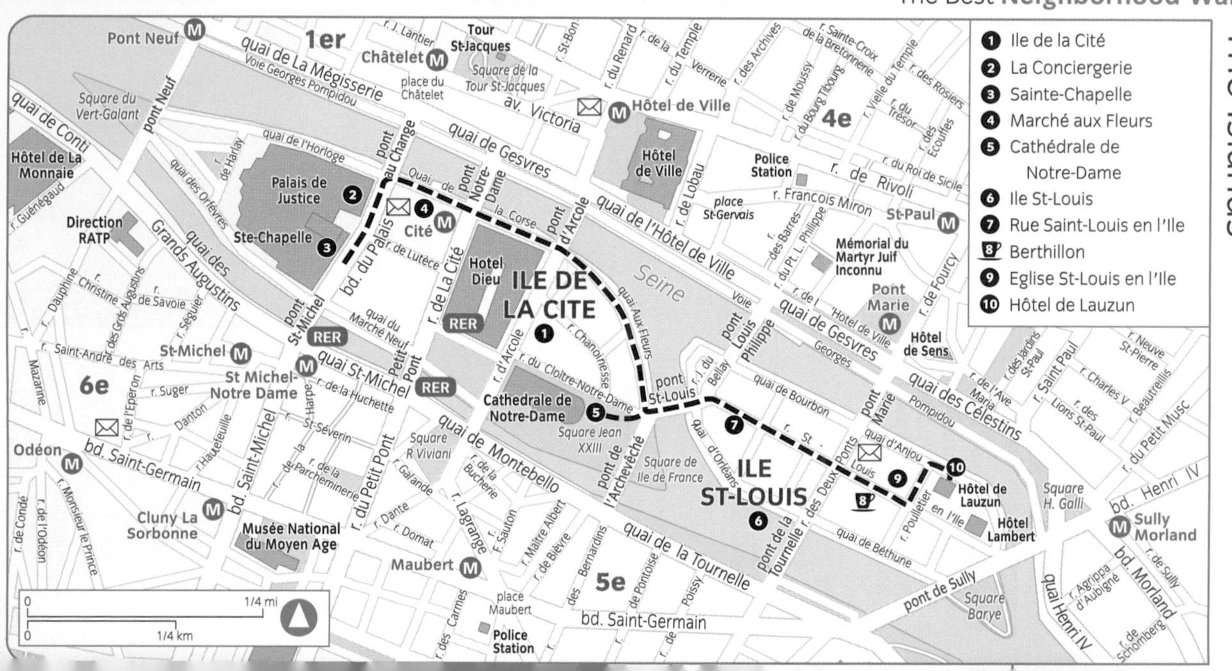
1 Ile de la Cité
2 La Conciergerie
3 Sainte-Chapelle
4 Marché aux Fleurs
5 Cathédrale de Notre-Dame
6 Ile St-Louis
7 Rue Saint-Louis en l'Ile
8 Berthillon
9 Eglise St-Louis en l'Ile
10 Hôtel de Lauzun
1er
4e
5e
6e
ILE DE LA CITE
ILE ST-LOUIS
Seine
Pont Neuf
Châtelet
Tour St-Jacques
Square de la Tour St-Jacques
place du Châtelet
quai de La Mégisserie
Voie Georges Pompidou
Square du Vert-Galant
quai de Conti
Hôtel de La Monnaie
Direction RATP
quai des Grands Augustins
Palais de Justice
Ste-Chapelle
quai de l'Horloge
quai des Orfèvres
pont au Change
pont Notre Dame
pont d'Arcole
quai de Gesvres
av. Victoria
Hôtel de Ville
Police Station
r. de Rivoli
place St-Gervais
St-Paul
Mémorial du Martyr Juif Inconnu
Pont Marie
Hôtel de Sens
quai de l'Hôtel de Ville
Cité
Hotel Dieu
RER
bd. du Palais
quai du Marché Neuf
pont St-Michel
St-Michel
St Michel-Notre Dame
quai St-Michel
Petit Pont
Cathedrale de Notre-Dame
Square Jean XXIII
quai Aux Fleurs
pont St-Louis
pont Louis Philippe
quai de Bourbon
quai d'Orléans
Square de Ile de France
pont de l'Archevêché
quai d'Anjou
quai de Béthune
Hôtel de Lauzun
Hôtel Lambert
quai des Célestins
Square H. Galli
Sully Morland
bd. Henri IV
bd. Morland
quai Henri IV
pont de Sully
Square Barye
pont de la Tournelle
quai de la Tournelle
quai de Montebello
Square R Viviani
Maubert
place Maubert
bd. Saint-Germain
bd. Saint-Michel
Musée National du Moyen Age
Cluny La Sorbonne
Odéon
0
1/4 mi
1/4 km

The Île de la Cité is where it all began, way before the Romans came in 53 B.C., when Paris was a small settlement populated by the Celtic Parisii tribe. Over the next 2,000 years, Paris was expanded by the Romans, Franks, Merovingians, and Capetian kings, but the city's soul remains here, around Notre-Dame cathedral. Across the bridge, Île Saint-Louis (former marshlands) is a coveted residential area filled with glorious 17th-century mansions. This tour takes you through both islands and along some of the loveliest stretches of the Seine. **START: Métro to Cité.**

❶ **Ile de la Cité.** By medieval times, this was a thriving island town with huddles of houses and narrow streets. It was all swept away, however, in the 19th century, by Baron Haussmann, when he evicted some 25,000 people to make way for the large administrative buildings we see today, such as the law courts and police station. Few have written more movingly about its heyday than Victor Hugo, who invited the reader "to observe the fantastic display of lights against the darkness of that gloomy labyrinth of buildings; cast upon it a ray of moonlight, showing the city in glimmering vagueness, with its towers lifting their great heads from that foggy sea." You have only to climb Notre-Dame's towers to see what he's talking about: on a cloudy day, the skies look dramatic and cast eerie light over the island. Linking the Ile de la Cité is the pont Neuf bridge, embellished by a statue of Henri IV. The name means "new bridge"—ironic considering that it's Paris's oldest bridge, dating back to the time of Catherine of Medici in the 16th century.

❷ ★ **La Conciergerie.** This intimidating building, originally a royal medieval palace, was converted into a prison during the Revolution, and became an object of terror to the public at a time when idle accusations could result in spontaneous executions. Marie Antoinette, Danton, and Robespierre all were held here before being guillotined. Today you can see the cells where they were held, and the

Pont des Arts, overlooking the Islands, is a copy of an original 19th-century bridge.

La Conciergerie, with a view toward the pont Neuf, was a palace in the Middle Ages.

rooms where they were tried and condemned. A strange and interesting place. *See p 23, bullet* ❸.

❸ ★ **Sainte-Chapelle.** Tucked away among the huge Conciergerie and the vast law courts of the Palais de Justice, this tiny church is as hard to find as a diamond in a coal mine—but persevere, because it's a precious place, made almost entirely of dazzling stained-glass windows. Unfortunately, it's not undiscovered, and I've found it in the past by following the crowds to a long line of people waiting to get in. *See p 23, bullet* ❸.

❹ **Marché aux Fleurs.** This vivid flower market is a photo opportunity simply crying out for your camera. It must be one of the most photographed places on Earth—and for good reason. On Sunday it's transformed into a bird market, but the standard of living for the animals presented is questionable. 🕘 ***30 min. Place Louis Lépine, quai de la Corse, quai des Fleurs, 4th. Mon–Sat 8am–7:30pm; Sun 8am–7pm. Métro: Cité.***

❺ ★★★ **Cathédrale Notre-Dame.** This world-famous cathedral is more beautiful in person than on film. Climb its towers to see malicious gargoyles and sweeping panoramas of the city. *See p 9, bullet* ❼.

❻ **Ile St-Louis.** Despite its central location, the Île St-Louis still feels like a tranquil backwater, removed, somehow, from the rest of the buzzing city. The 17th-century buildings lining the narrow streets are some of the city's most expensive properties; and many of them have hosted, at one point or another, French literary stars from Racine to Molière. A bourgeois arty crowd still frequents the many art galleries dotted around. It's a lovely place to wander, and so tiny it's almost impossible to get lost.

❼ **Rue St-Louis-en-L'Ile.** The Île St-Louis's central artery is gorgeous, narrow, and lined with restaurants and boutiques selling art, clothes, precious stones, and minerals, food, hats, and jewelry. Hôtel Chenizot, at no. 51, has fantastic carved dragons and bearded fauns on its facade. If you can, go through the door and admire the sculpted facade in the courtyard beyond. A second courtyard also contains craft shops and galleries. The end of the street closest to the Ile de la Cité is a great place to take a photo of Notre-Dame.

8 Berthillon. On Ile St-Louis, even the ice-cream stores are sophisticated. This place proves it, with polite crowds queuing outside for cones to go, and others perched at the tables inside to try the lemon, hazelnut, and mango flavors favored by the locals—the chocolate is especially divine. ***31 rue St-Louis-en-l'Ile, 4th. Métro: Pont Marie. $.***

9 Eglise St-Louis-en-l'Ile. This 17th-century church, overshadowed by its famous neighbor, has wonderful rococo baroque architecture, including a lovely sunburst above the altar. It's not as dramatic as Notre-Dame, but it's more intimate and enchanting. ***20 min. 19 rue St-Louis-en-l'Ile, 4th. ☎ 01-46-34-11-60. Tues–Sun 9am–noon, 3–7pm. Métro: Pont Marie.***

10 ★★ Hôtel Lauzun. This astonishing place, with fantastic drains in the shapes of sea serpents, was the scene of famously long, hazy hashish parties thrown by Baudelaire and Théophile Gautier. Baudelaire wrote *Les Fleurs Du Mal* while living here, although it's hard to see how he could have been so depressed living somewhere so pretty. The building takes its name from a former occupant, the duc de Lauzun. He was a favorite of Louis XIV until he asked for the hand of the king's cousin, the duchess of Montpensier. Louis refused and had Lauzun tossed into the Bastille. Eventually the duchess convinced Louis to release him, and they married secretly and moved here in 1682. ***17 quai d'Anjou. Generally closed to the public, although sometimes there are art exhibits here—check with the tourist office. Métro: Pont Marie.***

It's worth the wait for a glimpse inside Ste-Chapelle's stained glass interior.

The Marais

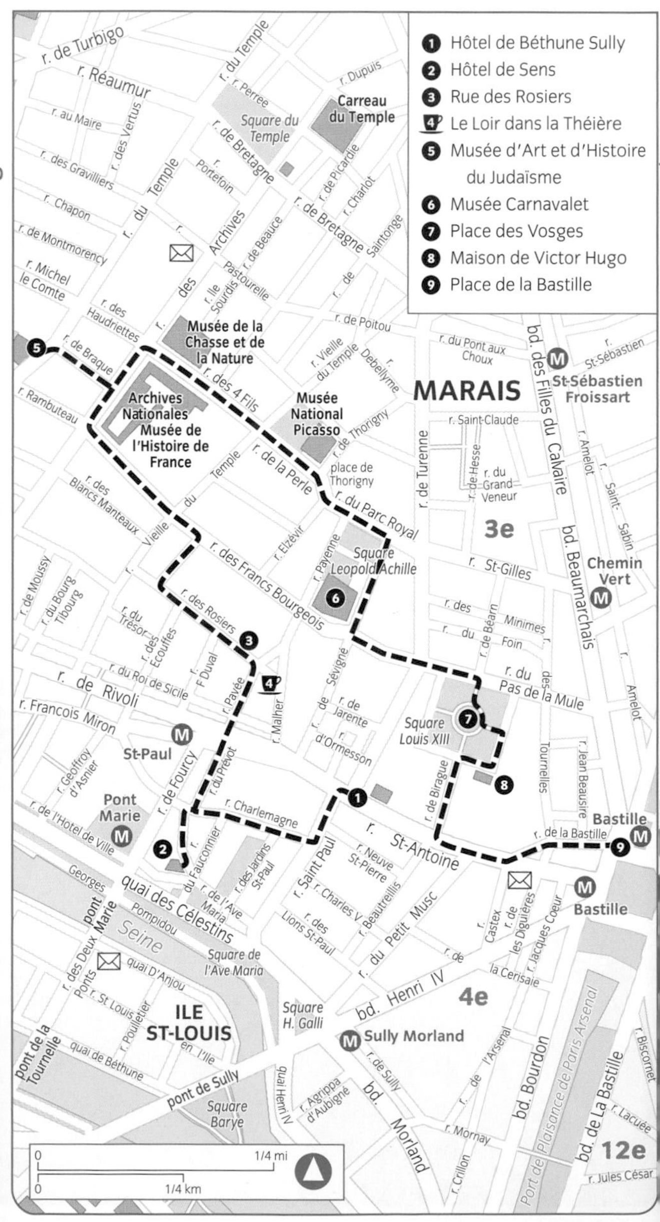
1 Hôtel de Béthune Sully
2 Hôtel de Sens
3 Rue des Rosiers
4 Le Loir dans la Théière
5 Musée d'Art et d'Histoire du Judaïsme
6 Musée Carnavalet
7 Place des Vosges
8 Maison de Victor Hugo
9 Place de la Bastille
MARAIS
3e
4e
12e
ILE ST-LOUIS
Carreau du Temple
Square du Temple
Musée de la Chasse et de la Nature
Archives Nationales Musée de l'Histoire de France
Musée National Picasso
place de Thorigny
Square Leopold Achille
Square Louis XIII
Square de l'Ave Maria
Square H. Galli
Square Barye
Seine
St-Sébastien Froissart
Chemin Vert
St-Paul
Pont Marie
Bastille
Sully Morland
r. de Turbigo
r. Réaumur
r. du Temple
r. de Bretagne
r. des Archives
r. de Rivoli
r. des Francs Bourgeois
r. des Rosiers
r. St-Antoine
r. du Pas de la Mule
r. du Parc Royal
r. de la Perle
r. des 4 Fils
r. Vieille du Temple
r. de Turenne
bd. des Filles du Calvaire
bd. Beaumarchais
r. de Birague
r. de la Bastille
r. Charlemagne
r. Saint Paul
r. du Petit Musc
bd. Henri IV
bd. Bourdon
bd. Morland
bd. de La Bastille
quai des Célestins
quai D'Anjou
quai de Béthune
pont de Sully
pont Marie
pont de la Tournelle
Port de Plaisance de Paris Arsenal
0 1/4 mi
0 1/4 km

When Ile de la Cité became overcrowded, it was here, to what had been swampland, that the wealthy Parisians moved, filling the streets with fashionable mansions called *hôtels.* Over the years it became the center of the city's Jewish community, though today the gay and lesbian community has adopted the area. Its many boutiques and diverse buildings make for excellent shopping and exploring. **START: Métro to St-Paul.**

1 Hôtel de Béthune Sully. Out of the Métro, turn right on rue St-Antoine and walk through the wooden doorway at no. 62. The relief-studded facade of this gracious mansion dazzles just as much as when it was first designed as the residence of the family of Maximilien de Béthune, Duke of Sully, Henri IV's famous minister in 1625. It stands as one of the finest Louis XIII buildings in Paris. Although the building is closed to the public, the charming, walled garden is open during office hours (and on weekends from 9am–6pm). A "secret" door leads to Place des Vosges (see bullet 7, below). *30 min. 62 rue St-Antoine, 4th. http://sully.monuments-nationaux.fr. Métro: St-Paul.*

The Hôtel de Béthune-Sully is one of the finest 17th-century buildings in Paris.

The Hôtel de Sens once housed the archbishops of Sens.

2 Hôtel de Sens. Given the leaded windows and fairy-tale turrets, you might not be surprised to find that this 15th-century mansion has a gloriously ornate courtyard in which you can wander at will most afternoons. Once a private home for archbishops and, later, queens, it now holds a fine arts library, the Bibliothèque Forney. *20 min. 1 rue du Figurier. ☎ 01-42-78-14-60. Courtyard open Tues, Fri–Sat 1:30–7:30pm; Wed–Thu 10am–7:30pm. Métro: St-Paul.*

3 Rue des Rosiers. Perhaps the most colorful and typical street remaining from the time when this was the city's Jewish quarter, rue des Rosiers (Street of the Rosebushes) meanders among the old buildings with nary a rose to be seen. It is jam-packed with falafel cafes and shops, though, and makes a plum spot for a cheap lunch.

4 ★ Le Loir dans la Théière. This bustling cafe serves some of the best homemade cakes in the Marais. There's usually a queue to get a table, but it's worth the wait—if only for the humongous lemon meringue pies (6.50€ a slice). The quiches and salads are good too (from 12€). *3 rue des Rosiers, 4th.* ☎ *01-42-72-90-61. $.*

5 ★ Musée d'Art et d'Histoire du Judaïsme. This museum was created in 1948 to protect the city's Jewish history after the Holocaust. It's a moving place, with excellent Jewish decorative arts from around Europe—German Hanukkah lamps, a wooden sukkah cabin from Austria—and documents related to Jewish history in Europe. There's also a memorial to the Jews who lived in the building in 1939—13 of whom died in concentration camps. *45 min. Hôtel de St-Aignan, 71 rue du Temple, 3rd.* ☎ *01-53-01-86-60. www.mahj.org. Mon–Fri 11am–6pm; Sun 10am–6pm. Admission 6.80€ ages 27 and over; free ages 26 and under. Métro: Rambuteau.*

6 Musée Carnavalet. The Renaissance palace that houses this museum was acquired by Mme. de Carnavalet, but is most associated with the letter-writing Mme. de Sévigné. She moved here in 1677 to be with her daughter and poured out nearly every detail of her life in her letters, virtually ignoring her son. Several salons cover the Revolution, others display furniture from the Louis XIV period to the early 20th century, including a replica of Marcel Proust's cork-lined bedroom. Also on view are the chessmen Louis XVI used to distract himself while waiting to go to the guillotine. *1 hr. 23 rue de Sévigné, 3rd.* ☎ *01-44-59-58-58. www.carnavalet.paris.fr. Tues–Sun 10am–6pm. Free admission. Métro: St-Paul or Chemin Vert.*

7 Place des Vosges. This is Paris's oldest square, and was once its most fashionable; today it's

Cafes and falafel shops line colorful rue de Rosiers.

The meticulously manicured topiary of the Renaissance-era Musée Carnavalet.

arguably its most adorable, with perfect brick-and-stone pavilions rising above covered arcades. Its perfect symmetry might be why so many writers and artists (Descartes, Pascal, Gautier, and Victor Hugo) chose to live here. *See p 14, bullet* ❺.

❽ Maison de Victor Hugo. The writer of *Les Misérables* lived here from 1832 to 1848, and his home has been turned into a small shrine with period rooms dedicated to his life and works. Room 3 is particularly impressive as an oriental-style medley of black, green, and red panels and porcelain based on the Chinese room at Hauteville Fairy in Guernsey; Hugo's mistress, Juliette Drouet, lived there during the couple's exile from France after Napoleon III's coup d'état. It won't take you more than half an hour to go around the rooms, but there are some interesting pieces, such as his inkwell and some of his furniture. The views from the windows also offer an interesting panorama over the pink-brick place des Vosges. ⌚ *30 min. 6 place des Vosges, 4th.* ☎ *01-42-72-10-16. Free admission. Tues–Sun 10am–6pm. Métro: St-Paul or Bastille.*

❾ ★ Place de la Bastille. Nothing but a few stones on Métro line 5 at Bastille station remain of the towered fortress that once stood here and held such prisoners as the "Man in the Iron Mask" and the Marquis de Sade. But it's worth a stop to commemorate the place where the Revolution began on July 14, 1789. *See p 14, bullet* ❻.

Life was hardly miserable for Victor Hugo when he lived in the rooms of what is now the Maison de Victor Hugo.

Montmartre & the Sacré Coeur

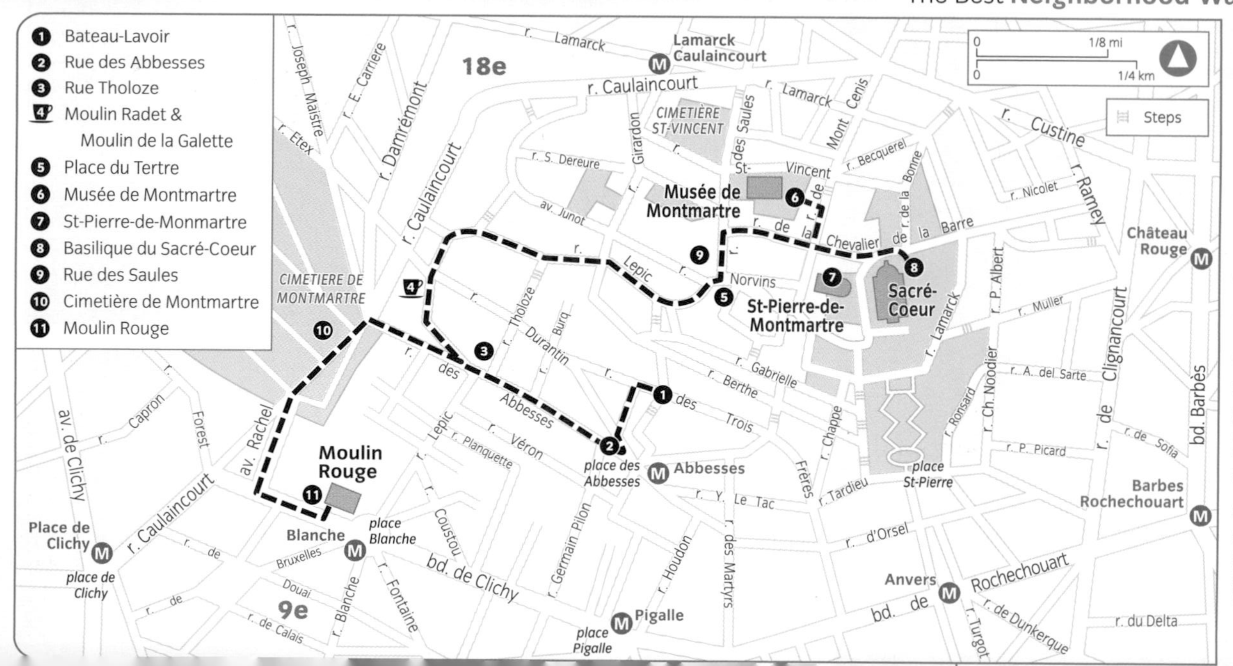

Artsy, graceful, undulating Montmartre does something to your heart. From the moment you see its narrow, tilting houses, still windmills, and steep streets, you're in love. This part of town—known as La Butte, or "the Hill" in the 18th arrondissement—was a rural village separate from Paris until 1860. Then, in the 1880s, Renoir and Toulouse-Lautrec helped to make it a lair of artists—a legacy that lives on today. It all starts at the Abbesses Métro station designed by French architect Hector Guimard—it's one of only two stations in Paris to still have its original Art Nouveau roof (the other is Porte Dauphine, in the 16th). **START: Métro to Abbesses.**

Views are sweeping from the steep streets and open-air staircases of Montmartre.

1 Bateau-Lavoir. From the station, take rue Ravignan to place Emile-Godeau, where you'll find this building, called the "cradle of cubism." While living here (1904–12), Picasso painted *The Third Rose* (of Gertrude Stein) and *Les Demoiselles d'Avignon*. Today it's filled with art studios, with some occasionally open to view. *10 min. 13 place Emile Goudeau. Métro: Abbesses.*

2 Rue des Abbesses. Backtrack to the station, turn right, and head down this street. The unusual rust-red church on the left with the turquoise mosaics is the neo-Gothic St-Jean-de-Montmartre, built early in the 20th century. Peek inside to see its delicately weaving arches. Many excellent cafes and dress shops line this street.

3 Rue Tholoze. Rue des Abbesses soon brings you to this steep, narrow street, with an adorable windmill at the top. Halfway up is Studio 28, which was the city's first proper art-house cinema, named after the year in which it opened. It showed Buñuel's *L'Age d'Or* in 1930, and outraged locals ripped the screen from the wall. Today it still shows arty flicks and has a tiny bar.

4 Moulin Radet & Moulin de la Galette. When you reach the windmill (La Bleute Fin), turn right down rue Lepic, which soon leads you to Moulin Radet. The windmill is a restaurant confusingly called Le Moulin de la Galette after the dance hall that once stood here, inspiring artists like Renoir. The food here is traditionally French and served at moderate prices. *83 rue Lepic.* ☎ *01-46-06-84-77. www.lemoulindelagalette.fr. $$.*

5 Place du Tertre. This old square would be lovely were it not for the tourists—and the artists chasing you around, threatening to draw your caricature. You can buy some very good original paintings

The neighborhood's history comes to life at the Musée de Montmartre.

here, but you'll have to barter to get a reasonable price. The perpetual hubbub can be entertaining—it's charming and awful all at once.

6 Musée de Montmartre. This isn't exactly a must-see, but if you're genuinely curious about the history of this neighborhood, it is an oasis of calm and will give you a good look at its past. There are pictures of 19th-century Montmartre, rural and lined with windmills, along with a few Toulouse-Lautrec posters and the like. *20 min. 12 rue Cortot, 8th. ☎ 01-49-25-89-37. www.museedemontmartre.fr. Admission 8€ ages 27 and over, 4€ ages 12–26, free for children 11 and under. Tues–Sun 11am–6pm. Métro: Abbesses.*

This moulin (windmill), atop rue Tholoze, is the subject of a recently authenticated Van Gogh painting.

7 St-Pierre-de-Montmartre. Follow the winding roads ever upward to this old Benedictine abbey, now a small, early Gothic church. This is one of the city's oldest churches (from 1133), as evidenced by its gradually bending columns. Its simplicity, in the shadow of an architectural giant, is refreshing. *15 min. Rue du Mont-Cenis.*

8 ★★ Basilique du Sacré Coeur. The creamy white domes of this basilica soar high above Paris. Inside is an artistic and archaeological explosion of color and form; out front are sweeping views of the gorgeous city in soft pastels. Unmissable. *See p 17, bullet* 2.

9 Rue des Saules. Head down rue des Saules, pausing to admire the oft-photographed nightclub Au Lapin Agile, which was a favorite hangout of Picasso's back when it was called Cabaret des Assassins. It's still usually crowded with tourists, strange fans of old French music, and those seeking Picasso's muse. Opposite, notice the small patch of vines, a throwback from the days when Montmartre was a winegrowing village separate from Paris. The Clos Montmartre harvest is celebrated annually in October over a very boozy weekend.

⑩ ★★ **Cimetière de Montmartre.** Retrace your steps and follow rue Lepic back down past no. 54, where van Gogh lived with his brother Theo. Turn right onto rue Joseph-de-Maistre, then left onto rue Caulaincourt to this quiet resting place. Get a map from the gatehouse (there's a stack on the desk)—it will help you find the graves of François Truffaut, Stendhal, Degas, and many others who rest here. But don't follow it too closely—it doesn't list most of the graceful statues of exquisitely tragic women draped across tombs, nor does it tell you where the most beautiful trees stand, or where the light dapples through, just so. You'll have to discover those treasures on your own. ⌚ ***1 hr. Access on rue Rachel by stairs from rue Caulaincourt, 18th. ☎ 01-53-42-36-30. Free admission. Mon–Sat 8am–6pm; Sun 9am–6pm (until 5:30pm Mar 16–Nov 5). Métro: Blanche.***

⑪ **Moulin Rouge.** From the cemetery, take avenue Rachel, then turn left onto boulevard de Clichy to place Blanche, where you'll find the bright red windmill we all somehow know so well. Immortalized by Toulouse-Lautrec (and more recently, Nicole Kidman), it hasn't changed much with time. Just as the windmill remains outside, the cancan still goes on inside. It's all just as tawdry and tacky as it was when Lautrec downed one absinthe after another to endure it, but it's the only place in Paris that still performs the real cancan. ***See p 133.***

Views are unrivaled from Sacré Coeur, crowning the highest summit in Paris.

The New Face of Paris

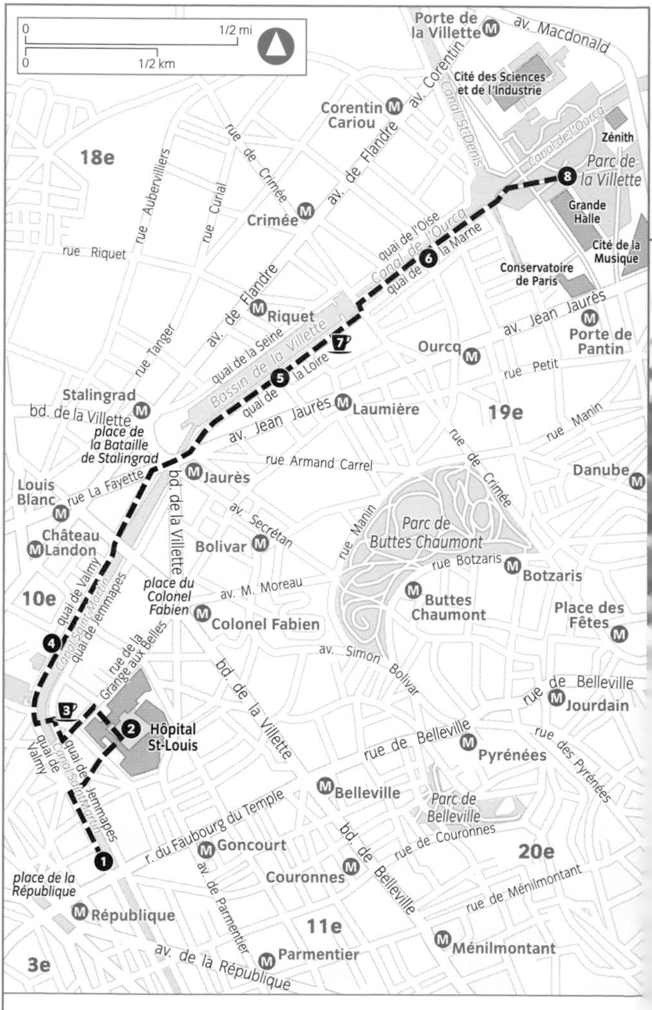

1. Canal St-Martin
2. Hôpital St-Louis
3. L'Hôtel du Nord
4. Quai Valmy shops
5. Bassin de la Villette
6. Canal de l'Ourcq
7. Bar Ourcq
8. Parc de la Villette

This tour will take you past legacies of early 20th-century industrialized Paris—its tree-lined quays, iron footbridges, old factories and warehouses—relics of the days when Piaf lifted the spirits of the nation with her soulful "La Vie en Rose" (1946). Today this area, both scruffy and cosmopolitan, is the most happening district in the city. Its bohemian vibe and new canal-side galleries, cafes, and shops make it a fun place to stroll. In summer the Parc de la Villette—with its science and music museums, IMAX cinema, and open-air film festival—is a hip place to see and be seen. **START: Métro to République.**

1 ★ Canal St-Martin. Walk up rue Faubourg du Temple past ethnic grocers and discount stores and turn left onto quai Valmy. The Canal St-Martin, built between 1805 and 1825, begins at Bastille but hides underground until boulevard Richard Lenoir nearby. This is the prettiest stretch, lined with chestnut trees and iron footbridges that beg to be photographed. In the film *Amélie,* it was here the title character skimmed stones.

At rue Beaurepaire, cross the footbridge and go up avenue Richerand.

2 Hôpital St-Louis. The St-Louis hospital was founded by Henri IV to house plague victims away from the city center. It's built in the same style as Place des Vosges (p 62). Enter, then leave via the left wing, past the chapel. ***Avenue Claude-Vellefaux.***

Turn left onto rue de la Grange aux Belles, where the 1233 Monfauchon gibbet was used to hang victims and leave them to the elements. Then turn right onto quai de Jemmapes.

An iron footbridge on the Canal St-Martin.

The rotunda on Place Stalingrad, at the start of Canal de l'Ourcq.

3 L'Hôtel du Nord. Director Marcel Carné's 1938 film *Hôtel du Nord* made this building, which still has its original facade, famous. Today it's a bistro serving hearty French cuisine with a typical 1930s interior, and a fine address for a spot of lunch. *102 quai de Jemmapes, 10th. ☎ 01-40-40-78-78. $$$.*

Cross back over the Canal onto quai Valmy.

4 ★ Quai Valmy shops. New boutiques keep appearing along this stretch of the canal (and along adjacent rue de Beaurepaire). The best ones are on quai de Valmy: **Dupleks** (no. 83; ☎ 01-42-06-15-08) is a women's clothes shop with a conscience, selling unusual, feminine garments made only from environmentally friendly and fair-trade materials; **Artazart** (also no. 83; ☎ 01-40-40-24-00) is a cutting-edge bookshop stocking glossy publications on fashion, art, and design. Farther up, at no. 93, you'll find girly designer offerings by **Stella Cadente** (☎ 01-42-09-27-00).

5 Bassin de la Villette. At the top of the Canal St-Martin, you reach the circular Barrière de la Villette, one of the few remaining 18th-century tollhouses designed by Nicolas Ledoux. The modernist fountains in front channel your view up the Canal de l'Ourcq past the twin MK2 art-house cinema complex. If you're a film buff, spend a few moments in the MK2's specialized bookshop (quai de la Loire,19th). If you fancy a film in English, look out for VO (*version originale)* written next to the title (providing the original version was in English of course).

Walk northward along the Canal de l'Ourcq.

6 Canal de l'Ourcq. Created in 1813 by Napoleon to provide drinking water and haulage, this stretch is characterized by the retro hue of 1960s and '70s tower blocks. It is separated from the Bassin de la Villette by an unusual 1885 hydraulic lifting bridge.

7 Bar Ourcq. Cheap drinks make this a popular bar with residents, especially on a hot day, when *boules* can be hired at the bar for a game of *pétanque* on the sand in front of the door. Be daring and challenge a local to a game. *68 quai de la Loire, 19th. ☎ 01-42-40-12-26. $.*

A barge on the Canal de l'Ourcq.

8 kids ★★★ Parc de la Villette. The city's former abattoir district is now a vast, retro-futurist park with wide-open lawns and play areas for children. Onsite is also the excellent **Cité des Sciences** (☎ 01-40-05-70-00; www.cite-sciences.fr), with a section entirely dedicated to kids (Cité des Enfants); the **Cité de la Musique** music museum and concert hall (☎ 01-44-84-44-84; www.cite-musique.fr; p 29); the **Zenith concert hall** (www.le-zenith.com), where international bands play; and the Geode 3D-IMAX movie theater, whose silver dome sparkles in the sunlight. In August the park becomes a great outdoor cinema (cinéma en plein-air) with Europe's biggest inflatable screen. *Av. Corentin-Cariou, 19th. ☎ 01-40-03-75-75. www.villette.com. Métro: Porte de la Villette or Porte de Pantin.*

The Géode in the Parc de la Villette is a 3D-IMAX cinema.

Montparnasse

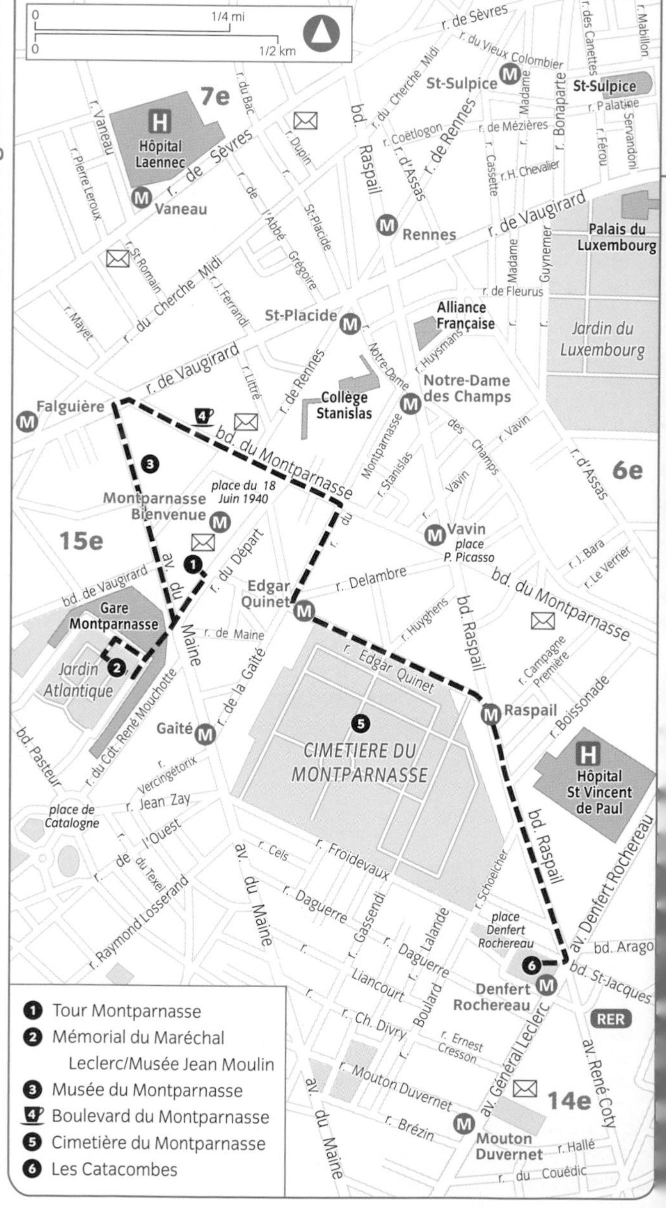

When Montmartre artists did their jobs so well that the neighborhood became popular and rents shot up, they all moved to Montparnasse. Before long Picasso, Léger, and Chagall had joined Man Ray, Henry Miller, and Gertrude Stein on its somewhat forbidding streets. In terms of beauty, the two areas don't compare—concrete is abundant in Montparnasse, but it offers plenty of sights to keep you busy. **START: Métro to Montparnasse-Bienvenue.**

The view of the city's radial streets from the Tour Montparnasse.

1 kids ★ Tour Montparnasse. Completed in 1973 and rising 210m (689 ft.) above the skyline, Paris's most famous innercity skyscraper was denounced by some as "bringing Manhattan to Paris." The city soon outlawed any further structures of this size in the heart of Paris. Today it is frequented for its panoramic viewing platform on the 56th floor, which affords the best views over the whole city including the Eiffel Tower. Feel your ears pop as you go up in the elevator, before splurging on a cocktail or dinner in the touristy **Ciel de Paris** restaurant (☎ 01-40-64-77-64), famed for its views. *33 av. de Maine, 15th. ☎ 01-45-38-52-56. www.tourmontparnasse56.com. Admission 10€ adults, 7€ students ages 16–20, 4.20€ ages 7–15, free for children 6 and under. Apr–Sept daily 9:30am–11:30pm; Oct–Mar Sun–Thurs 9:30am–10:30pm, Fri–Sat & the eve of public holidays 9:30am–11pm. Last lift 30 min. before closing. Métro: Montparnasse-Bienvenüe.*

2 Mémorial du Maréchal Leclerc/Musée Jean Moulin. This rooftop museum fills you in on World War II France and the French

The Tour Montparnasse inspired a law against additional skyscrapers in Paris.

Resistance. The absorbing film archives and the art—which includes posters exhorting residents of occupied France to work in Germany—show what the French endured. 🕘 *1 hr. 23 allée de la 2e DB Jardin Atlantique (above Grandes Lignes of Gare Montparnasse), 15th.* ☎ *01-40-64-39-44. www.ml-leclerc-moulin.paris.fr. Free admission. Tues–Sun 10am–6pm. Métro: Montparnasse-Bienvenue.*

3 Musée du Montparnasse. This small gallery, located down a pretty, cobbled lane, feels like a secret. It used to be an atelier-cum-canteen frequented by Picasso, Modigliani, and other artists. Nowadays it hosts interesting temporary art exhibitions by artists from across the world. *21 av. du Maine, 15th.* ☎ *01-42-22-91-96. www.museedumontparnasse.net. Admission 6€ adults, 5€ students, free for children under 12. Tues–Sun 12:30–7pm. Métro: Montmarnasse or Edgar Quinet.*

4 Boulevard du Montparnasse. Just a block from the train station, this well-traveled street gets busiest at night, when its brasseries and cinemas are aglow, but at any time of day the enticing aromas may lure you to one of its many creperies or cafes. Succumb to a full meal at no.108, **Le Dôme,** now a seafood restaurant, *$$;* or at no.102, **La Coupole,** a fabulous Art Deco brasserie, *$$;* or, a bit farther along, at no. 171, **La Closerie des Lilas,** which includes among its former fans Picasso, Trotsky, Lenin, and Hemingway, *$$$.*

Six million skeletons stretch 910m (2,986 ft.) through underground tunnels in Les Catacombes beneath Paris.

5 ★ Cimetière du Montparnasse. A short walk down boulevard Edgar Quinet, past its many attractive cafes, takes you to this well-known burial ground. For literary types and philosophical sorts, it's a must-see. The graves of Samuel Beckett, Charles Baudelaire, and photographer Man Ray are here, as well as the shared grave of Simone de Beauvoir and Jean-Paul Sartre, usually covered in tiny notes of intellectual affection from fans. *3 bd. Edgar-Quenet, 14th.* ☎ *01-44-10-86-50. There's a map posted to the left of the main gate. Free admission. Mon–Fri 8am–6pm; Sat 8:30am–6pm; Sun 9am–6pm. Métro: Edgar Quinet.*

6 ★★ kids Les Catacombes. Just before the Revolution, Paris's cemeteries were bursting at the seams, spreading disease. To solve the problem, millions of bones were transferred underground into the quarried tunnels that sprawl beneath the Denfert Rochereau district. These Catacombes, 18m underground, can be visited today. It feels incredibly strange seeing miles of neatly stacked bones and skulls; and it's surprisingly rather moving. The sign at the appropriately eerie entrance reads STOP! THIS IS THE EMPIRE OF DEATH! Older kids will love it; younger ones will probably have nightmares. 🕘 *1 hr. 1 place Denfert Rochereau, 14th.* ☎ *01-43-22-47-63. Admission 8€ ages 27 and older, 4 € ages 14–26, free for children 13 and under. Tues–Sun 10am–5pm. Last ticket sold at 4pm. Métro/RER: Denfert-Rochereau.* ●

4 The Best **Shopping**

Shopping Best Bets

Best **Haute Vintage**
★★★ Didier Ludot, *20-24 Galerie de Montpensier, 1st (p 85)*

Best **Flea Market**
Marché aux Puces de St-Ouen, *rue des Rosiers, 94300 Saint Ouen (p 82)*

Best **Contemporary Art**
★ Artcurial, *7 rond-point des Champs-Elysées, 8th (p 82)*

Best **Art Supplies**
★ Viaduc des Arts, *9–147 av. Daumesnil, 12th (p 82)*

Best **Children's Clothing**
★ Bonpoint, *15 rue Royale, 8th (p 83);* and Carabosse, *11 rue de Sevigne, 4th (p 83)*

Best **Toy Store**
Au Nain Bleu, *5 bd. Malesherbes, 8th (p 83)*

Best **Picnic Lunch**
★★★ Poilâne, *8 rue du Cherche-Midi, 6th (p 87)*

Best **Jewelry**
★★ Cartier, *23 place Vendôme, 1st (p 88)*

Best **Kitchenware**
E. Dehillerin, *18 rue Coquilliére, 2nd (p 88)*

Most **High-Minded Concept Store**
★★★ Merci, *111 bd. Beaumarchais, 3rd (p 85)*

Best **English-Language Books & Magazines**
Village Voice Bookshop, *6 rue Princesse, 6th (p 83)*

Best **Shop for Gifts**
★ Baccarat, *11 place de la Madeleine, 8th (p 84)*

Best **Gourmet Food**
★ Fauchon, *26–30 place de la Madeleine, 8th (p 87)*

Best **Porcelain**
★★ Manufacture Nationale de Sèvres, *4 place André Malraux, 1st (p 84)*

Best **Accessories Boudoir**
★★★ Pring, *29 rue Charlot, 3rd (p 86)*

Best **Makeovers**
By Terry, *30 rue La Trémoille, 8th (p 88)*

The Passage Jouffroy, one of the city's 19th-century shopping arcades. Previous page: Le Bon Marché is Paris's oldest department store, from 1852.

Right Bank (8th & 16th–17th)

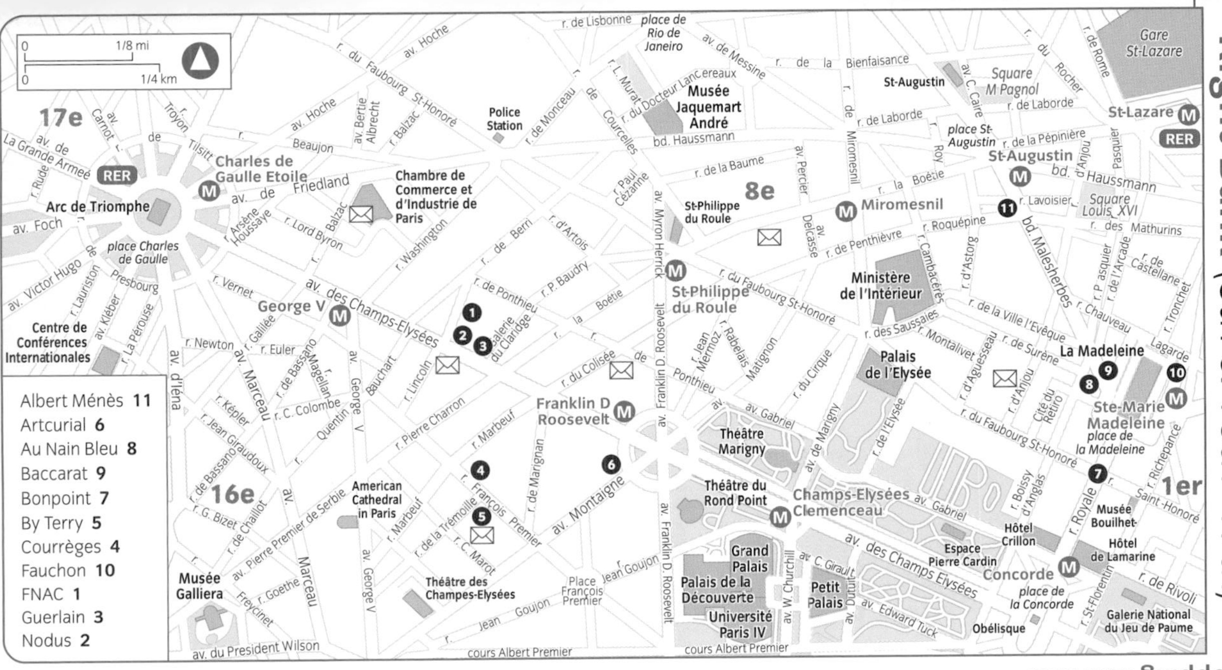

Right Bank (1st–4th & 9th–11th)

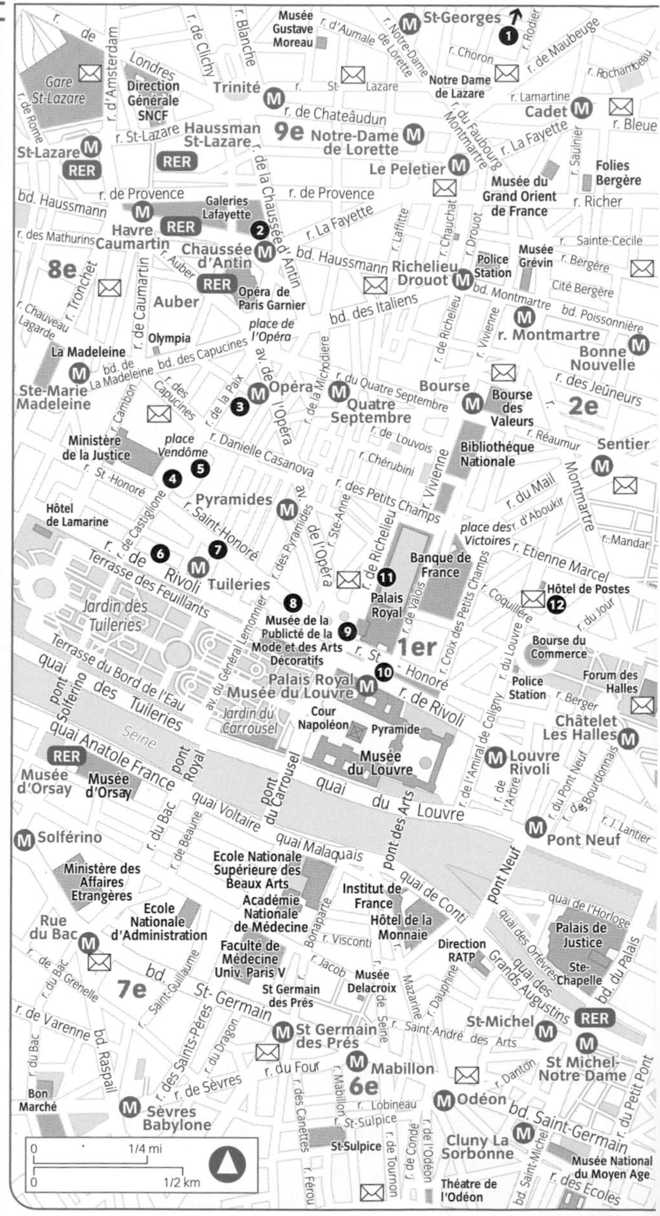

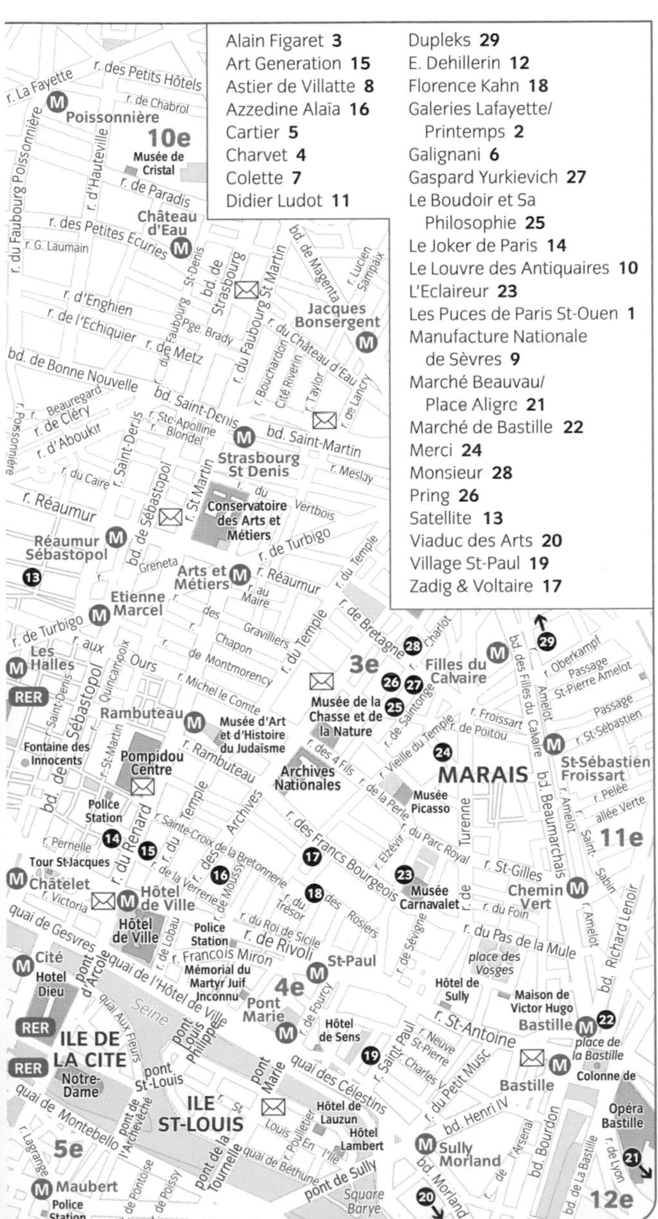
Alain Figaret 3
Art Generation 15
Astier de Villatte 8
Azzedine Alaïa 16
Cartier 5
Charvet 4
Colette 7
Didier Ludot 11
Dupleks 29
E. Dehillerin 12
Florence Kahn 18
Galeries Lafayette/ Printemps 2
Galignani 6
Gaspard Yurkievich 27
Le Boudoir et Sa Philosophie 25
Le Joker de Paris 14
Le Louvre des Antiquaires 10
L'Eclaireur 23
Les Puces de Paris St-Ouen 1
Manufacture Nationale de Sèvres 9
Marché Beauvau/ Place Aligre 21
Marché de Bastille 22
Merci 24
Monsieur 28
Pring 26
Satellite 13
Viaduc des Arts 20
Village St-Paul 19
Zadig & Voltaire 17
10e
3e
4e
5e
11e
12e
MARAIS
ILE DE LA CITE
ILE ST-LOUIS
Poissonnière
Château d'Eau
Jacques Bonsergent
Strasbourg St Denis
Réaumur Sébastopol
Arts et Métiers
Etienne Marcel
Les Halles
Rambuteau
Filles du Calvaire
St-Sébastien Froissart
Chemin Vert
Châtelet
Hôtel de Ville
Cité
St-Paul
Pont Marie
Bastille
Sully Morland
Maubert
Musée de Cristal
Conservatoire des Arts et Métiers
Musée de la Chasse et de la Nature
Musée d'Art et d'Histoire du Judaïsme
Archives Nationales
Pompidou Centre
Fontaine des Innocents
Musée Picasso
Musée Carnavalet
Tour St-Jacques
Mémorial du Martyr Juif Inconnu
Hôtel de Sens
Hôtel de Sully
Maison de Victor Hugo
place des Vosges
place de la Bastille
Colonne de
Opéra Bastille
Hotel Dieu
Notre-Dame
Hôtel de Lauzun
Hôtel Lambert
Square Barye
Police Station
Seine

Left Bank (5th–6th)

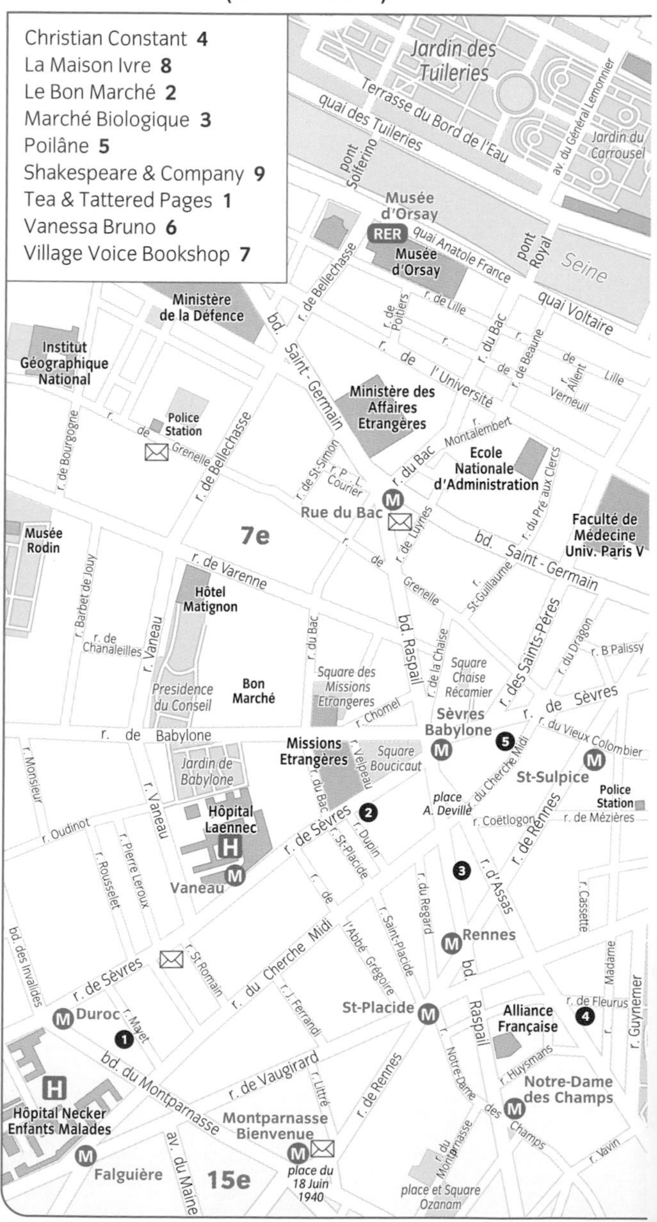

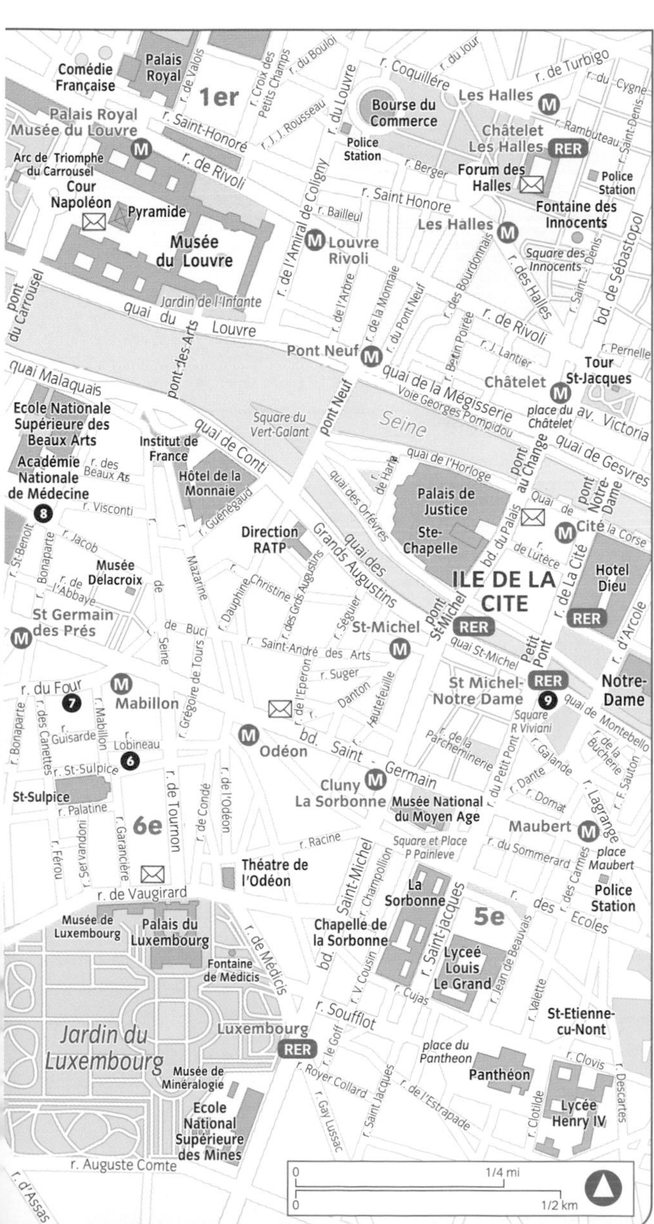
Comédie Française
Palais Royal
1er
Palais Royal Musée du Louvre
Arc de Triomphe du Carrousel
Cour Napoléon
Pyramide
Musée du Louvre
Jardin de l'Infante
Bourse du Commerce
Police Station
Les Halles
Châtelet Les Halles
RER
Forum des Halles
Police Station
Fontaine des Innocents
Square des Innocents
Louvre Rivoli
Pont Neuf
Tour St-Jacques
Châtelet
place du Châtelet
Seine
Square du Vert-Galant
Ecole Nationale Supérieure des Beaux Arts
Institut de France
Académie Nationale de Médecine
Hôtel de la Monnaie
Palais de Justice
Ste-Chapelle
Cité
Hotel Dieu
Direction RATP
Musée Delacroix
ILE DE LA CITE
St Germain des Prés
St-Michel
St Michel-Notre Dame
Notre-Dame
Square R Viviani
Mabillon
Odéon
Cluny La Sorbonne
Musée National du Moyen Age
Maubert
place Maubert
St-Sulpice
6e
Square et Place P Painleve
Théatre de l'Odéon
La Sorbonne
Police Station
5e
Musée de Luxembourg
Palais du Luxembourg
Fontaine de Médicis
Chapelle de la Sorbonne
Lyceé Louis Le Grand
St-Etienne-cu-Nont
Jardin du Luxembourg
Luxembourg
place du Pantheon
Panthéon
Lycée Henry IV
Musée de Minéralogie
Ecole National Supérieure des Mines
r. de Valois
r. Croix des Petits Champs
r. du Bouloi
r. du Jour
r. Coquillère
r. de Turbigo
r. du Cygne
r. Saint-Honoré
r. J. J. Rousseau
r. du Louvre
r. Rambuteau
r. Saint-Denis
r. de Rivoli
r. Berger
r. Saint Honore
r. Bailleul
r. de l'Amiral de Coligny
r. des Bourdonnais
r. des Halles
bd. de Sébastopol
pont du Carrousel
quai du Louvre
pont des Arts
r. de l'Arbre
r. de la Monnaie
r. du Pont Neuf
r. Bertin Poirée
r. de Rivoli
r. J. Lantier
r. Pernelle
quai Malaquais
quai de la Mégisserie
Voie Georges Pompidou
av. Victoria
pont Neuf
quai de Conti
quai de l'Horloge
pont au Change
quai de Gesvres
r. des Beaux Arts
r. de Harlay
quai des Orfèvres
pont Notre-Dame
r. Visconti
r. Guénégaud
Quai de la Corse
r. Jacob
quai des Grands Augustins
bd. du Palais
r. de Lutèce
r. St-Benoit
r. Bonaparte
r. de l'Abbaye
r. de Seine
r. Mazarine
r. Dauphine
r. Christine
r. des Grds Augustins
r. Séguier
pont St-Michel
r. de La Cité
r. d'Arcole
r. de Buci
r. Saint-André des Arts
quai St-Michel
Petit Pont
r. du Four
r. des Canettes
r. Mabillon
r. Grégoire de Tours
r. Suger
r. de l'Eperon
r. Danton
r. Hautefeuille
quai de Montebello
r. Guisarde
r. Lobineau
bd. Saint Germain
r. de la Parcheminerie
r. Galande
r. de la Bucherie
r. St-Sulpice
r. du Petit Pont
r. Dante
r. F. Sauton
r. Palatine
r. de Tournon
r. de Condé
r. de l'Odéon
r. Domat
r. Lagrange
r. Servandoni
r. Garancière
r. Racine
r. du Sommerard
r. Férou
r. de Vaugirard
r. Saint-Michel
r. Champollion
r. des Carmes
r. des Ecoles
r. de Médicis
bd. Saint-Michel
r. Saint-Jacques
r. V. Cousin
r. Jean de Beauvais
r. Valette
r. Cujas
r. Soufflot
r. le Goff
r. Clovis
r. Royer Collard
r. Saint Jacques
r. de l'Estrapade
r. Descartes
r. Gay Lussac
r. Clotilde
r. Auguste Comte
r. d'Assas
0 1/4 mi
0 1/2 km

Paris Shopping **A to Z**

Lighting and other housewares on display at Marché aux Puces de St-Ouen.

Antiques & Collectibles

Le Louvre des Antiquairies PALAIS ROYAL Across from the Louvre, this palace of antiquity holds 250 vendors selling quality antiques from the centuries gone by. Just the place if you seek 30 matching 19th-century Baccarat crystal champagne flutes, or a Sèvres tea set from 1773. Its selection of antique jewelry and clocks absolutely sparkles. *2 place du Palais Royal, 1st. ☎ 01-42-97-27-27. www.louvre-antiquaires.com. MC, V. Métro: Palais Royal. Map p 78.*

Les Puces de Paris St-Ouen NORTH OF MONTMARTRE This massive, permanent site, one of the largest flea markets in Europe, contains many 18th- and 19th-century treasures, but you'll have to haggle for them. Beware of pickpockets. *All around rue des Rosiers in St-Ouen 94300. From the Métro walk north along av. de la Porte de Clignancourt, (18th) then av. Michelet and turn right. ☎ 01-40-12-32-58. www.parispuces.com. MC, V (some stalls cash only). Métro: Porte de Clignancourt. Map p 78.*

Village St-Paul MARAIS This cluster of antiques and art dealers spreads across interlocking courtyards, and sells quality early-20th-century furniture, bric-a-brac, and art. *23–27 rue St-Paul, 4th. www.levillagesaintpaul.com. No phone. MC, V (some boutiques cash only). Métro: St-Paul. Map p 78.*

Art

★ **Artcurial** CHAMPS-ELYSEES This is the best, most prestigious place in Paris for contemporary art, from jewelry to sculpture to tapestry. *Centre d'Art Contemporain, 7 Rond-Point des Champs-Elysées, 8th. ☎ 01-42-99-20-20. www.artcurial.com. MC, V. Métro: Franklin-D.-Roosevelt. Map p 77.*

Art Generation MARAIS In this all-white gallery, contemporary works (photography, paintings, sculpture, video, or drawings) created by up-and-coming artists, are accessible whatever your budget. Prices range from 60€ to 2,800€ for original, cutting-edge art. Who knows, the value of the pieces you buy might be worth much more money one day. *67 rue de la Verrerie, 4th. ☎ 01-53-01-83-88. www.artgeneration.fr. MC, V. Métro: Hôtel de Ville. Map p 78.*

★ **Viaduc des Arts** BASTILLE This complex of 51 boutiques and crafts shops fills the vaulted space beneath a disused 19th-century viaduct with furniture makers, potters, jewelers, and weavers. *9–147 av. Daumesnil, 12th. ☎ 01-44-75-80-66. www.viaducdesarts.fr. Most places accept MC, V. Métro: Bastille or Gare de Lyon. Map p 78.*

Books

Galignani TUILERIES This venerable wood-paneled bookstore,

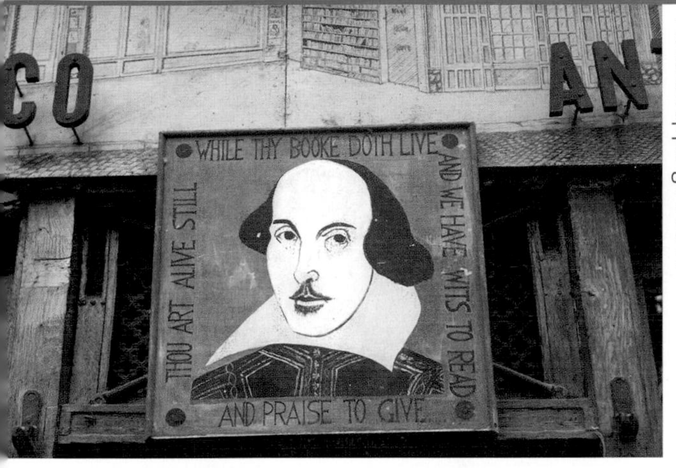

After nearly 100 years in business, Shakespeare & Company is still a hub for English-speaking expats.

established in 1801, sells a vast selection of books in French and English. *224 rue de Rivoli, 1st.* ☎ *01-42-60-76-07. www.galignani.com. MC, V. Métro: Tuileries. Map p 78.*

★★★ Shakespeare & Company LATIN QUARTER The most famous bookstore in Paris was, in its early days, the literary home of Sylvia Beach, Hemingway, Fitzgerald, and Gertrude Stein. Expats still gather here to swap books and catch readings. *37 rue de la Bucherie, 5th.* ☎ *01-43-25-40-93. www.shakespeareco.org. No credit cards. Métro: Maubert-Mutualité. Map p 80.*

★★ Tea and Tattered Pages SAINT-GERMAIN If you fancy a cup of tea while you read, this homely English-language bookshop fits the bill nicely. *24 rue Mayet, 6th.* ☎ *01-40-65-94-35. www.teaandtatteredpages.com. MC, V. Métro: Duroc. Map p 80.*

Village Voice Bookshop LEFT BANK This quirky shop, another hangout of the expat literati, is an excellent source of English-language books and magazines with around 18,000 titles. *6 rue Princesse, 6th.* ☎ *01-46-33-36-47. www.villagevoicebookshop.com. AE, DC, MC, V. Métro: Mabillon. Map p 80.*

Children's Fashion & Toys

Au Nain Bleu MADELEINE The olde-worlde "Bleu Dwarf" has been selling children's toys since 1836. You'll find cuddly teddies, dolls, pirate ships, and wooden puppets. *5 bd. Malesherbes, 8th.* ☎ *01-42-65-20-20. http://boutique.aunainbleu.com. AE, MC, V. Métro: Madeleine. Map p 77.*

★ Bonpoint CONCORDE The clothing here borders on haute couture for kids, so be warned. The diminutive outfits are tailored, traditional, expensive, and irresistible. *15 rue Royale, 8th.* ☎ *01-47-42-52-63. www.bonpoint.com. AE, MC, V. Métro: Concorde. Map p 77.*

Le Joker de Paris MARAIS Fun for adults as well as kids, this tiny boutique is packed to the gills with board games, toy soldiers, card tricks, puzzles, chess sets, and even dart boards. *77 rue de la Verrerie,*

A marionette from Au Nain Bleu.

4th. ☎ 01-42-71-21-25. www.lejokerdeparis.fr. MC, V. Métro: Hôtel de Ville. Map p 78.

China, Crystal & Porcelain

★ **Astier de Villatte** PALAIS ROYAL Napoleon's silversmith used to live here. Nowadays, it sells precious handmade ceramics and knickknacks inspired by 17th- and 18th-century designs. *173 rue St-Honoré, 1st. ☎ 01-42-60-74-13. www.astierdevillatte.com. MC, V. Métro: Palais-Royal. Map p 78.*

★ **Baccarat** MADELEINE Baccarat, one of Europe's best-known purveyors of full-lead crystal, ensures that every pricey piece sparkles. But can your wallet take it? *11 place de la Madeleine, 8th. ☎ 01-42-65-36-26. www.baccarat.com. AE, MC, V. Métro: Madeleine. Map p 77.*

La Maison Ivre ST-GERMAIN-DE-PRES Handmade, country-style pottery fills this adorable shop. There's an emphasis on Provençal and artisanal ceramics. *38 rue Jacob, 6th. ☎ 01-42-60-01-85. www.maison-ivre.com. MC, V. Métro: St-Germain-des-Prés. Map p 80.*

★★ **Manufacture Nationale de Sèvres** PALAIS ROYAL This is where the world-famous porcelain giant Sèvres sells the plates off which kings and presidents dine. *4 place André Malraux, 1st. ☎ 01-47-03-40-20. www.sevresciteceramique.fr. MC, V. Métro: Palais Royal. Map p 78.*

Colette sells music, housewares, and art alongside designer clothing.

Concept and Department Stores

Colette LOUVRE This swank fashion citadel sells men's and women's fashions by some of the city's most promising young talent, including Marni and Lucien Pellat-Finet. It's for sophisticated shoppers with high credit card limits. For a reprieve, try the excellent downstairs water bar. *213 rue St-Honoré, 1st. ☎ 01-55-35-33-90. www.colette.fr. AE, MC, V. Métro: Tuileries or Pyramides. Map p 78.*

Galeries Lafayette/Printemps OPERA Though separate entities, these flagship department stalls, with Art Nouveau cupolas and rooftop views over Paris, stand like twin temples to shopping along the boulevard Haussmann. Galeries Lafayette stocks over 90 designers, and has five fashion and beauty consultants and a sumptuous food gallery (Lafayette Gourmet). Printemps has a vast shoe department (over 200 brands) and six floors of high-street and designer fashion.

Galeries Lafayette: 40 bd. Haussmann, 9th. ☎ 01-42-82-34-56. www.galerieslafayette.com. AE, MC, V. Printemps: 64 bd. Haussmann, 9th. ☎ 01-42-82-50-00. www.printemps.com. AE, MC. Métro for both: Opéra or Chausée d'Antin Lafayette. RER: Auber. Map p 78.

★ **Le Bon Marché** INVALIDES Paris's oldest department store is jammed with luxury boutiques from Dior to Chanel, for both men and women. If you grow weary of the clothes, the Grande Epicerie food hall will dazzle you. ***22–24 rue de Sevres, 7th.*** *☎ 01-44-39-80-00. www.lebonmarche.fr. AE, DC, MC, V. Métro: Sèvres-Babylone. Map p 80.*

★★★ **Merci** MARAIS/BASTILLE This is Paris's first ever charity concept store. Items aren't always secondhand (some clothes, furniture lines, and other items have been created especially for the shop), and prices aren't always low, but there are bargains to be had. The money raised goes to humanitarian organizations. There's also a funky cafe. ***111 bd. Beaumarchais, 3rd.*** *☎ 01-42-77-01-90. MC, V. Métro: St-Sébastien–Froissart. Map p 78.*

Fashion

Alain Figaret OPERA One of France's foremost designers of men's shirts offers a broad range of fabrics and elegant silk ties. ***21 rue de la Paix, 2nd.*** *☎ 01-42-65-04-99. www.alain-figaret.fr. AE, MC, V. Métro: Opéra. Map p 78.*

Sunday Shopping

Most shops close on Sundays, except in the Marais (Métro: St-Paul), at Bercy Village (Métro: Cour St-Emilion), and in the Carousel du Louvre underneath the Louvre Museum, 99 rue de Rivoli (Métro: Palais Royal–Musée du Louvre).

Galeries Lafayette's stained-glass cupola is classified as a historic monument.

Azzedine Alaïa MARAIS Alaïa, known for bringing body consciousness back to French fashion (as if it had ever left), makes sexy clothes for skinny girls. If you can't swing the price tags, try the stock shop around the corner at 18 rue de Verrerie. ***7 rue de Moussy, 4th.*** *☎ 01-42-72-19-19. MC, V. Métro: Hôtel-de-Ville. Map p 78.*

Charvet OPERA Charvet made shirts for fashionable Frenchmen for years before he was discovered by English royalty. (He now makes shirts for the duke of Windsor.) Shop here for crisp designs and lush fabrics for men and women. ***28 place Vendôme, 1st.*** *☎ 01-42-60-30-70. MC, V. Métro: Opéra. Map p 78.*

Courrèges CONCORDE Little white vinyl go-go boots, silver disco purses—here, it's the designer '70s again, dominated by bold colors, plastic, and glitter. ***40 rue François-1er, 8th.*** *☎ 01-53-67-30-00. www.courreges.com. MC, V. Métro: Franklin-D.-Roosevelt. Map p 77.*

★★★ **Didier Ludot** PALAIS-ROYAL Recent and rare vintage haute couture and buyers with an

The proceeds on goods sold at Merci benefit children's charities.

eye for young talent (i.e., sussing out the vintage clothes of the future) make Didier Ludot an exceptional address for women with money to spend on an Audrey Hepburn wardrobe (Chanel, Hermes, and Dior). *20–24 Galerie de Montpensier, Palais Royal, 1st.* ☎ *01-42-96-06-56. MC, V. Métro: Palais Royal–Musée du Louvre. Map p 78.*

Dupleks CANAL ST-MARTIN This small, one-off boutique, offers fun and ethical commerce brands, organic lingerie, and recycled leather bags for women with an eccentric edge. *83 quai de Valmy, 10th.* ☎ *01-42-06-15-08. MC, V. Métro: Jacques Bonsergent. Map p 78.*

Dressing to the Nines

Gaspard Yurkievich MARAIS This tiny store sells end-of-season, ready-to-wear native Parisian design for men and women, plus a range of smoking shoes. Stock turns over regularly, so you just never know what stuff you'll find. *38 rue Charlot, 3rd.* ☎ *01-42-77-42-48. MC, V. Métro: Filles du Calvaire. Map p 78.*

L'Eclaireur MARAIS This swish futuristic looking boutique stocks outfits by cool urban couturiers like Dries Van Noten, Comme des Garçons, and Carpe Diem, as well as exclusive one-offs by lesser known (but talented) designers. Its wild interior is worth seeing even if you don't buy. *40 rue de Sevigné, 3rd.* ☎ *01-48-87-10-22. www.leclaireur.com. MC, V. Métro: St-Paul. Map p 78.*

Nodus CHAMPS ELYSEES This men's shirts specialist has floor to ceiling displays of shirts in every color under the sun, as well as a few accessories, cufflinks, and ties. *74 avenue des Champs Elysées (Claridge mall), 8th.* ☎ *01-43-59-32-53. www.nodus.fr. AE, DC, MC, V. Métro: Georges V. Map p 78.*

★★★ **Pring** MARAIS Amid minimalist art galleries and progressive designer boutiques, this woman's accessories boudoir provides gorgeous, rainbow arrays of neo-Cinderella shoes (with attitude) and matching purses. *29 rue Charlot, 3rd.* ☎ *01-42-72-71-87. www.pringparis.com. Métro: Saint-Sébastien-Froissart. Map p 78.*

Vanessa Bruno SAINT-GERMAIN-DES-PRES Bruno's unique clothes are deeply feminine, without being frilly. Her years in Japan gave her an appreciation for sleek lines and simple, clean fabrics. Great bags, too. *25 rue St-Sulpice, 6th.* ☎ *01-43-54-41-04. www.vanessabruno.com. AE, DC, MC, V. Métro: Odéon. Map p 78.*

Zadig & Voltaire MARAIS This is one of several Z&V branches in Paris. Shelves are stocked with hip clothes in classic styles for men and women. Cotton tops, cashmere sweaters, and faded jeans are big sellers. *42 rue des Francs-Bourgeois, 3rd.* ☎ *01-44-54-00-60. www.zadig-et-voltaire.com. AE, MC, V. Métro: St-Paul or Hôtel-de-Ville. Map p 78.*

Food

Albert Ménès MADELEINE One of Paris's most prestigious small-scale purveyors of foodstuffs prides itself on selling only goods that were picked, processed, and packaged by hand. Everything from sugared almonds to Breton sardines, terrines, jams, pâtés, and more. ***41 bd. Malesherbes, 8th.*** ☎ ***01-42-66-95-63. www.albertmenes.fr. MC, V. Métro: St-Augustin or Madeleine. Map p 77.***

Christian Constant LATIN QUARTER Chocoholics rejoice. The chocolates at this divine shop are made with exotic ingredients and sold by the kilo. ***37 rue d'Assas, 6th.*** ☎ ***01-53-63-15-15. www.christianconstant.com. No credit cards. Métro: St-Placide. Map p 80.***

★ **Fauchon** MADELEINE This fabulous, upscale, megadelicatessen will fill your stomach as fast as it empties your wallet. Must be seen to be believed. ***26–30 place de la Madeleine, 8th.*** ☎ ***01-70-39-38-00. www.fauchon.com. MC, V. Métro: Madeleine. Map p 77.***

★ **Florence Kahn** MARAIS This Jewish bakery, one of the best in the city, has all the heavy cakes, poppy seeds, apples, and cream cheese you could want. ***24 rue des Ecouffes, 4th.*** ☎ ***01-48-87-92-85. http://florence-kahn.fr. No credit cards. Métro: St-Paul. Map p 78.***

★★★ **Poilâne** ST-GERMAIN-DES-PRES One of the city's best-loved bakeries, with irresistible apple tarts, butter cookies, and crusty croissants. Get in line. ***8 rue du Cherche-Midi, 6th.*** ☎ ***01-45-48-42-59. www.poilane.fr. No credit cards. Métro: St-Sulpice. Map p 80.***

Markets

Marché Beauvau/Place Aligre

LEDRU ROLLIN This is one of Paris's cheapest markets—and one of the best (Tues–Sun 7am–2pm). The Marché Beauvau offers uncompromisingly good meat, fish, and cheese too. ***Place Aligre, 12th. Cash only. Métro: Ledru-Rollin. Map p 78.***

Marché Biologique SAINT-GERMAIN This organic market (Sun 9am–3pm) sells top-notch produce, often locally sourced, plus hot soups, crêpes, and oysters to go. ***Bd. Raspail (between rue du Cherche-Midi and rue de Rennes), 6th. Cash only. Métro: Rennes. Map p 78.***

★★ **Marché de Bastille** BASTILLE This huge market (Thurs 7:30am–2:30pm; Sun 7am–3pm) is an excellent source for local cheese, meats, and fresh fish. Street performers usually liven up the shopping experience here. ***Bd. Richard Lenoir, 11th. Cash only. Métro: Bastille. Map p 78.***

Gifts & Jewelry

Le Boudoir et Sa Philosophie

MARAIS This great boudoir-themed

Beneath the covered stalls of the Marché Beauvau on Place Aligre.

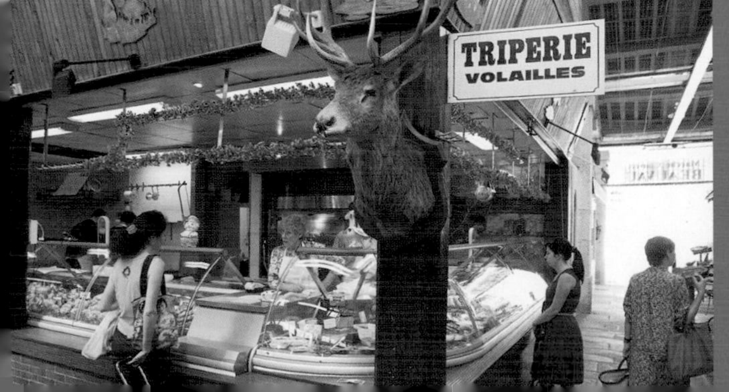

shop sells wonderful little gifts plus eccentricities like portraits of dogs in human clothes. Bring a photo of your own Fido and commission a portrait. *18 rue Charlot, 3rd.* ☎ *01-48-04-89-79. MC, V. Métro: St Sébastien Froissart. Map p 78.*

★★ **Cartier** CONCORDE One of the most famous jewelers in the world, Cartier has glamorous gems to match its sky-high prices. *23 place Vendôme, 1st.* ☎ *01-44-55-32-20. www.cartier.fr. AE, MC, V. Métro: Opéra or Tuileries. Map p 78.*

Monsieur MARAIS You could almost miss this tiny jewelry shop, where creator Nadia Azoug concocts striking, unisex, gold and silver bands and chains. *53 rue Charlot.* ☎ *01-42-71-12-65. www.monsieur-paris.com. MC, V. Métro: Filles du Calvaire. Map p 78.*

★ **Satellite** LES HALLES Stylist Sandrine Dulon uses high-quality stones from Bavaria in intricate earrings, bracelets, and necklaces priced from 10€ to 700€. *10 rue Dussoubs, 2nd (near rue Marie Stuart).* ☎ *01-55-34-95-77. http://satelliteparis.com. AE, MC, V. Métro: Réaumur-Sébastopol. Map p 78.*

All the produce is organic at Marché Biologique in Saint-Germain.

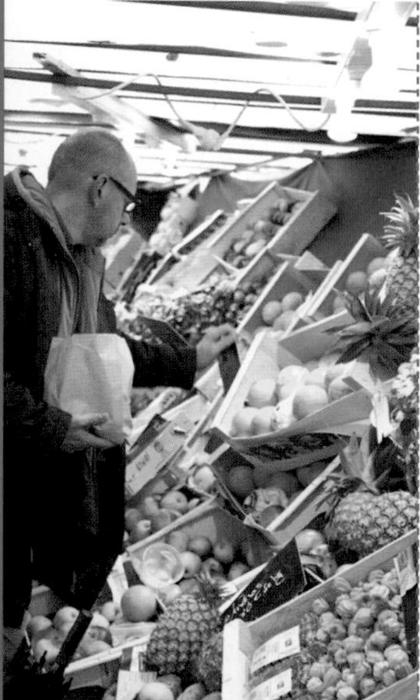

Kitchen

E. Dehillerin LES HALLES This shop has outfitted great chefs for more than a century. Nothing here comes cheap, but a Dehillerin sauté pan is forever. *18 rue Coquillière, 1st.* ☎ *01-42-36-53-13. www.e-dehillerin.fr. MC, V. Métro: Les Halles. Map p 78.*

Perfume & Makeup

By Terry CHAMPS-ELYSEES Founded by former YSL make-up artist Terry de Gunzburg. Capture that catwalk look or create your own style with this shop's *"haute-couleur"* cosmetic ranges. *10 av. Victor Hugo, 16th.* ☎ *01-55-73-00-73. www.byterry.fr. AE, DC, MC, V. Métro: Victor Hugo. Map p 77.*

Guerlain CHAMPS-ELYSEES This adorable Belle Epoque boutique sells the famous French brand's skin cream, perfume, cosmetics, and more. Divine. *68 av. des Champs-Elysées, 8th.* ☎ *01-45-62-52-57. www.guerlain.fr. AE, MC, V. Métro: Franklin-D.-Roosevelt. Map p 77.*

Music & Tickets

FNAC CHAMPS-ELYSEES This supermarket of culture is where you can pick up CDs of French and international artists, DVDs, computer games, and electronic equipment. It's also a convenient place to buy tickets for concerts, plays, sports events, and museums. The branch on the Champs-Elysées stays open until midnight. *74 av. des Champs-Elysées, 8th.* ☎ *08-25-02-00-02. AE, DC, MC, V. Métro: George-V. Map p 77.* ●

5 The Best of the **Outdoors**

Jardin des Tuileries

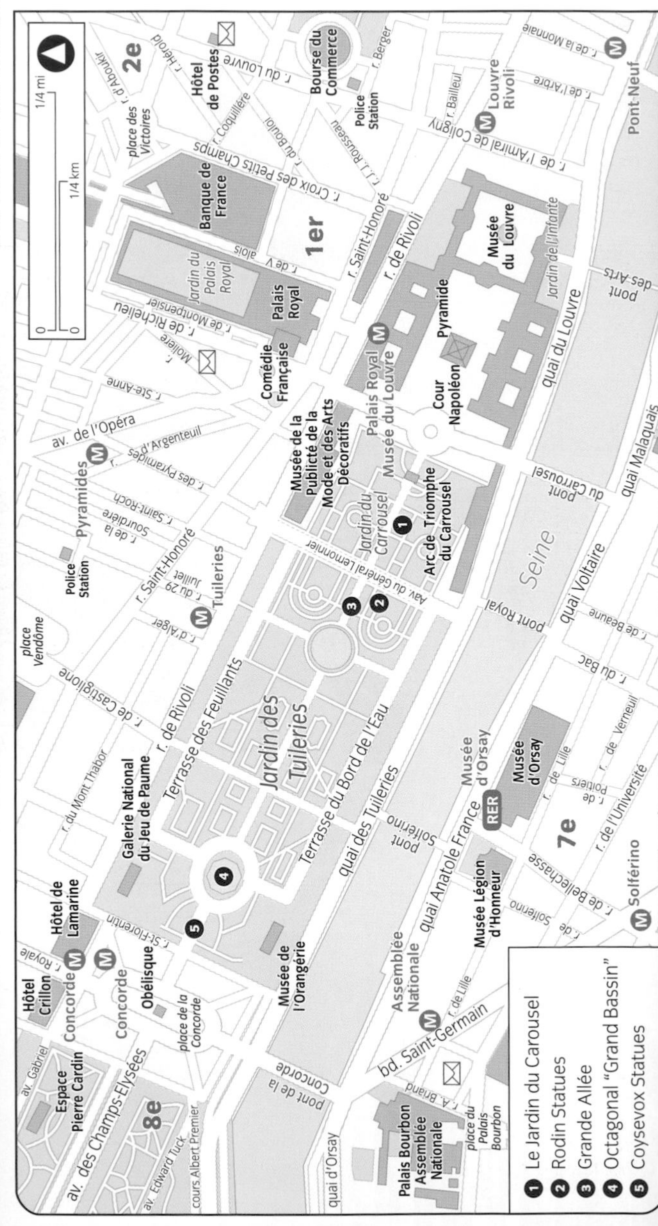

Previous page: Sculpture in the Jardin des Tuileries.

More a statue garden than, as its name implies, a "garden of tiles" (the clay earth here was once used to make roof tiles), the Tuileries stretch from the Louvre all the way down to the place de la Concorde. Under lacy chestnut trees, paths curl and stretch off the dusty main *alleé* (alley), and each seems to hold something to charm you—statues, ice-cream stands, and ponds surrounded by chairs you can move to the water's edge in order to read and contemplate the beauty around you. It's open daily, from 7am to 9pm in summer, and from 7am to 5:45pm in winter. **START: Métro to Tuileries or Concorde.**

1 Le Jardin du Carousel. Start by the glass pyramid and walk past the Arc de Triomphe du Carousel—an elaborate arch ordered by Napoleon in 1806 and copied from the Septimus Severus Arch in Rome—into the eastern edge of the Tuileries, the Carousel gardens. The gold-tipped obelisk you see gleaming at the end (the Luxor Obelisk, a gift from Egypt) marks place de la Concorde. As you walk into the garden you'll pass buskers selling cheap, imported Eiffel Towers—poor copies of the real deal visible beyond the tree tops. But look around you and you'll find beautiful boxed hedges, among which twenty graceful statues by Maillol seemingly play hide and seek.

2 Rodin Statues. Extricate yourself from the crowds and keep walking until you cross avenue du Général-Lemonnier. Four typically graceful statues by Rodin (*The Kiss, Eve, Meditation,* and *The Shadow*) flank the paths. The glimmering, golden statue in the distance at place des Pyramides is *Joan of Arc;* she assembled her army against the British from a spot not far from here on avenue de l'Opéra.

3 Grande Allée. Off to the sides of the Grande Allée, a number of modern statues peek at you from the greenery—Henry Moore's *Figure Couchée* lounges leisurely, and Alberto Giacometti's *Grande Femme II* sits near Jean Dubuffet's dazzling *Le Bel Costume.* Particularly beguiling is *The Welcoming Hands*—a collage of intertwined hands, by Louise Bourgeois.

Eighteen enormous bronzes by Aristide Maillol adorn the Jardin du Carousel.

4 Octagonal "Grand Bassin." The statues surrounding this pond date to the days when this was a royal park fronting the ill-fated Palais Tuileries, which burned to the ground during a battle in 1871. But its layout has changed little since La Nôtre first designed the gardens in the 17th century. The statues are all allegories—of the seasons, of French rivers, of the Nile, and of the Tiber.

5 Coysevox Statues. At the end of the garden, at the gates facing the place de la Concorde, are copies of a set of elaborate statues originally created by Louis XIV's sculptor, Charles-Antoine Coysevox (1640–1720). They depict the gods Mercury and Fame riding winged horses.

Cimetière du Père-Lachaise

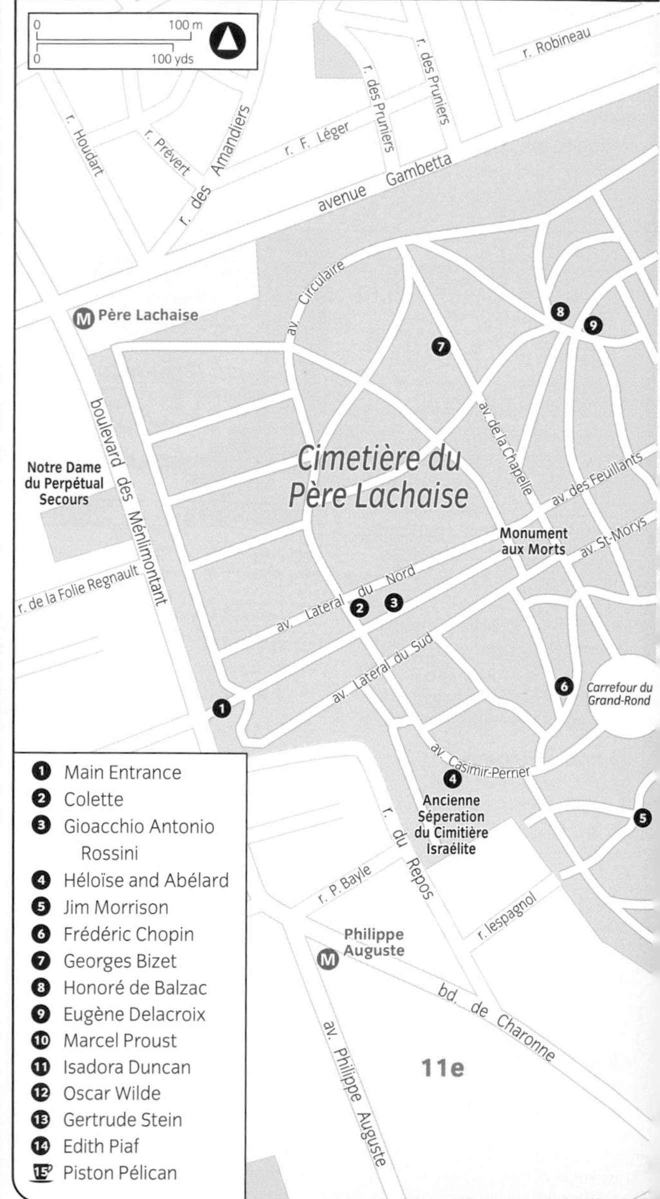

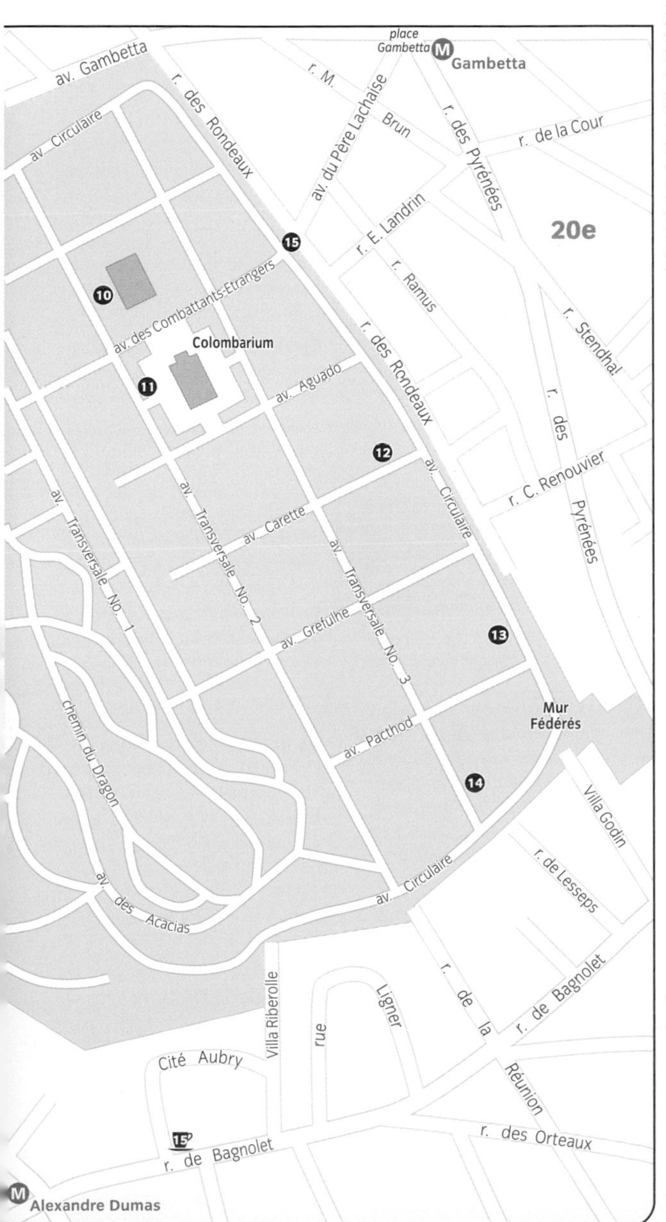
place Gambetta
Gambetta
av. Gambetta
r. M. Brun
av. du Père Lachaise
r. des Pyrénées
r. de la Cour
r. des Rondeaux
av. Circulaire
r. E. Landrin
20e
15
10
av. des Combattants-Etrangers
r. Ramus
r. Stendhal
Colombarium
11
av. Aguado
r. des Rondeaux
r. des Pyrénées
12
av. Circulaire
r. C. Renouvier
av. Transversale No. 1
av. Transversale No. 2
av. Carette
av. Transversale No. 3
av. Grefulhe
13
Mur Fédérés
av. Pacthod
chemin du Dragon
14
Villa Godin
av. Circulaire
r. de Lesseps
av. des Acacias
r. de Bagnolet
Villa Riberolle
rue Ligner
r. de la Réunion
Cité Aubry
r. des Orteaux
15
r. de Bagnolet
Alexandre Dumas

Père-Lachaise became one of the world's most famous cemeteries when Jim Morrison died (or didn't die, as some fans believe) in 1971. Almost immediately Morrison's grave became a site of pilgrimage, and the place filled with tourists, most of whom you can avoid if you stay away from Morrison's grave. Aside from its VIP RIPs, Père-Lachaise is a peaceful place in which to get away from the hubbub of city life. It's also a magnet for art lovers who can admire some of Europe's most intricately sculpted and beautiful 19th-century tombstones. **START: Métro to Philippe-Auguste or Père-Lachaise.**

The city acquired the cemetery in 1804; 19th-century sculpture abounds.

1 Main Entrance. Start by picking up a free map at the gate. *Bd. de Ménilmontant & rue de la Roquette. ☎ 01-40-33-85-89. Free admission. Daily 8:30am (9am Sun and public holidays)–6pm (until 5:30pm in winter). Métro: Philippe-Auguste or Père-Lachaise.*

2 Colette. French writer Sidonie-Gabrielle Colette published 50 novels. Her most famous story, *Gigi,* became a successful Broadway play and film. When she died in 1954, she was given a state funeral but was refused Roman Catholic rites because of her naughty lifestyle. *Section 4.*

3 Gioacchio Antonio Rossini. The Italian musical composer is best known for *The Barber of Seville* and *William Tell,* the overture of which is one of the most famous in the world. His dramatic style led to his nickname among other composers—"Monsieur Crescendo." *Section 4.*

4 Héloïse and Abelard. If you turn right down avenue du Puits, near Colette's grave, you soon come to the oldest inhabitants of the cemetery. These star-crossed medieval lovers were kept apart their entire lives by Héloïse's family. Their passionate love letters to one another were published and have survived the ages. Abelard died first. Local lore maintains that when Héloïse died, a romantic abbess opened Abelard's grave to put Héloïse's body inside, and his corpse opened its arms to embrace his long-lost love. *Section 7.*

5 Jim Morrison. If you must visit Morrison's grave, follow the crowds. The bust that once stood at the head of the tomb was stolen years ago by one of his "fans." The cigarette butts stubbed out on the grave are also courtesy of his "fans." As are the graffiti and the stench of old beer. What a mess! *Section 6.*

6 Frédéric Chopin. Retrace your steps across avenue Casimir-Perier to section 11, where you'll find the appropriately elaborate grave of Chopin marked with a statue of Erato, the muse of music. *Section 11.*

7 Georges Bizet. The bespectacled 19th-century composer of

Carmen was a child prodigy who entered the prestigious Paris Conservatory of Music at age 9. *Section 68.*

8 Honoré de Balzac. The passionate French novelist wrote for up to 15 hours a day, drinking prodigious quantities of coffee to keep him going. His writing was often sloppy and uninspired, but it makes an excellent record of 19th-century Parisian life. *Section 48.*

9 Eugène Delacroix. This dramatic and intensely romantic painter's *Liberty Leading the People* is a lesson in topless inspiration. His bizarre phallic tomb puzzles and vaguely horrifies me each time I see it. *Section 49.*

10 Marcel Proust. The wistful 19th-century novelist died before he could finish editing his famous series of books, *A la Recherche du Temps Perdu (Remembrance of Things Past),* yet he's considered one of the world's great writers. *Section 85.*

11 Isadora Duncan. The tragic death of this marvelous modern dancer is legendary. She favored long, dramatic scarves and convertibles, and one day one of those wrapped around the other and that was the end of Isadora. *Section 87.*

12 Oscar Wilde. The bluntly named avenue des Etrangers Morts pour la France (Avenue of Dead Foreigners, basically) leads you to the fantastical tomb of this gay 19th-century wit and writer. The size of the member with which the artist equipped the statue was quite the buzz in Paris until a vengeful woman knocked it off. *Section 89.*

13 Gertrude Stein. The early-20th-century writer and unlikely artistic muse shares a simple, double-sided tomb with her longtime companion, Alice B. Toklas. *Section 94.*

14 Edith Piaf. Just one more stop before you collapse—the resting place of famed French songbird Edith Piaf, beloved by broken-hearted lovers and gay men everywhere. *Section 97.*

15 Exit. Leave the cemetery at rue de la Réunion, and from there head right down rue de Bagnolet to the Alexandre Dumas Métro station. On the way, shabby-chic bar **Piston Pélican,** 15 rue de Bagnolet, 20th (☎ 01-43-71-15-76; www.piston pelican.com), serves decent coffee and wine to arty crowds.

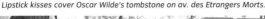

Lipstick kisses cover Oscar Wilde's tombstone on av. des Etrangers Morts.

Exploring the **Bois de Boulogne**

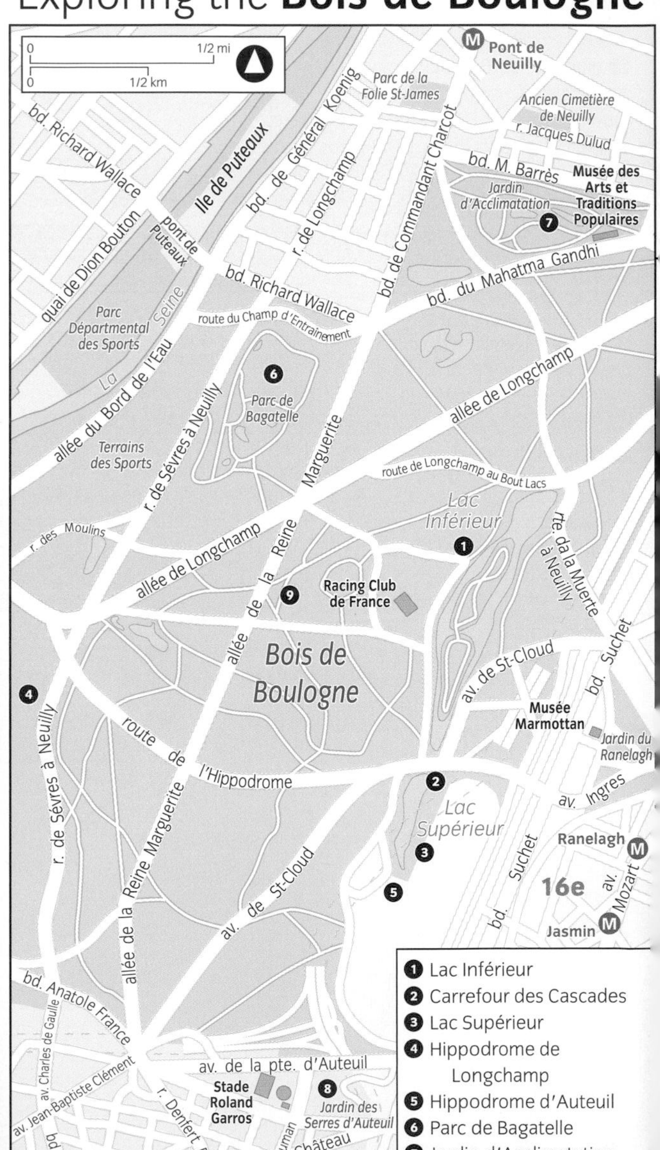

This former forest, once used for royal hunts, has two personalities. By day it's a family park where children gambol and ride ponies, while walkers and cyclists take in the beauty of its lakes and waterfalls. By night it's one of the city's busiest prostitution districts and a hub for other nefarious activities, so make sure you get out before sundown. While you're there, however, you're in for a bucolic day amid birds, woodlands, and 19th-century tropical greenhouses. Between May and September, you can even take in classical theater (in English and French), among the sweet-scented roses of the Jardin de Shakespeare. **START: RER to avenue Foch.**

❶ Lac Inférieur. Most easily accessed by way of avenue Foch, This unfairly named lake (it's the larger of the two) has two picturesque islands connected by fanciful footbridges. You can rent a boat and paddle across to the islands' cafes and restaurants. On a hot summer day, it's also a perfect spot for a picnic.

❷ Carrefour des Cascades. The scenic walkway between the upper and lower lakes is an attraction in itself, with willows dipping their branches languorously in the water, and a handsome, man-made waterfall creating a gorgeous backdrop. You can even walk under the waterfall.

❸ Lac Supérieur. The smaller of the two lakes has more of everything you find on the larger lake, with lots of boats to paddle and several restaurants and cafes dotted about.

❹ Hippodrome de Longchamp. If your euros are burning a hole in your pocket, head to the southern end of the park, where two horse-racing courses—the excellent Hippodrome de Longchamp and the smaller Hippodrome d'Auteuil (see next stop)—offer galloping action. The Grand Prix held at Longchamp each June is a major derby and gets the ladies out to the track in their finest hats. *Route des Tribunes, 16th.* ☎ *01-44-30-75-00. www.france-galop.com. Métro:*

Bois de Boulogne is known as the green lung of the French capital.

Bois de Boulogne: Practical Matters

Bois de Boulogne is open daily from dawn to dusk. Because it's such a large park, there are several entrances and several public transportation options. Nearby Métro stops include Les Sablons (north, on av. Charles de Gaulle), Porte Maillot (northeast, on av. de la Grande Armée), Porte Dauphine (northeast, on av. Foch), or Porte d'Auteuil (southeast, on av. de la Porte d'Auteuil). Take the RER to avenue Foch or avenue Henri Martin. In the park are numerous cafes and restaurants. A miniature train runs to the Jardin d'Acclimatation from Porte Maillot—a fun touch for kids. You won't be able to do the whole of the Bois in one day, but to see a maximum of sites, bikes can be hired near the Jardin d'Acclimatation and the Lac Inférieur. They cost around 10€ for half a day and there are plenty of cycle paths to follow.

Porte Maillot then bus 244 to Carrefour de Longchamp.

❺ **Hippodrome d'Auteuil.** This racetrack, the smaller of the two in Bois de Boulogne, is known for its heart-pounding steeplechases and obstacle courses. *Route d'Auteuil aux Lacs, 16th.* ☎ *01-40-71-47-47. www.france-galop.com. Métro: Porte d' Auteuil-Hippodrome.*

❻ **Parc de Bagatelle.** This romantic 18th-century park-within-a-park in the northwest of Bois de Boulogne is a riot of colorful tulips in spring, and the rose garden blooms spectacularly by late May. A sequence of little bridges, grottoes, and water features also make it one of Paris's most popular trysting spots. ☎ *01-40-67-97-00. Métro: Porte d'Auteuil or Jasmin.*

❼ ★★ **kids Jardin d'Acclimatation.** Those with small children may want to head straight to this amusement park on the north end of Bois de Boulogne, which boasts colorful rides, a small zoo, and a kid-size train. *See p 29, bullet* ❻.

❽ ★★ **Jardin des Serres d'Auteuil.** These elegant glass and iron greenhouses (built in 1898 and strewn among beautiful landscaped English and Japanese gardens) are a botanist's dream, with rows of tropical plants each bigger and more colorful than the next. *1 av. Gorden Bennet, 16th.* ☎ *01-40-71-74-00. Métro: Porte d'Auteuil.*

❾ ★★ **Jardin de Shakespeare.** This has to be one of the most beautiful open-air theaters in the world—a lawn encircled by bright, buzzing flowerbeds and draping trees. Every summer it becomes the idyllic stage for Shakespeare and classical French theatre productions. ☎ *01-40-19-95-33. http://jardinshakespeare.fr. In the Jardin Pré-Catelan. Métro: Porte de la Muette.* ●

6 The Best Dining

Dining Best Bets

Best **for Perfect Soufflés**
★ La Cigalle-Récamier $$$$$ *4 rue Récamier, 7th (p 110)*

Best **for High Teas**
★ Angélina $$ *226 rue de Rivoli, 1st (p 106)*

Best **for Kids**
★ Breakfast in America $ *17 rue des Ecoles, 5th (p 108)*

Best **Cheap Meal in 19th-Century Surroundings**
★ Chartier $ *7 rue du Faubourg Montmartre, 9th (p 108)*

Best **Comfort Food**
★★ Astier *$$$$ 44 rue Jean-Pierre Timbaud, 11th (p 106)*

Best **Vegetarian**
★★ Le Potager du Marais $$ *22 rue Rambuteau, 3rd (p 111)*

Best **Seafood**
★ Les Fables de la Fontaine $$$$ *131 rue St-Dominique, 7th (p 109)*

Best **Rabbit**
★★★ Monsieur Lapin (Chez Franck Enée) $$$$ *11 rue Raymond Losserand, 14th (p 112)*

Best **Gourmet Asian**
Shangri-La $$$$$ *10 avenue d'Iéna, 16th (p 112)*

Best **for Food Critics**
★★★ Le Grand Véfour $$$$$ *17 rue de Beaujolais, 2nd (p 110)*

Best **Home-Style Cooking**
★ Aux Lyonnais $$ *32 rue St-Marc, 2nd (p 107)*

Best **Romantic Meal**
Le Restaurant $$$$$ *Inside L'Hôtel, 13 rue des Beaux-Arts, 6th (p 111)*

Best **Cheap Lunch**
Higuma $ *32bis rue Sainte Anne, 2nd (p 109)*

Best **Open-Air Summer Meal**
Le Lasserre $$$$$ *17 av. Franklin Roosevelt, 8th (p 110)*

Best **Celebrity-Chef Restaurant**
★★★ Chez Jean-François Piège $$$$$ *In the Hôtel Thoumieux, 79 rue Sainte Dominique, 7th (p 111)*

Best **Trendy Pizzas**
★★ Pink Flamingo $ *67 rue Bichat, 10th (p 112)*

Best **Green & Gourmet**
★★★ L'Arpège $$$$$ *84 rue Varenne, 7th (p 110)*

Previous page: A mural at Le Grand Véfour.
Kids are always welcome at the Pink Flamingo pizza parlor.

Right Bank (8th & 16th–17th)

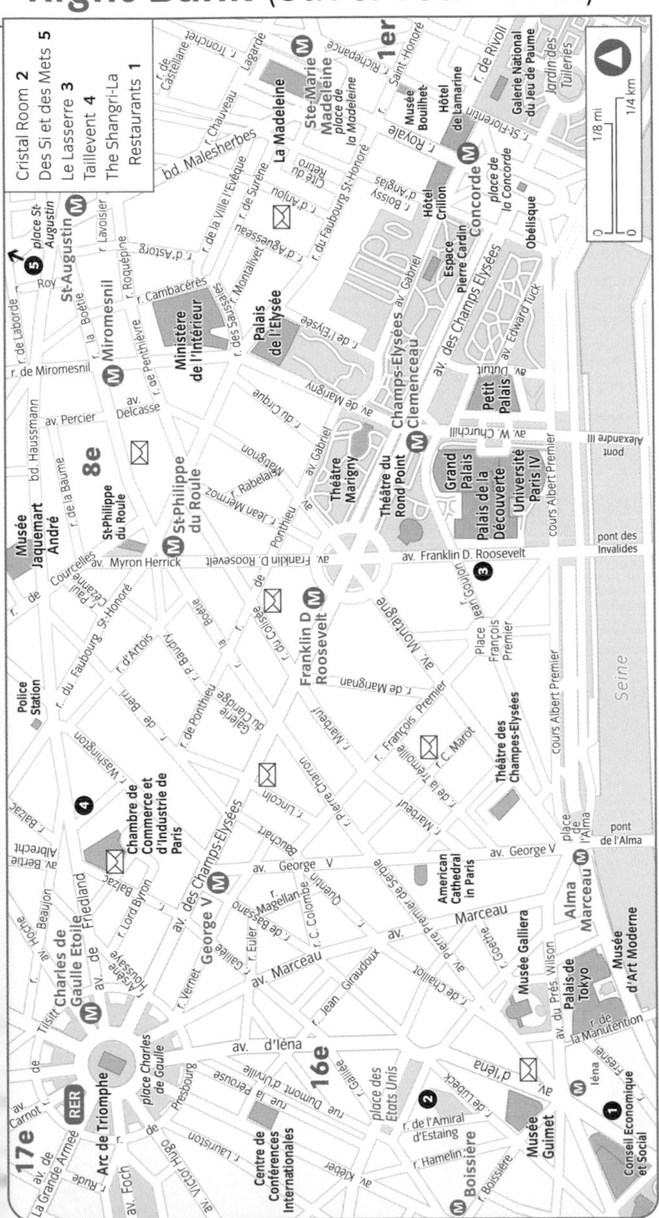

Right Bank (1st–4th & 9th–11th)

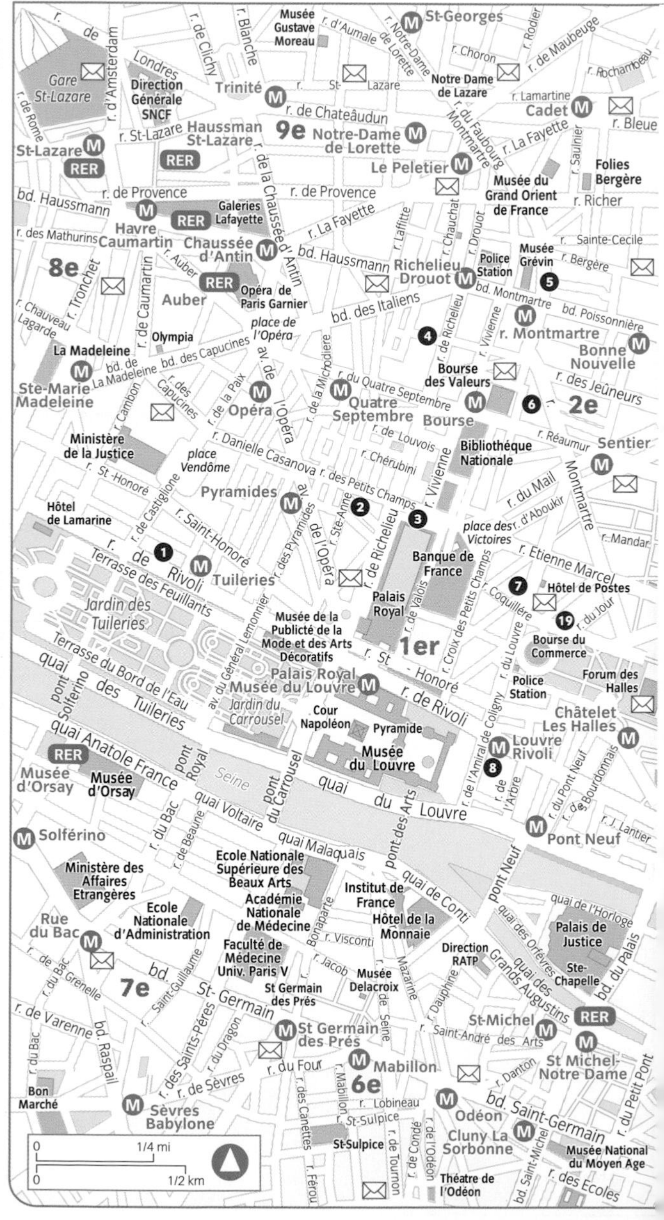

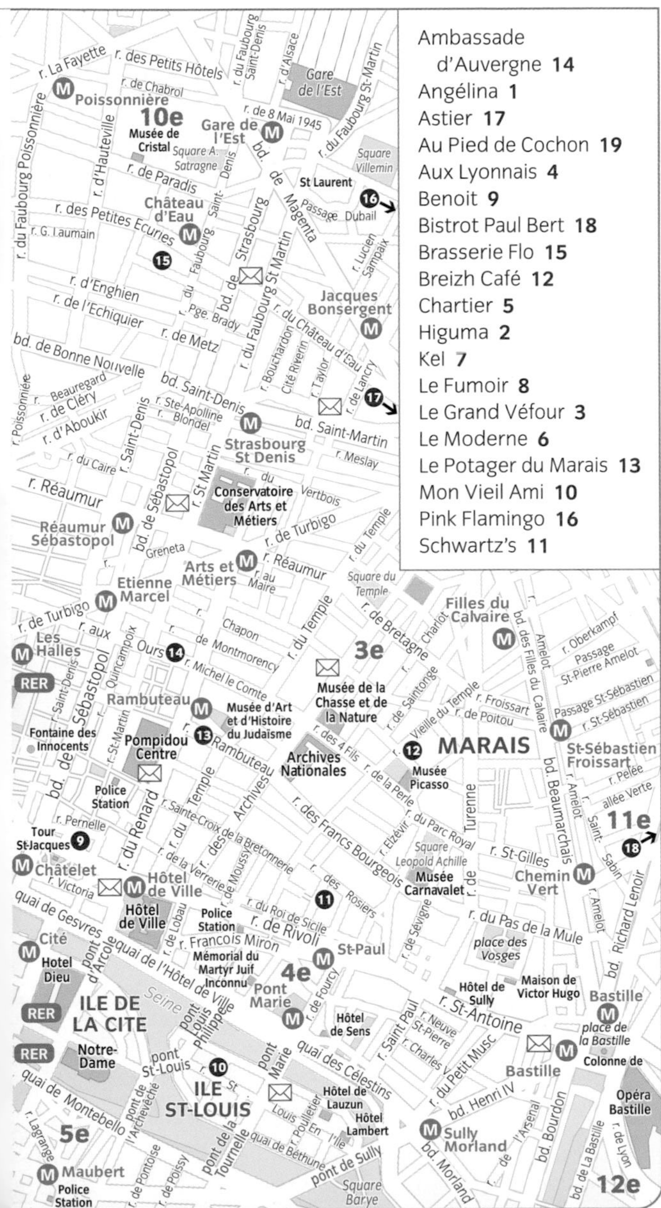
Ambassade d'Auvergne 14
Angélina 1
Astier 17
Au Pied de Cochon 19
Aux Lyonnais 4
Benoit 9
Bistrot Paul Bert 18
Brasserie Flo 15
Breizh Café 12
Chartier 5
Higuma 2
Kel 7
Le Fumoir 8
Le Grand Véfour 3
Le Moderne 6
Le Potager du Marais 13
Mon Vieil Ami 10
Pink Flamingo 16
Schwartz's 11
10e
3e
4e
5e
11e
12e
MARAIS
ILE DE LA CITE
ILE ST-LOUIS
Seine
Gare de l'Est
Poissonnière
Château d'Eau
Jacques Bonsergent
Strasbourg St Denis
Réaumur Sébastopol
Arts et Métiers
Etienne Marcel
Les Halles
Rambuteau
Filles du Calvaire
St-Sébastien Froissart
Chemin Vert
Châtelet
Hôtel de Ville
Cité
St-Paul
Pont Marie
Bastille
Sully Morland
Maubert
Musée de Cristal
Conservatoire des Arts et Métiers
Musée de la Chasse et de la Nature
Musée d'Art et d'Histoire du Judaïsme
Pompidou Centre
Archives Nationales
Musée Picasso
Musée Carnavalet
place des Vosges
Maison de Victor Hugo
Hôtel de Sully
Hôtel de Sens
Hôtel de Lauzun
Hôtel Lambert
Mémorial du Martyr Juif Inconnu
Notre-Dame
Hotel Dieu
Tour St-Jacques
Fontaine des Innocents
Police Station
Opéra Bastille
Colonne de
place de la Bastille
Square Villemin
Square du Temple
Square Leopold Achille
Square Barye
Square A. Satragne

Left Bank (5th–6th)

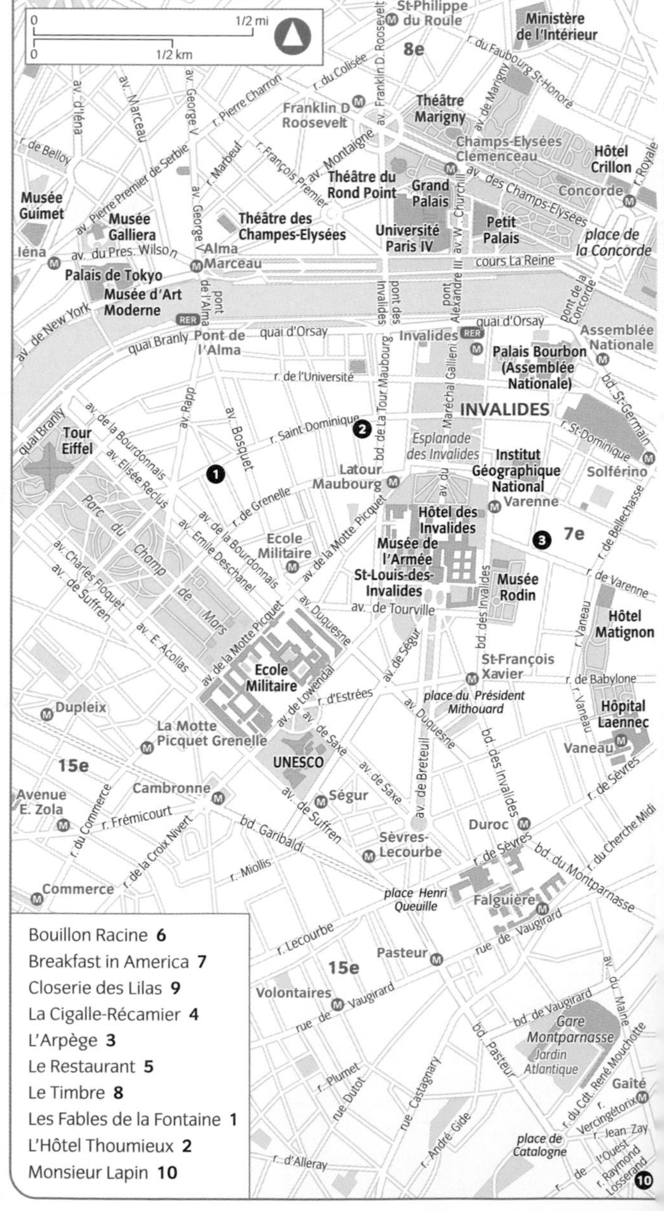

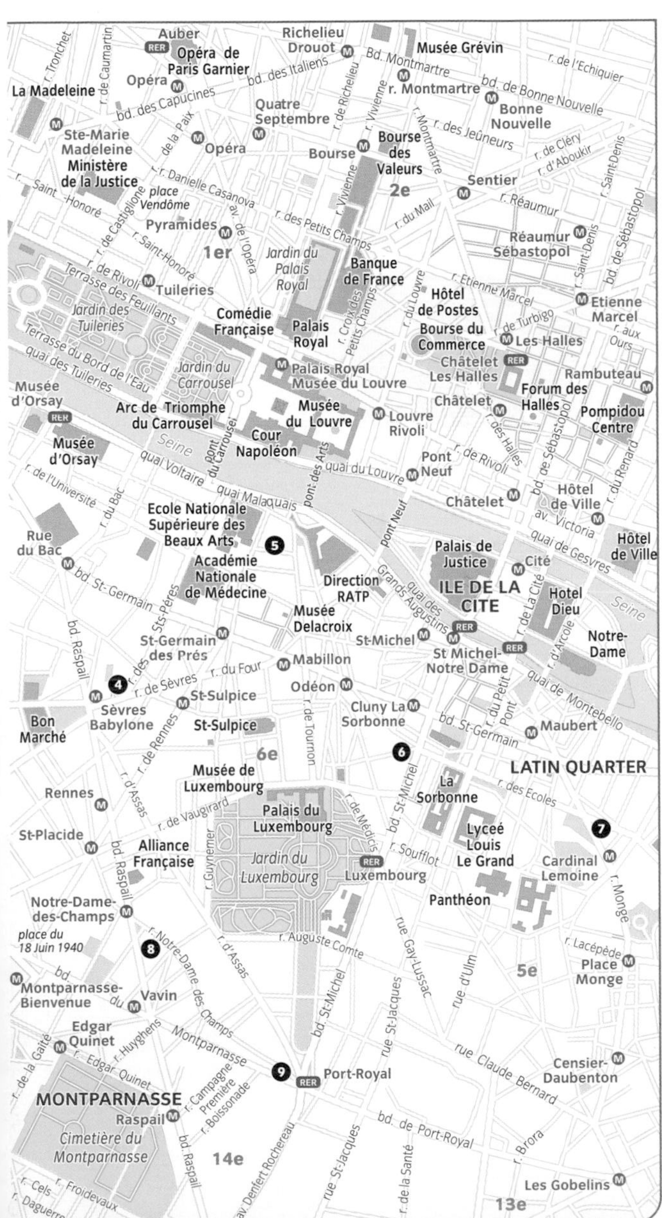
Auber
RER
Opéra de Paris Garnier
Opéra
La Madeleine
r. Tronchet
r. de Caumartin
bd. des Capucines
bd. des Italiens
Richelieu Drouot
Bd. Montmartre
Musée Grévin
r. de l'Echiquier
r. Montmartre
bd. de Bonne Nouvelle
Bonne Nouvelle
Quatre Septembre
r. de Richelieu
r. Vivienne
r. Montmartre
r. des Jeûneurs
Ste-Marie Madeleine
Ministère de la Justice
de la Paix
Opéra
Bourse
Bourse des Valeurs
r. de Cléry
r. d'Aboukir
r. Saint-Denis
r. Danielle Casanova
place Vendôme
r. Saint-Honoré
Sentier
2e
r. Réaumur
r. du Mail
r. Vivienne
r. des Petits Champs
av. de l'Opéra
r. de Castiglione
Pyramides
1er
r. Saint-Honoré
Réaumur Sébastopol
bd. de Sébastopol
r. Saint-Denis
Jardin du Palais Royal
Banque de France
r. de Rivoli
Terrasse des Feuillants
Tuileries
Jardin des Tuileries
r. Etienne Marcel
Hôtel de Postes
Etienne Marcel
r. du Louvre
r. Croix des Petits Champs
Comédie Française
Palais Royal
Bourse du Commerce
r. de Turbigo
Les Halles
r. aux Ours
Terrasse du Bord de l'Eau
quai des Tuileries
Jardin du Carrousel
Palais Royal Musée du Louvre
Châtelet Les Halles
RER
Rambuteau
Musée d'Orsay
RER
Arc de Triomphe du Carrousel
Musée du Louvre
Louvre Rivoli
Châtelet
Forum des Halles
Pompidou Centre
Cour Napoléon
Musée d'Orsay
Seine
pont du Carrousel
quai Voltaire
pont des Arts
quai du Louvre
Pont Neuf
r. de Rivoli
r. des Halles
bd. de Sébastopol
r. du Renard
r. de l'Université
r. du Bac
quai Malaquais
Châtelet
Hôtel de Ville
av. Victoria
Ecole Nationale Supérieure des Beaux Arts
Rue du Bac
5
pont Neuf
Palais de Justice
quai de Gesvres
Hôtel de Ville
Académie Nationale de Médecine
Direction RATP
Cité
bd. St-Germain
r. des Sts-Pères
Grands Augustins
quai des
ILE DE LA CITE
Hotel Dieu
Seine
Musée Delacroix
bd. Raspail
St-Germain des Prés
St-Michel
RER
St Michel-Notre Dame
RER
r. de la Cité
r. d'Arcole
Notre-Dame
r. des
r. du Four
Mabillon
4
r. de Sèvres
St-Sulpice
Odéon
quai de Montebello
Sèvres Babylone
r. de Tournon
Cluny La Sorbonne
r. du Petit Pont
Bon Marché
St-Sulpice
bd. St-Germain
Maubert
r. de Rennes
6e
6
LATIN QUARTER
Musée de Luxembourg
bd. St-Michel
La Sorbonne
r. des Ecoles
Rennes
r. d'Assas
r. de Vaugirard
Palais du Luxembourg
r. de Médicis
7
St-Placide
Alliance Française
Lycée Louis Le Grand
bd. Raspail
r. Guynemer
Jardin du Luxembourg
RER
Luxembourg
r. Soufflot
Cardinal Lemoine
r. Monge
Notre-Dame-des-Champs
Panthéon
place du 18 Juin 1940
8
r. Notre-Dame des Champs
r. d'Assas
r. Auguste Comte
rue Gay-Lussac
r. Lacépède
Place Monge
bd. du Montparnasse
Montparnasse-Bienvenue
Vavin
bd. St-Michel
rue St-Jacques
rue d'Ulm
5e
Edgar Quinet
r. Huyghens
r. de la Gaîté
r. Edgar Quinet
r. Campagne Première
r. Boissonade
9
RER
Port-Royal
rue Claude Bernard
Censier-Daubenton
MONTPARNASSE
Raspail
Cimetière du Montparnasse
bd. Raspail
14e
av. Denfert Rochereau
rue St-Jacques
bd. de Port-Royal
r. de la Santé
r. Broca
Les Gobelins
13e
r. Cels
r. Froidevaux
r. Daguerre

Paris Dining A to Z

You're likely to catch fashion-industry mavens taking tea at Angélina.

★★ **Ambassade d'Auvergne** BEAUBOURG *TRADITIONAL FRENCH* The Auvergne is a region known for its hearty cuisine. And this friendly restaurant does it justice with large tasty portions of specials like lentils cooked in goose fat (which tastes better than it sounds), beef stewed in red wine, and rich and gooey *aligot* (potatoes, garlic, and cheese). *22 rue du Grenier St-Lazare, 3rd.* ☎ *01-42-72-31-22. www.ambassade-auvergne.com. Entrees 16€–24€; Prix fixe menu 28€; 3-course average 45€. MC, V. Lunch & dinner daily; closed Sun July 14–Aug 15. Métro: Rambuteau. Map p 102.*

★ **Angélina** TUILERIES *TEA SHOP* This traditional *salon de thé* serves its high-society patrons tea, pastries, and sandwiches on silver platters. If you have a sweet tooth, try the house special Mont Blanc, a gooey meringue cream and chestnut cake. *226 rue de Rivoli, 1st.* ☎ *01-42-60-82-00. Tea 6€–11€; entrees 12€–15€. AE, MC, V. Breakfast, lunch & tea daily. Métro: Tuileries or Concorde. Map p 102.*

★★ **Astier** OBERKAMPF *FRENCH* This red and white chequered dining institution is where chef Christophe Kestler reworks vintage staples like smoked herrings and potato salad, wild boar terrine, and braised Charolais beef with modern flair. The staff is friendly, the wine list long, and the managers also own the next-door Italian restaurant and *épicerie;* so if there's no room at Astier, you won't go hungry. *44 rue Jean-Pierre Timbaud, 11th.* ☎ *01-43-57-16-35. http://restaurant-astier.com. 3-course average 35–45€. Lunch & dinner daily. MC, V. Métro: Oberkampf. Map p 102.*

★ **Au Pied de Cochon.** Where else in Paris can you get such a good meal at 3am? Specialties include onion soup, grilled pigs' feet with béarnaise sauce, and *andouillettes.* On the street outside, you can buy some of the freshest oysters in town. *6 rue Coquillière, 1st.* ☎ *01-40-13-77-00. www.pieddecochon.com. Main courses 17€–48€. AE, DC, MC, V. Open daily 24 hr. Métro: Les Halles or Louvre. Map p 112.*

Diners under the vaulted arcades of the Marais district.

Au Pied de Cochon is open 24 hours daily serving revelers til dawn.

★ **Aux Lyonnais** GRANDS BOULEVARDS *LYONNAIS* Famed chef Alain Ducasse, the best in Paris at Lyonnais cuisine, creates dishes like parsleyed calf's liver, pike dumplings, skate *meunière,* and peppery *coq au vin* in a restaurant designed to look like a 19th-century bistro. *32 rue St-Marc, 2nd.* ☎ *01-42-96-65-04. www.alain-ducasse.com. Reservations required. Prix fixe menu from 28€ (lunch); 3-course av 50€. AE, DC, MC, V. Lunch & dinner Tues–Fri, dinner Sat. Métro: Grands Boulevards. Map p 102.*

★ **Benoit** MARAIS *TRADITIONAL FRENCH* Since 1912, every mayor of Paris has dined at Benoit; perhaps that explains the air of gravitas here. Time-tested classics fill the menu—my favorites are the escargot, cassoulet, and, for dessert, Sainte-Eve (pears with cream). *20 rue St-Martin, 4th.* ☎ *01-42-72-25-76. www.benoit-paris.com. Reservations required. Entrees 50€–120€; prix fixe lunch 34€. AE, MC, V. Lunch & dinner daily. Métro: Hôtel-de-Ville. Map p 102.*

★★★ **kids** **Bistrot Paul Bert** FAIDHERBE *FRENCH* This locals' haunt has old tiled floors and a real zinc bar—just as a Parisian bistro should. The food is just as authentic and delicious: crispy duck confit with garlicky potatoes, homemade pâtés, and possibly the best *île flottante* (whisked egg whites in a vanilla sauce) in town. *11 rue Paul Bert, 12th.* ☎ *01-43-72-24-01. Entrees 20€. 3-course menu 35€–40€. MC, V. Lunch & dinner Tues–Sat. Métro: Faidherbe-Chaligny. Map p 102.*

★★★ **Bouillon Racine** ST-MICHEL *FRENCH* This jewel-box dining room is the best example of baroque Art Nouveau in Paris—a magnificent affair of swirling iron and woodwork,

Parisians flock to Bistrot Paul Bert for île flottantes, *homemade pâtés, and other bistro staples in a classic setting.*

Lunch is a bargain at Bouillon Racine, an Art Nouveau time capsule in the 6th.

with twinkling stained glass, mirrors, and tiles. The brasserie fare includes carpaccio of beef with basil, lemon, and Parmesan; scallop risotto; and chicken blanquette. The two-course lunch menu is a steal at 15.50€. *3 rue Racine, 6th. ☎ 01-44-32-15-60. www.bouillon-racine.com. Entrees 18€. 3-course menu 35€. MC, V. Lunch & dinner daily. Métro: Odéon. Map p 104.*

★★ **Brasserie Flo** NORTHEAST PARIS *TRADITIONAL FRENCH* This well-known restaurant is a bit hard to find, down a discreet, cobbled passage, but you'll be glad you tracked it down when you try the onion soup, sole *meunière,* or guinea hen with lentils. *7 cour des Petites-Ecuries, 10th. ☎ 01-47-70-13-59. www.flobrasseries.com. Reservations recommended. Entrees 16€–28€; prix fixe lunch 24€–40€, dinner from 34€. AE, DC, MC, V. Lunch & dinner daily. Métro: Château d'Eau or Strasbourg-St-Denis. Map p 102.*

★ kids **Breakfast in America** LATIN QUARTER *AMERICAN* Homesick Americans make a beeline to this diner, which could have been transported here straight from the streets of Chicago. The menu features favorites like pancakes with maple syrup, fresh-squeezed OJ, burgers with grilled onions and fries, and brownies. *17 rue des Ecoles, 5th. ☎ 01-43-54-50-28. www.breakfast-in-america.com. Entrees 8€–17€. MC, V. Breakfast, lunch & dinner daily. Métro: Cardinal Lemoine. Map p 104.*

★ kids **Breizh Café** MARAIS *CREPERIE* You could be in Brittany at this upbeat, modern creperie, which uses top-notch, mostly organic produce in its unusual and delicious fillings: think potato and smoked herring, or 70% cocoa solids in the chocolate dessert crêpes. You can wash it all down with one of 15 artisanal ciders. *109 rue Vieille-du-Temple, 3rd. ☎ 01-42-72-13-77. www.breizhcafe.com. Crêpes 6€–14€. MC, V. Lunch & dinner Wed–Sun. Métro: Filles du Calvaire. Map p 102.*

★ kids **Chartier** LES HALLES *TRADITIONAL FRENCH* This unpretentious, affordable, *fin-de-siècle* restaurant has soaring ceilings, fabulous brasswork, and straightforward cooking—try the beef bourguignon (in red-wine sauce), the *pavé* (thick steak), or the fish. *7 rue du Faubourg Montmartre, 9th. ☎ 01-47-70-86-29. www.restaurant-chartier.com. Entrees 9.50€–14€. MC, V. Lunch & dinner daily. Métro: Grands Boulevards. Map p 102.*

★ **Closerie des Lilas** MONTPARNASSE *TRADITIONAL FRENCH* This restaurant and brasserie was a favorite of Gertrude Stein and Picasso (not to mention Lenin and Trotsky—a revolution marches on its stomach, apparently). Have a champagne julep before stuffing yourself with veal ribs with cider or filet of beef in peppercorn sauce. *171 bd. du Montparnasse, 6th. ☎ 01-40-51-34-50. www.closeriedeslilas.fr. Reservations far in advance for the restaurant, not needed for the brasserie. Restaurant* *entrees 35€–45€; brasserie entrees 19€–24€. AE, DC, V. Lunch & dinner daily. Métro: Port Royal or Vavin. Map p 104.*

Cristal Room CHAMPS-ELYSEES *HAUTE CUISINE* You have to climb a red carpet encrusted with crystals to get to Baccarat's chic dining room. Once you're inside, chef Thomas L'Hérisson's cuisine lives up to the grand entrance with fillets of red mullet in a chickpea and coriander crust, or perfect pan-fried veal cutlet with tandoori gnocchi. A meal here also includes a trip around the tiny but stunningly beautiful Baccarat museum. *11 place des Etats-Unis, 16th. ☎ 01-40-22-11-10. www.baccarat.fr. Lunch menu 38€–58€. 3-course menu 100€. MC, V. Lunch & dinner Mon–Sat. Métro: Boissière or Iéna. Map p 101.*

Des Si et des Mets MONTMARTRE *GLUTEN-FREE FRENCH* Traditional seafood blanquette, lemon and ginger lamb, and *boeuf bourguignon* with macaroni gratin are just some of the mouth-watering, gluten-free dishes prepared for you in this smart Montmartrois restaurant. *63 rue Lepic, 18th. ☎ 01-42-55-19-61. www.dessietdesmets.com. Entrees 16€. 3-course menu 26€; brunch 22€ (Sun noon–2:30pm). MC, V. Lunch Sat–Sun, dinner Tues–Sun. Métro: Abbesses or Blanche. Map p 101.*

The chandelier in the Cristal Room promises more to come in the onsite Baccarat museum.

★ Les Fables de la Fontaine EIFFEL TOWER *SEAFOOD* One of the city's best seafood restaurants draws crowds with its fresh fried shrimp, baked sea bass with a rich, creamy sauce, big bowls of mussels, and fine oysters. There are only 20 places inside, so book the second sitting if you want to linger. *131 rue St-Dominique, 7th. ☎ 01-44-18-37-55. www.lesfablesdelafontaine.net. Entrees 33€–40€. Lunch menus from 30€. MC, V. Lunch & dinner Tues–Sat. Métro: Ecole Militaire. Map p 104.*

Higuma OPERA *JAPANESE* This no-frills Japanese canteen is always full, so get here early if you don't want to queue in the street at mealtimes. The reasons behind its popularity are the quirky open kitchen, which fills the air with delicious-smelling steam, and the low prices—around 8€ for a giant bowl of soup, rice, or noodles, piled high with meat, seafood, or stir-fried vegetables. *32bis rue St-Anne, 1st. ☎ 01-47-03-38-59. http://higuma.fr. Fixed-price menu from 13€. Entrees 9€. MC, V. Lunch & dinner daily. Métro: Pyramides. Map p 102.*

★★ Kei CHÂTELET *TRADITIONAL FRENCH* In this sophisticated dining room that feels like someone's parlor, Kei, a Japanese chef who trained with Alain Ducasse, serves haute French cuisine like lobster with pepper emulsion and veal rib with egg-plant caviar. The presentation is very feng shui, with each dish looking like a modern artwork. *5 rue Coq Héron, 1st. ☎ 01-42-33-14-74. www.restaurant-kei.fr. Prix fixe lunch 38€, prix fixe dinner from 75€. DC, MC, V. Métro: Louvre Rivoli. Map p 102.*

★★ **L'Arpège** INVALIDES *FRENCH* Supplies for this exclusive eaterie come from chef Alain Passard's own farms in the Sarthe, Eure, and Mont-St-Michel regions, where horses replace polluting machinery, and pesticides (when necessary) are vegetable-based. Expect Michelin-starred dishes like roasted Brittany Turbot with smoked potatoes and blue lobster in honey. ***84 rue de Varenne, 7th.*** ☎ ***01-47-05-09-06. www.alain-passard.com. Entrees 60€–140€. AE, MC, V. Mon–Fri noon–2:30pm and 7:30–10:30pm. Métro Varenne. Map p 104.***

★★ **La Cigalle-Récamier** ST-GERMAIN-DES-PRES *SOUFFLES* Whatever flavor you order, be they savory or sweet, La Cigalle's soufflés are perfect every time, and the most delicious in Paris. Perhaps that's why the restaurant is favored by the crème de la crème of St-Germain's society. On a sunny day, the terrace is a special treat. ***4 rue Récamier, 7th.*** ☎ ***01-45-48-86-58. Entrees 20€–45€. MC, V. Lunch & dinner Mon–Sat. Métro: Sèvres-Babylone. Map p 104.***

Low prices, an open kitchen, and delicious soups draw crowds to Higuma.

★ **Le Fumoir** LOUVRE *BISTRO* This handy spot near the Louvre and Arts Décoratifs museums has a faithful following from Paris's literary and media crowd. Sink into a Chesterfield armchair and order a refreshing fruit cocktail; or fill up on salads, steak, or vegetarian risotto. ***6 rue de l'amiral Coligny, 1st.*** ☎ ***01-42-92-00-24. Entrees average at 17€. Métro: Louvre-Rivoli. Lunch menus from 18.50€. AE, MC, V. Lunch & dinner daily. Métro: Louvre-Rivoli. Map p 102.***

★★★ **Le Grand Véfour** TUILERIES *TRADITIONAL FRENCH* This romantic, historic, expensive place is a favorite of food critics. Specialties include lamb cooked with sweet wine, Breton lobster, and cabbage sorbet in dark-chocolate sauce. ***17 rue de Beaujolais, 1st.*** ☎ ***01-42-96-56-27. www.grand-vefour.com. Reservations far in advance. Entrees 65€–90€; prix fixe lunch 80€, dinner 240€. AE, DC, MC, V. Lunch & dinner Mon–Thurs, lunch Fri. Closed Aug. Métro: Louvre-Palais Royal or Pyramides. Map p 102.***

★★ **Le Lasserre** CHAMPS-ELYSEES *HAUTE FRENCH* The experience of dining here—with gold cutlery and fine porcelain, waiters plying to your every whim, and Michelin-starred food on your plate—is a treat available to only a lucky few. If you can afford it, do it, especially in summer when the restaurant roof opens to let in the warm breeze. Lunch is less than half the price of dinner, for the same food. ***17 av. Franklin Roosevelt, 8th.*** ☎ ***01-43-59-02-13. www.restaurant-lasserre.com. Reservations recommended. Prix fixe lunch 75€; prix fixe dinner 185€; entrees 75€–90€. MC, V. Lunch & dinner Thurs–Fri, dinner Sat–Wed. Métro: Champs Elysée Clémenceau. Map p 101.***

★★ **Le Moderne** BOURSE *CONTEMPORARY FRENCH* This narrow,

An elegant table awaits discerning diners at Le Grand Véfour.

black and beige restaurant is the place to go for inventive cuisine like Brittany fish in cardamom *jus,* beef with braised vegetables, and a lip-smacking praline and vanilla *mille-feuille* (layers of sweet pastry and cream). The wine list is good too. ***40 rue Notre-Dame des Victoires, 2nd. ☎ 01-53-40-84-10. Prix fixe menus 28€–40€. MC, V. Lunch & dinner Mon–Fri, dinner only Sat. Métro: Bourse. Map p 102.***

★ Le Potager du Marais MARAIS *VEGETARIAN* Vegetarians flock to this organic offering, arguably the best vegetarian restaurant in Paris. Dishes are so tasty, meat eaters won't complain. The welcome is warm, and many items are gluten free. ***22 rue Rambuteau, 3rd. ☎ 01-42-74-24-66. Entrees 9€–16€. MC, V. Lunch & dinner daily. Métro: Rambuteau. Map p 102.***

★★ Le Restaurant ST-GERMAIN DES PRES *HAUTE CUISINE* Inside L'Hôtel, where Oscar Wilde died impoverished, in the shadow of Les Beaux Arts, Le Restaurant's intimate, rococo dining room is pure romance. Bring a special person along to enjoy chef Philippe Bélissante's unusual take on French cuisine served in a stylish, hip atmosphere. He's just been awarded his first Michelin star for dishes such as crab meat with argan oil and hot bisque. ***13 rue des Beaux-Arts, 6th. ☎ 01-44-41-99-00. www.l-hotel.com. Reservations recommended. Prix fixe 42€–155€. AE, DC, MC, V. Lunch & dinner Mon–Sat. Métro: St-Germain-des-Prés. Map p 104.***

★★ Le Timbre LUXEMBOURG *FRENCH* "The Stamp" is, as its name implies, a tiny restaurant. But what it lacks in space, it makes up for in the kitchen with delicious dishes like asparagus and crumbled Parmesan, pork with red onions, and *moelleux au chocolat* (squishy chocolate cake). There's an appetizing wine list, too. ***3 rue Ste-Beuve, 6th. ☎ 01-45-49-10-40. www.restaurantletimbre.com. Lunch menu 26€. 3-course menu 40€. MC, V. Lunch & dinner Tues–Sat. Métro: Vavin. Map p 104.***

★★★ L'Hôtel Thoumieux INVALIDES *CONTEMPORARY FRENCH/BRASSERIE* This is possibly the most exciting place to eat in Paris. There's the Art Deco–inspired downstairs brasserie, *Le Thoumieux,* which serves dishes like scallops and cheese macaroni and hot churros in sticky chocolate sauce to well-healed Parisians. Upstairs chef Jean-François Piège (in the restaurant of the same name), creates dreamy dishes for real foodies like asparagus latticed with black truffle cream, coated in Cantal cheese emulsion; or crayfish in a herby broth with foie-gras. ***In the Hôtel Thoumieux, 79 rue St-Dominique, 7th. ☎ 01-47-05-79-00. www.thoumieux.fr. Reservations required in advance. Brasserie 3-course average 50€; Chez Jean-François Piège prix fixe menus 70€–150€. AE, DC, MC, V. Daily lunch & dinner. Métro: La Tour-Maubourg. Map p 104.***

★ **Monsieur Lapin** (chez Franck Enée) MONTPARNASSE *FRENCH* There is no better place to eat rabbit in Paris than Monsieur Lapin, where chef Franck Enée serves it in terrines, tajines, and all sorts of delicious sauces. He's also a big fish fan, so you'll find dishes on the menu like cod roasted with artichokes. Dessert-wise, the praline soufflé is to die for. ***11 rue Raymond Losserand, 14th. ☎ 01-43-20-21-39. Reservations recommended. Prix fixe menu 28€; 3-course average 80€. AE, MC, V. Lunch Tue–Fri, Sun & dinner Tue–Sun. Closed 1st week March. Métro: Montparnasse. Map p 104.***

★★ **Mon Vieil Ami** ILE SAINT-LOUIS *CONTEMPORARY FRENCH* This slice of gastronomy is where chef Antoine Westermann prepares traditional French cuisine with a modern twist. Vegetables take pride of place alongside perfect meat and fish, creating wonderful *plats* like slow-braised roebuck with celery, quince, and chestnuts; and seafood casserole topped with tomatoes and tender baby squid. ***65 rue St-Louis-en-L'Île, 4th. ☎ 01-40-46-01-35. www.mon-vieil-ami.com. Reservations required. Prix fixe menu 41€. AE, MC, V. Lunch & dinner Wed–Sun, dinner Tues. Métro: Pont Marie. Map p 102.***

kids **Pink Flamingo** CANAL ST-MARTIN *PIZZA* Not only are the Pink's pizzas quirky (try the Poulidor, with goat cheese and sliced duck breast), they're also put together with the best, freshest ingredients, and the crusts are made with organic flour. If you picnic by the canal, take a pink helium balloon, find your spot, and wait for the pizza delivery boy to cycle to you. There are other locations at 105 rue Vieille du Temple, 3rd, 23 rue d'Aligre, 12th, and 30 rue Muller, 18th. ***67 rue Bichat, 10th. ☎ 01-42-02-31-70. www.pinkflamingopizza.com. Pizzas from 10.50€. MC, V. Lunch & dinner Tues–Sun. Métro: Jacques Bonsergent. Map p 102.***

★ **kids** **Schwartz's** MARAIS *JEWISH* This New York–style Jewish deli bustles throughout the day with hungry folk looking to fill up on smoked herring, pastrami, chunky bagels, burgers, and hotdogs. The cheese-cake is a treat too. Reserve in advance if possible. ***16 rue des Ecouffes, 4th. ☎ 01-48-87-31-29. www.schwartzsdeli.fr. Entrees 9€–19€. AE, DC, MC, V. Lunch & dinner Mon–Sat, brunch Sun. Métro: St-Paul. Map p 102.***

★★★ **The Shangri-La Restaurants** CHAILLOT *FRENCH & ASIAN* The palatial Hôtel Shangri-La (p 148) gives you no less than three fabulous, high-end eating opportunities: *Shang Palace,* the city's first ever gourmet Cantonese restaurant; *L'Abeille,* a fabulous *gastronomique* French restaurant overlooking the interior garden; and in the hotel's epicenter (set beneath a 1930's Eiffel-style cupola), *La Bauhinia* Brasserie, which serves lip-smacking Chinese and French dishes. ***10 avenue Iéna, 16th. ☎ 01-53-67-19-98. www.shangri-la.com. Entrees 60€–90€; prix fixe lunch from 80€. AE, DC, MC, V. Lunch & dinner daily. Métro: Iéna. Map p 101.***

★★★ **Taillevent** CHAMPS-ELYSEES *MODERN FRENCH* Occupying a 19th-century town house off the Champs-Elysées with paneled rooms and crystal chandeliers, this is one of the city's best gastronomic restaurants. Try the sausage of Breton lobster, the watercress soup with Sevruga caviar, or the salmon in sea salt. ***15 rue Lamennais, 8th. ☎ 01-44-95-15-01. www.taillevent.com. Reservations 6 weeks in advance. Prix fixe 70€–190€. AE, DC, MC, V. Lunch & dinner Mon–Fri. Closed Aug. Métro: George-V. Map p 101.*** ●

7 The Best Nightlife

Nightlife Best Bets

Best Bohemian Bar
★ Chez Prune, *71 quai de Valmy, 10th (p 122)*

Best Chic Cocktails
★★★ Bar Hemingway, *In the Hôtel Ritz, 15 place Vendôme, 1st (p 121)*

Best Place to Steal a Kiss
★★ La Palette, *43 rue de Seine, 6th (p 122)*

Best Wine Bar
★★ Le Baron Rouge, *1 rue Théophile-Roussel, 12th (p 120)*

Best Nikka Bar Outside Japan
Le Curio Parlour, *16 rue des Bernardins (p 123)*

Best for Students
★ Académie de la Bière, *88 bd. du Port Royal, 5th (p 121)*

Best for Fans of Papa
★★★ Harry's Bar, *5 rue Daunou, 2nd (p 122)*

Best for Dinner and a Boogie
★ L'ARC, *12 rue Presbourg, 16th (p 123)*

Best Hip Hangout
★★ Chez Jeanette, *47 rue du Faubourg St-Denis, 10th (p 121)*

Best Cocktails and Frites
Dédé La Frite, *135 rue Montmartre, 2nd (p 122)*

Best Waterfront Location
★★ Batofar, *11 quai François Mauriac,13th (p 123)*

Best Urban Culture and Cupcakes
★★ Horror Picture Tea, *95 rue St-Honoré, 8th (p 122)*

Best for the Latest Electro Sounds
★★ Machine du Moulin Rouge, *90 bd. de Clichy, 18th (p 124)*

Best Gay Bars
Open Café & Café Cox, *15 & 17 rue des Archives, 4th (p 124)*

Best Lesbian Bar
La Champmeslé, *4 rue Chabanais, 2nd (p 124)*

Best Boudoir
★★★ Le Bar de L'Hôtel, *13 rue des Beaux-Arts, 6th (p 122)*

The cocktails served at Le Curio Parlour are hard to find outside Japan.

Previous page: Celebrities frequent the bar at L'Arc in the 16th arrondissement.

Right Bank (8th & 16th–17th)

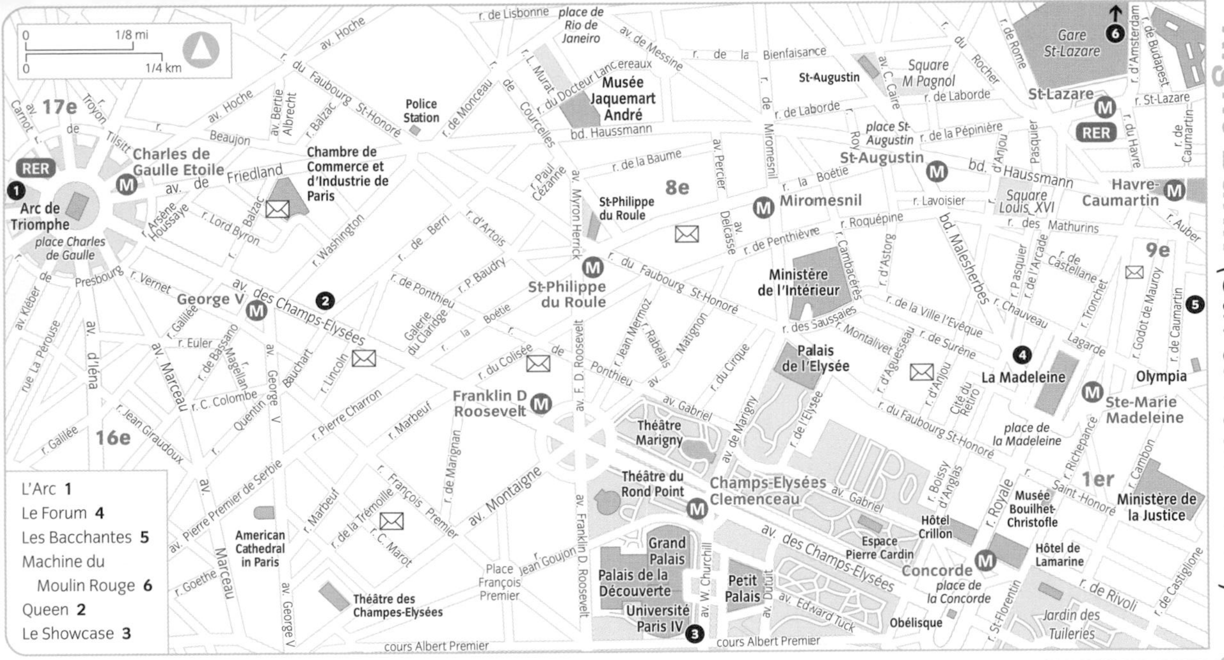

Right Bank (1st–4th & 9th–11th)

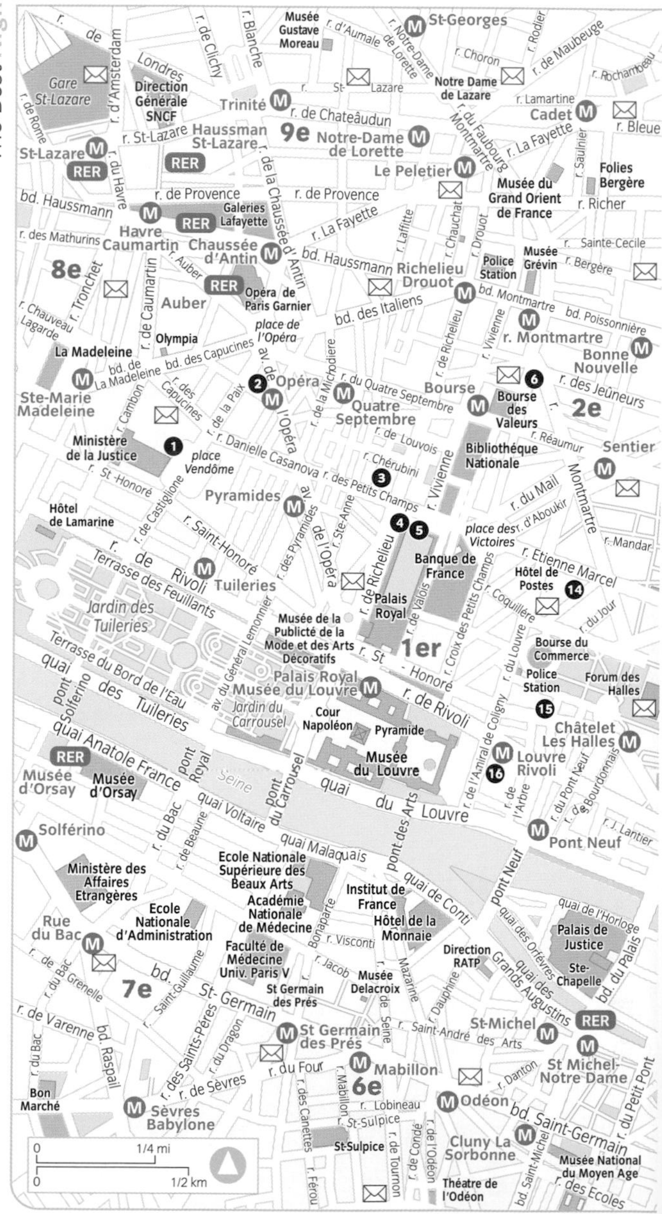

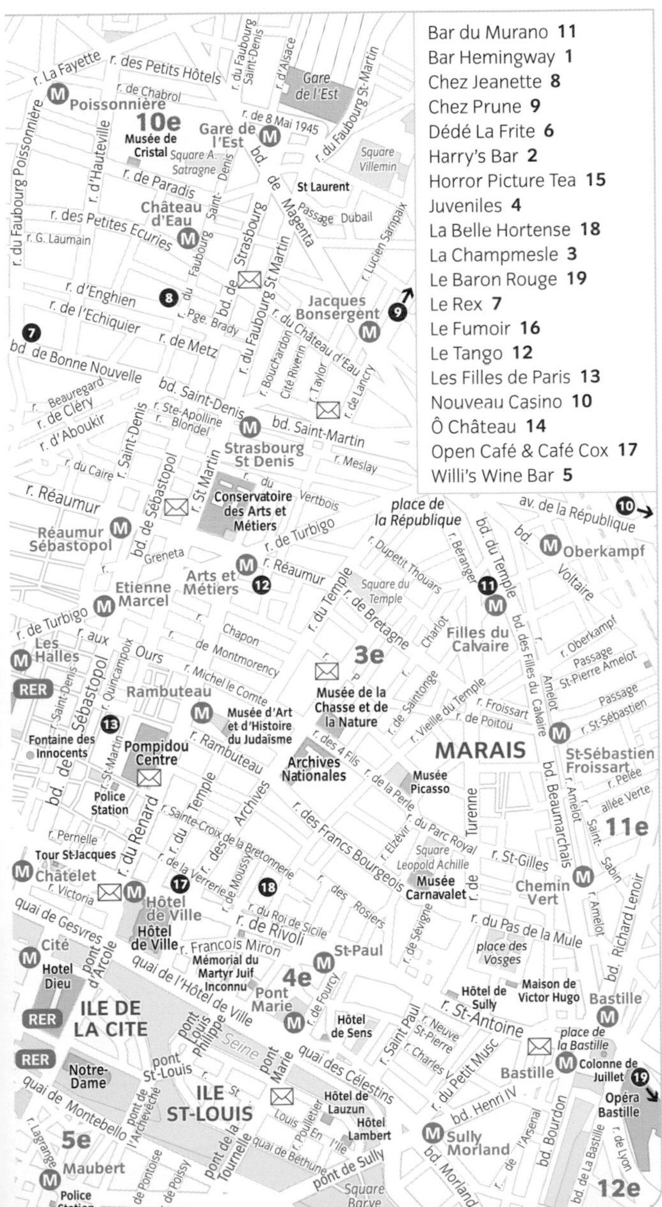
Bar du Murano 11
Bar Hemingway 1
Chez Jeanette 8
Chez Prune 9
Dédé La Frite 6
Harry's Bar 2
Horror Picture Tea 15
Juveniles 4
La Belle Hortense 18
La Champmesle 3
Le Baron Rouge 19
Le Rex 7
Le Fumoir 16
Le Tango 12
Les Filles de Paris 13
Nouveau Casino 10
Ô Château 14
Open Café & Café Cox 17
Willi's Wine Bar 5
10e
3e
4e
5e
11e
12e
MARAIS
ILE DE LA CITE
ILE ST-LOUIS
Gare de l'Est
Poissonnière
Musée de Cristal
Square A. Satragne
Château d'Eau
St Laurent
Passage Dubail
Square Villemin
Jacques Bonsergent
Strasbourg St Denis
Conservatoire des Arts et Métiers
place de la République
Oberkampf
Réaumur Sébastopol
Arts et Métiers
Etienne Marcel
Square du Temple
Filles du Calvaire
Les Halles
RER
Rambuteau
Musée d'Art et d'Histoire du Judaïsme
Musée de la Chasse et de la Nature
Fontaine des Innocents
Pompidou Centre
Archives Nationales
Musée Picasso
St-Sébastien Froissart
Police Station
Tour St-Jacques
Square Leopold Achille
Musée Carnavalet
Châtelet
Hôtel de Ville
Chemin Vert
Cité
Hotel Dieu
Mémorial du Martyr Juif Inconnu
St-Paul
place des Vosges
Pont Marie
Hôtel de Sully
Maison de Victor Hugo
Bastille
Hôtel de Sens
place de la Bastille
Colonne de Juillet
Opéra Bastille
Notre-Dame
Hôtel de Lauzun
Hôtel Lambert
Sully Morland
Maubert
Square Barye
Seine

Left Bank (5th–6th)

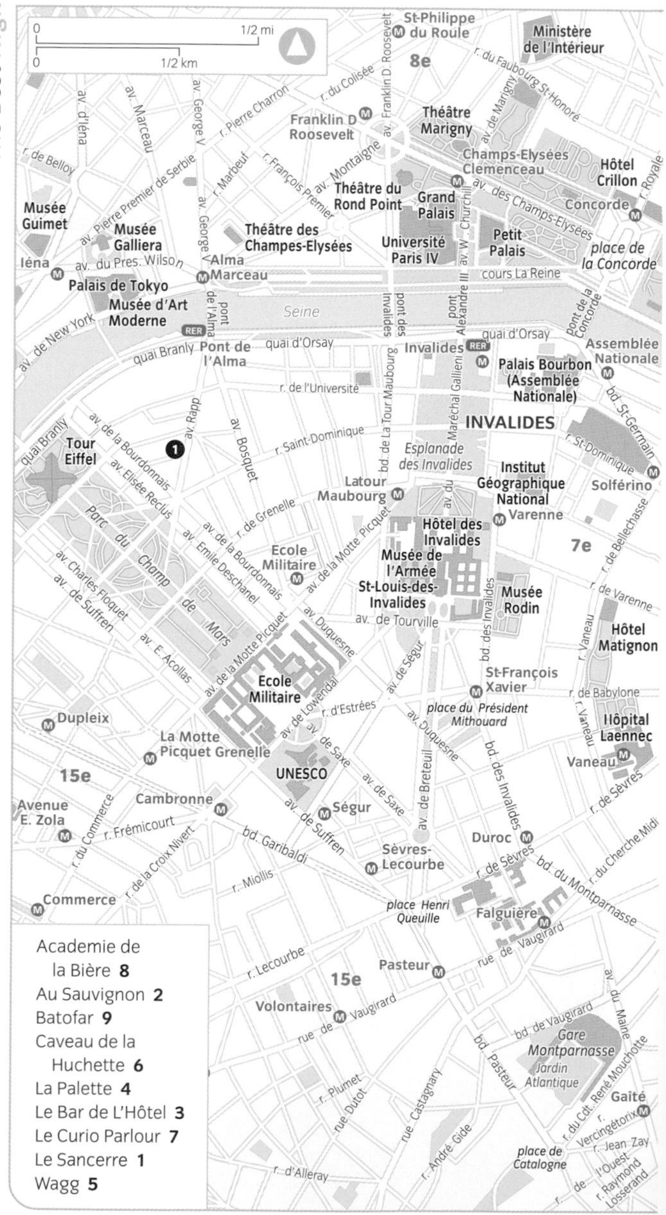

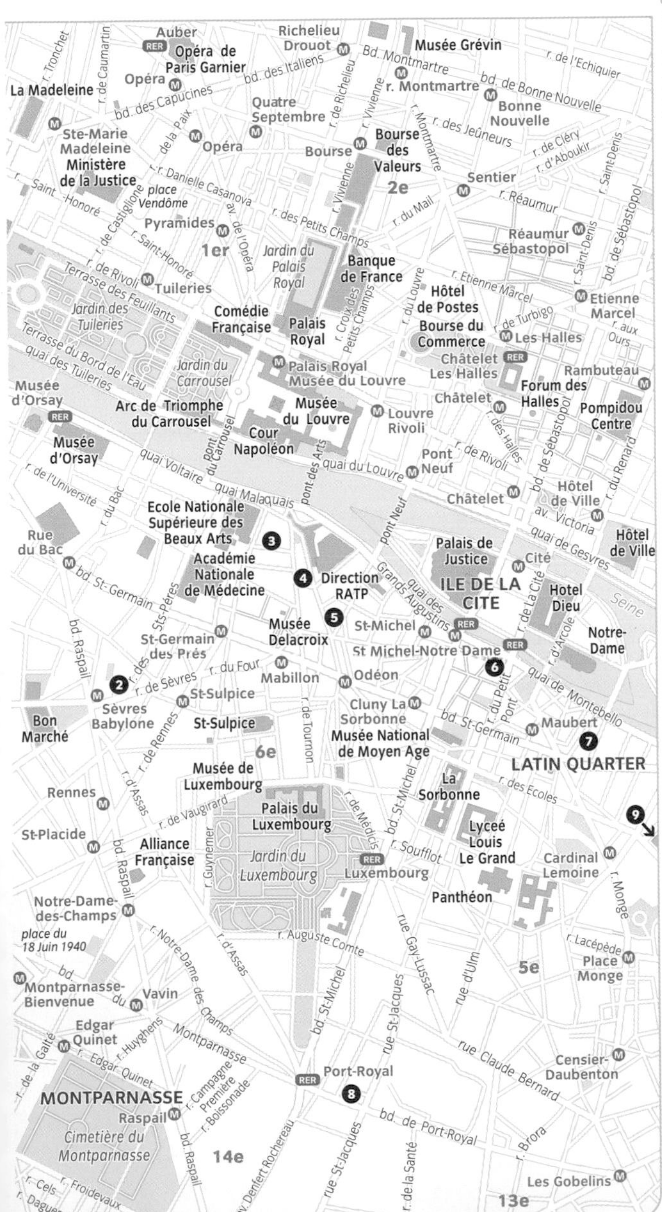
Auber
Opéra de Paris Garnier
Richelieu Drouot
Musée Grévin
La Madeleine
Opéra
Quatre Septembre
r. Montmartre
Bonne Nouvelle
Ste-Marie Madeleine
Ministère de la Justice
place Vendôme
Opéra
Bourse
Bourse des Valeurs
2e
Sentier
Pyramides
1er
Jardin du Palais Royal
Banque de France
Réaumur Sébastopol
Tuileries
Jardin des Tuileries
Comédie Française
Palais Royal
Hôtel de Postes
Bourse du Commerce
Etienne Marcel
Les Halles
Jardin du Carrousel
Palais Royal Musée du Louvre
Châtelet Les Halles
Rambuteau
Musée d'Orsay
Arc de Triomphe du Carrousel
Musée du Louvre
Cour Napoléon
Louvre Rivoli
Châtelet
Forum des Halles
Pompidou Centre
Musée d'Orsay
Pont Neuf
Châtelet
Hôtel de Ville
Ecole Nationale Supérieure des Beaux Arts
Rue du Bac
Académie Nationale de Médecine
Direction RATP
Palais de Justice
ILE DE LA CITE
Cité
Hôtel de Ville
Hotel Dieu
Seine
St-Germain des Prés
Musée Delacroix
St-Michel
St Michel-Notre Dame
Notre-Dame
Mabillon
Odéon
Sèvres Babylone
St-Sulpice
Cluny La Sorbonne
Musée National de Moyen Age
Bon Marché
St-Sulpice
Maubert
6e
LATIN QUARTER
Musée de Luxembourg
La Sorbonne
Rennes
Palais du Luxembourg
St-Placide
Alliance Française
Jardin du Luxembourg
Luxembourg
Lycée Louis Le Grand
Cardinal Lemoine
Panthéon
Notre-Dame-des-Champs
place du 18 Juin 1940
Place Monge
5e
Montparnasse-Bienvenue
Vavin
Edgar Quinet
Censier-Daubenton
Port-Royal
MONTPARNASSE
Raspail
Cimetière du Montparnasse
14e
Les Gobelins
13e
r. Tronchet
r. de Caumartin
bd. des Capucines
bd. des Italiens
Bd. Montmartre
r. de l'Echiquier
bd. de Bonne Nouvelle
r. de Richelieu
r. Vivienne
r. Montmartre
r. des Jeûneurs
r. de Cléry
r. d'Aboukir
r. Saint-Denis
r. Saint-Honoré
r. de la Paix
r. Danielle Casanova
av. de l'Opéra
r. des Petits Champs
r. du Mail
r. Réaumur
bd. de Sébastopol
r. de Castiglione
r. Saint-Honoré
r. de Rivoli
Terrasse des Feuillants
r. Croix des Petits Champs
r. du Louvre
r. Etienne Marcel
r. de Turbigo
r. aux Ours
Terrasse du Bord de l'Eau
quai des Tuileries
pont du Carrousel
r. des Halles
r. de Rivoli
r. du Renard
quai Voltaire
pont des Arts
quai du Louvre
r. de l'Université
quai Malaquais
r. du Bac
pont Neuf
av. Victoria
quai de Gesvres
bd. St-Germain
r. des Sts-Pères
quai des Grands Augustins
r. de la Cité
bd. Raspail
r. d'Arcole
r. des Sèvres
r. du Four
r. de Sèvres
r. du Petit Pont
quai de Montebello
r. de Tournon
bd. St-Germain
r. de Rennes
r. d'Assas
r. des Ecoles
r. de Vaugirard
r. de Médicis
bd. St-Michel
bd. Raspail
r. Soufflot
r. Guynemer
r. Monge
r. Notre-Dame des Champs
r. d'Assas
r. Auguste Comte
rue Gay-Lussac
rue d'Ulm
r. Lacépède
bd. du Montparnasse
r. de la Gaîté
r. Huyghens
r. Edgar Quinet
bd. St-Michel
rue St-Jacques
rue Claude Bernard
r. Campagne Première
r. Boissonade
bd. de Port-Royal
r. Broca
bd. Raspail
av. Denfert Rochereau
rue St-Jacques
r. de la Santé
r. Cels
r. Froidevaux
r. Daguerre
RER
M

Paris Nightlife A to Z

Wine Bars

★ **Au Sauvignon** ST-GERMAIN-DES-PRES This tiny bar, with ceramic tiles and colorful frescoes, has tables overflowing onto the terrace, where a cheerful crowd downs wines from the cheapest Beaujolais to the priciest Grand Cru. *80 rue des St-Pères, 7th.* ☎ *01-45-48-49-02. Métro: Sévres-Babylone. Map p 118.*

★ **Juveniles** BOURSE This sleek place prides itself on its enormous wine cellar with labels from around the world. The trendy crowd stays busy watching itself in the mirror. *47 rue des Richelieu, 1st.* ☎ *01-42-97-46-49. Métro: Palais Royal. Map p 116.*

★★ **La Bacchantes** MADELEINE This place just down the road from Printemps department store is a top spot for a post-shopping tipple. Around 50 wines grace the board, so be prepared for indecision. Exposed beams and tiles add character, and chalkboards list special vintages and platters. *21 rue Caumartin, 9th.* ☎ *01-42-65-25-35. www.lesbacchantes.fr. Métro: Opéra or Madeleine. Map p 116.*

★ **La Belle Hortense** MARAIS The fact that this quirky bar has a bookshop within its walls makes it a perpetual favorite for bookish wine lovers. The crowd of regulars can discuss the finer points of Gertrude Stein at the drop of a *chapeau. 31 vieille du Temple, 4th.* ☎ *01-48-04-71-60. www.cafeine.com. Métro: Hôtel-de-Ville. Map p 116.*

★ **La Sancerre** INVALIDES This charmingly old-fashioned cafe is a veritable podium for Sancerre wines (red, white, and rosé). Staff are friendly and there are plenty of tasty omelets, cheese, and salads to soak up the juices. *22 av. Rapp, 7th.* ☎ *01-45-51-75-91. www.sancerredegustation.com. Métro: Alma-Marceau or Ecole Militaire. Map p 118.*

★★ **Le Baron Rouge** BASTILLE Be prepared to fight for elbow room at this popular locals' haunt, opposite the Aligre market, where excellent wine is sold by the glass and drunk on wine barrels posing as tables. If you're hungry, grab a plate of charcuterie or oysters (when in season). *24 rue de Rivoli, 4th.* ☎ *01-42-72-76-85. Métro: St-Paul. Map p 116.*

★ **Ö Château** LOUVRE A quality wine list, screens for rugby matches, *Vinomatic* wine dispensers that let

The book-lined walls inspire rich conversation at La Belle Hortense in the Marais.

The decor of Chez Jeanette, in the 10th arrondissement, is vintage 1940s.

you dose how much you taste, and good food platters make this a huge draw for lovers of the vine. You can follow tasting lessons here too. ***68 rue Jean-Jaques Rousseau, 1st.*** ☎ ***01-44-73-97-80. www.o-chateau.fr. Métro: Louvre-Rivoli. Map p 116.***

★★ Willi's Wine Bar BOURSE A favorite of journalists and stockbrokers, this place in the city's financial district has a bit of an English touch, thanks to its expat owner. Still, it's all about wine, with 250 labels and plenty to try by the glass. ***13 rue des Petits-Champs, 1st.*** ☎ ***01-42-61-05-09. www.williswinebar.com. Métro: Bourse, Pyramides, or Palais Royal. Map p 116.***

Pubs & Bars

★ Académie de la Bière LATIN QUARTER The decor in this academy of beer is subdued enough, with a wood-paneled, rustic look, but the mood can nonetheless be raucous. Most of the beers on tap come from Belgium. Soak it up with delicious *moules-frites*. ***88 bd. du Port Royal, 5th.*** ☎ ***01-43-54-66-65. www.academie-biere.com. RER: Port Royal. Map p 118.***

Bar du Murano MARAIS Inside the Uber-cool Murano Urban Resort, this hotel bar, frequented by the fashion set, serves a decadent 140 types of vodka and almost as many types of cocktails. If you're feeling flush, dine in the excellent hotel restaurant with its sheltered courtyard. ***13 bd. du Temple, 3rd.*** ☎ ***01-42-71-21-01. www.muranoresort.com. Métro: Filles du Calvaire or Oberkampf. Map p 116.***

★★★ Bar Hemingway PLACE VENDOME One of the best bars on Earth has been commemorated in book, film, and song for more than half a century. In 1944, Hemingway and Allied soldiers famously liberated it from the Nazis and ordered a round of martinis. Today it's just as you might expect—book-filled, wood-paneled, and loaded with memorabilia. Expect well-mixed drinks, an excellent staff, and high prices. ***In the Hôtel Ritz, 15 place Vendôme, 1st.*** ☎ ***01-43-16-30-30. www.ritzparis.com. Métro: Opéra. Map p 116.***

Chez Jeanette STRASBOURG-ST-DENIS The decor in this bar hasn't changed since the 1940s. Nowadays, crowds of trendy 30-somethings lap up the cheap wine and concentrate on being cool, while the occasional old regular sweeps in, Jack Russell in tow, oblivious to the change of clientele. ***47 rue du Faubourg St-Denis, 10th.***

With its frescoes in the back room, La Palette is a magnet for art students.

☎ *01-47-70-30-89. Métro: Strasbourg-St-Denis or Château Eau. Map p 116.*

★ **Chez Prune** CANAL ST-MARTIN This bobo magnet serves excellent, well-priced food, including some vegetarian dishes (from 13€), coffee, beer, and wine to local arty types and cool do-littlers taking in the canal-side view. *71 quai de Valmy, 10th.* ☎ *01-42-41-30-47. Métro: République. Map p 116.*

Dédé La Frite BOURSE In the shadow of the stock exchange, Dédé serves beers and cocktails to after-work crowds. Just when you fancy a nibble, the wafting aroma of fries and burgers fills the air. Then later on, the music is cranked up a notch. *135 rue Montmartre, 2nd.* ☎ *01-40-41-99-90. Métro: Bourse. Map p 116.*

★★★ **Harry's Bar** OPERA This place is sacred to Hemingway disciples as the place where he and the rest of the ambulance corps drank themselves silly during the Spanish Civil War. This bar is responsible for the White Lady and the Sidecar, along with numerous damaged livers. A pianist plays in the cellar; upstairs is somewhat more sophisticated. Filled with expats, this place is more fun than you might think. *5 rue Daunou, 2nd.* ☎ *01-42-61-71-14. www.harrys-bar.fr. Métro: Opéra or Pyramides. Map p 116.*

★★ **Horror Picture Tea** LOUVRE This hotbed of urban culture has the fashionistas talking. Nowhere else in Paris can you tuck into delicious cupcakes, admire an art exhibition, get a tattoo, and listen to top-quality rock in the basement all under one roof. *95 rue St-Honoré, 1st. No phone. Métro: Louvre Rivoli. Map p 116.*

★ **La Palette** ST-GERMAIN-DES-PRES This is a favorite rendezvous for students from the nearby fine-arts school. It's also rather romantic (especially the fresco-painted back room). A drink here means following in the steps of Hemingway and Jim Morrison; and if you can find a seat on the leafy terrace, you may well want to sit there long enough to watch their ghosts go by. A handy base for exploring St-Germain's art galleries. *43 rue de Seine, 6th.* ☎ *01-43-26-68-15. Métro: Odéon. Map p 118.*

★★★ **Le Bar de L'Hôtel** ST-GERMAIN-DES-PRES This place is appropriately theatrical—with lots of marble, a Victorian color scheme, and baroque touches—when you consider that the regulars tend to be in the film industry—or want to be. When you take into account that this was the hotel where Oscar

Wilde died, impoverished and abandoned, it takes on a kind of poignancy. It's a lovely historic place for a drink and a ponder. *13 rue des Beaux-Arts, 6th. ☎ 01-44-41-99-00. www.l-hotel.com. Métro: St-Germain-des-Prés. Map p 118.*

Le Curio Parlour LATIN QUARTER This is one of the only Nikka bars outside Japan, serving 138° Bitter Truth to the very brave. Tequila and whisky cocktails are also house specialties, as are a myriad of other concoctions that you won't find anywhere else in town. *16 rue des Bernardins, 5th. ☎ 01-47-07-12-47. Métro: St-Germain-des-Prés. Map p 118.*

★ **Le Forum** MADELEINE This business-crowd favorite is like a London private club—all oak paneling, single malts, and brass. Try a champagne cocktail and soak up the atmosphere. On Saturdays (1–3pm) you can learn how to make (and drink) your own cocktails at the Bar School. *4 bd. Malesherbes, 8th. ☎ 01-42-65-37-86. www.bar-le-forum.com. Métro: Madeleine. Map p 115.*

★★ **Le Fumoir** LOUVRE An intriguing mix of hip Parisians and Euro-loungers comes to linger over wine and cocktails or eat good food in a setting of book-lined walls that recalls the great cafes of French colonial Indochina in the 1930s. *6 rue de l'Admiral de Coligny, 1st. ☎ 01-42-92-00-24. www.lefumoir.com. Métro: Louvre-Rivoli. Map p 116.*

Dance Clubs

★★ **Batofar** BIBLIOTHEQUE Virtually everybody views this club, which sits on a converted barge that floats on the Seine, as hip. Batofar attracts hundreds of 20- and 30-year old followers of the rotating DJs. In the summer, the quayside turns into an extension of the boat, with food, a bar, and deck chairs. *11 quai François Mauriac, 13th. ☎ 09-71-25-50-61. www.batofar.org. Cover free–15€. Métro: Quai de la Gare. Map p 118.*

Caveau de la Huchette LATIN QUARTER This rocking club fosters good times, partying, and loud music. The crowd tends to be in their 30s and above, with a taste for funk, jazz, and classic rock. *5 rue de la Huchette, 5th. ☎ 01-43-26-65-05. www.caveaudelahuchette.fr. Cover 10€–14€. Métro: St-Michel. Map p 118.*

L'ARC CHAMPS ELYSEES Dine on tasty French cuisine alongside celebrity A-listers, before burning off the calories on the dance floor at this smart Champs Elysées institution. Dress for the occasion and smile sweetly if you want to get in. *12 rue de Presbourg, 16th. ☎ 01-45-00-78-70. http://larc-paris.com. Cover free–30€. Métro/RER: Charles-de-Gaulle-Etoile. Map p 115.*

★★ **Le Rex** CLUB GRANDS BOULEVARDS This place is known for its cutting-edge electronic music, with top DJs playing weekly, and frequent free nights. Check local listings to see who's at the helm. *5 bd. Poissonnière, 2nd. ☎ 01-42-36-10-96. www.rexclub.com. Cover up to 16€. Métro: Bonne Nouvelle. Map p 116.*

Le Showcase CHAMPS ELYSEES Underneath the arches of Pont Alexandre III inside an old boat hangar, this happening club packs in the young and energetic for nightly jams to French and international rock, pop, funk, and renowned DJs. *Pont Alexandre III, 8th. ☎ 01-45-61-25-43. www.showcase.fr. Cover up to 20€. Métro: Champs-Elysées Clémenceau. Map p 115.*

★★ Machine du Moulin Rouge MONTMARTRE Set in the nightclub adjoining Paris's most famous cabaret, this is the latest hotspot for electronic music lovers. Expect cool DJ sets by famous names, a big dance floor, and youthful fauna soaking up the vibes. A great place to party. *90 bd. de Clichy, 18th. ☎ 01-53-41-88-89. Cover free–30€. Métro: Blanche. Map p 115.*

★★ Nouveau Casino OBERKAMPF This is one of the city's hottest clubs from Wednesday to Saturday, when local collectives and international names take over the DJ booth. From club to techno with stop-offs at jungle, it's a good place to see how the French get down. *102 rue Oberkampf, 11th. ☎ 01-43-57-57-40. http://www.nouveaucasino.net. Cover free–20€. Métro: Parmentier. Map p 116.*

Queen BOURSE Once a gay club (which explains the name), this very-late-night club attracts a mixed crowd of corporate workers kicking back, ladies out for a night of dancing, and tourists in the know. Occasionally attracts international DJs. *102 av. des Champs-Elysées, 8th. ☎ 01-53-89-08-90. www.queen.fr. Cover free–20€. Métro: George-V. Map p 115.*

★★ Wagg ST-GERMAIN-DES-PRES This was once the Whisky Go Go, a favorite of Jim Morrison during his last days. Now it lures technoholics and funk lovers from around the world. *62 rue Mazarine, 6th. ☎ 01-55-42-22-01. www.wagg.fr. Cover 5€–12€. Métro: Odéon. Map p 118.*

Gay & Lesbian Bars & Clubs

La Champmeslé BOURSE Dim lighting, background music, and banquets set the scene at this cozy meeting place for lesbians and gays. The 300-year-old building features exposed stone, ceiling beams, and 1950s-style furnishing. There's a cabaret every Thursday and Saturday at 10pm, and art exhibits every month. *4 rue Chabanais, 2nd. ☎ 01-42-96-85-20. www.lachampmesle.com. Métro: Pyramides or Bourse. Map p 116.*

Les Filles de Paris MARAIS This kitschy, lesbian-friendly bar doubles up as a restaurant and club, so you can party all night. Gays and straights are welcome too, so it's a fun spot for a wild night with a mixed group of friends. *57 rue Quincampoix, 4th. ☎ 01-42-71-72-20. Métro: Hôtel-de-Ville. Map p 116.*

Le Tango (aka La Boite à Frissons) REPUBLIQUE This wacky gay and lesbian dance hall plays cheesy Madonna songs and accordion music alike. Couples practice dancing the foxtrot and tango early on, then a DJ takes over and plays everything except techno. *13 rue au Maire, 2nd. ☎ 01-42-72-17-78. www.boite-a-frissons.fr. Cover 8€ (free Thurs). Métro: Arts et Métiers. Map p 116.*

Open Café & Café Cox MARAIS This pair of gay men's bars are two independent businesses, but there's so much traffic between them they're often thought of as a single place. You'll find the most mixed gay crowd in Paris here. *15 & 17 rue des Archives, 4th. ☎ 01-42-72-26-18 & www.opencafe.fr; ☎ 01-42-72-08-00 & www.cox.fr. Métro: Hôtel-de-Ville. Map p 116.*

8 The Best Arts & Entertainment

Arts & Entertainment Best Bets

Best **Theater for Musicals**
★★★ Théâtre du Châtelet *1 place du Châtelet, 1st (p 131)*

Best **Place to Walk in the Phantom's Footsteps**
★★★ Opéra Garnier *place de l'Opéra, 9th (p 132)*

Best **Place to Hear Classical Music**
Théâtre des Champs-Elysées *15 av. Montaigne, 8th (p 132)*

Best **Theater**
★ Comédie Française p*lace Colette, 1st (p 131)*

Best **Drag Show**
Cabaret Michou *80 rue des Martyrs, 18th (p 132)*

Best **Place to Hear Modern French Chanson**
★ Les Trois Baudets *64 bd. de Clichy, 18th (p 136)*

Best **Place to See the Cancan**
★ Moulin Rouge *place Blanche, 18th (p 133)*

Best **Chic Cabaret**
★★ Lido *116 bis av. des Champs-Elysées, 8th (p 132)*

Best **Place for 20-Somethings**
★ La Flêche d'Or *102 bis rue de Bagnolet, 20th (p 134)*

Best **Place to See & Be Seen**
★ New Morning *7–9 rue des Petites-Ecuries, 10th (p 136)*

Best **Jazz Club**
★★★ Au Duc des Lombards *42 rue des Lombards, 1st (p 134)*

Best **Nouvelle Orleans Jazz**
★★★ Le Sunset/Le Sunside *60 rue des Lombards, 1st (p 135)*

Best **Live Dinner Music**
La Bellevilloise *19 rue Boyer, 20th (p 134)*

Best **Indie Rock Concerts**
La Boule Noire, *120 bd. de Rochechouart,18th (p 134)*

The Opéra Bastille was inaugurated in 1989 for the Revolution's bicentennial. Previous page: The Grand Staircase and rococo interior of the Opéra Garnier.

Right Bank (8th & 18th)

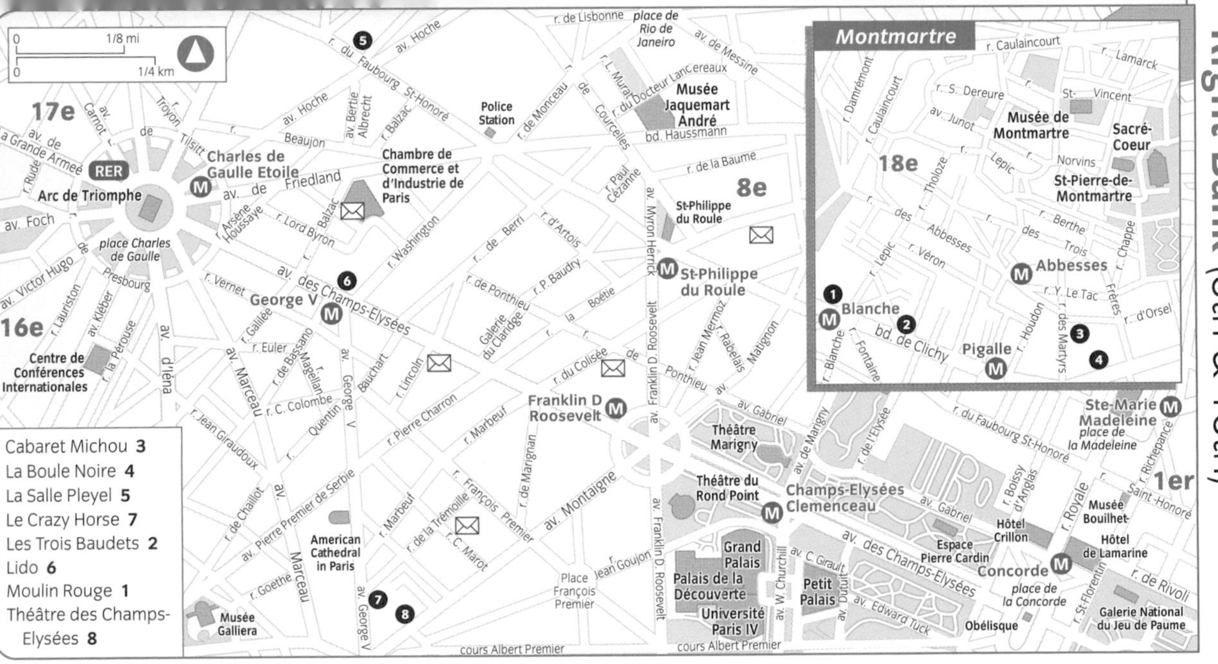

Right Bank (1st–4th & 9th–11th)

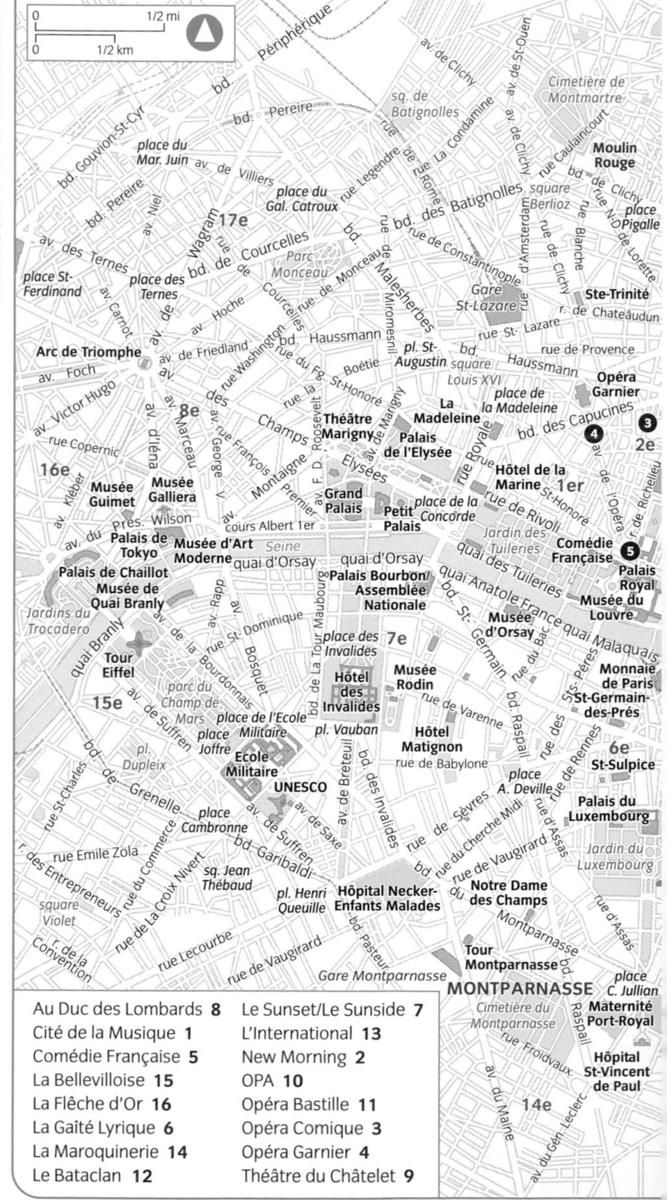

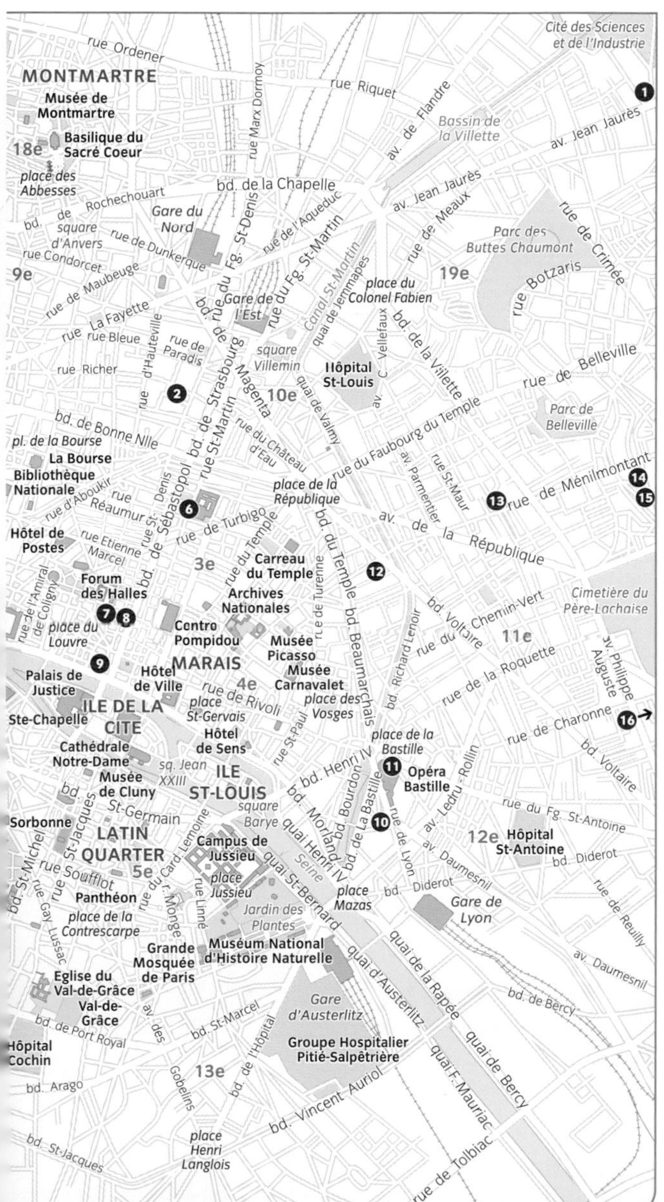
MONTMARTRE
Musée de Montmartre
Basilique du Sacré Coeur
18e
place des Abbesses
bd. de Rochechouart
square d'Anvers
Gare du Nord
rue Ordener
rue Marx Dormoy
rue Riquet
av. de Flandre
Bassin de la Villette
Cité des Sciences et de l'Industrie
av. Jean Jaurès
bd. de la Chapelle
rue de Dunkerque
rue Condorcet
9e
rue de Maubeuge
rue La Fayette
rue Bleue
rue Richer
rue d'Hauteville
rue de Paradis
rue du Fg. St-Denis
rue de l'Aqueduc
rue du Fg. St-Martin
Canal St-Martin
quai de Jemmapes
av. de Meaux
place du Colonel Fabien
19e
Parc des Buttes Chaumont
rue de Crimée
rue Botzaris
Gare de l'Est
bd. de Magenta
square Villemin
Hôpital St-Louis
av. C. Vellefaux
bd. de la Villette
rue de Belleville
Parc de Belleville
10e
quai de Valmy
bd. de Strasbourg
rue St-Martin
bd. de Bonne Nlle
pl. de la Bourse
La Bourse
Bibliothèque Nationale
rue d'Aboukir
rue Réaumur
rue St-Denis
bd. de Sébastopol
rue du Château d'Eau
rue du Faubourg du Temple
place de la République
av. Parmentier
rue St-Maur
rue de Ménilmontant
av. de la République
Hôtel de Postes
rue Etienne Marcel
rue de Turbigo
rue du Temple
Carreau du Temple
3e
bd. du Temple
Forum des Halles
Archives Nationales
rue de Turenne
rue de l'Amiral de Coligny
place du Louvre
Centre Pompidou
Musée Picasso
bd. Beaumarchais
bd. Voltaire
rue du Chemin-Vert
11e
Cimetière du Père-Lachaise
bd. Richard Lenoir
rue de la Roquette
av. Philippe Auguste
Palais de Justice
Hôtel de Ville
MARAIS
4e
Musée Carnavalet
rue de Rivoli
place St-Gervais
place des Vosges
Ste-Chapelle
ILE DE LA CITE
rue de Charonne
Hôtel de Sens
rue St-Paul
place de la Bastille
Cathédrale Notre-Dame
sq. Jean XXIII
ILE ST-LOUIS
bd. Henri IV
Opéra Bastille
av. Ledru-Rollin
bd. Voltaire
Musée de Cluny
bd. St-Germain
square Barye
bd. Morland
bd. Bourdon
bd. de La Bastille
rue du Fg. St-Antoine
Sorbonne
LATIN QUARTER
rue St-Jacques
bd. St-Michel
rue Soufflot
5e
rue du Card. Lemoine
Campus de Jussieu
quai Henri IV
Seine
rue de Lyon
av. Daumesnil
12e
Hôpital St-Antoine
bd. Diderot
place Jussieu
quai St-Bernard
place Mazas
Gare de Lyon
rue de Reuilly
Panthéon
rue Gay Lussac
place de la Contrescarpe
r. Monge
rue Linné
Jardin des Plantes
Grande Mosquée de Paris
Muséum National d'Histoire Naturelle
quai d'Austerlitz
quai de la Rapée
av. Daumesnil
bd. de Bercy
Eglise du Val-de-Grâce
Val-de-Grâce
av. des Gobelins
bd. St-Marcel
Gare d'Austerlitz
bd. de Port Royal
bd. de l'Hôpital
Groupe Hospitalier Pitié-Salpêtrière
quai de Bercy
quai F. Mauriac
Hôpital Cochin
13e
bd. Arago
bd. Vincent Auriol
bd. St-Jacques
place Henri Langlois
rue de Tolbiac
1
2
6
7
8
9
10
11
12
13
14
15
16

Left Bank (5th–6th)

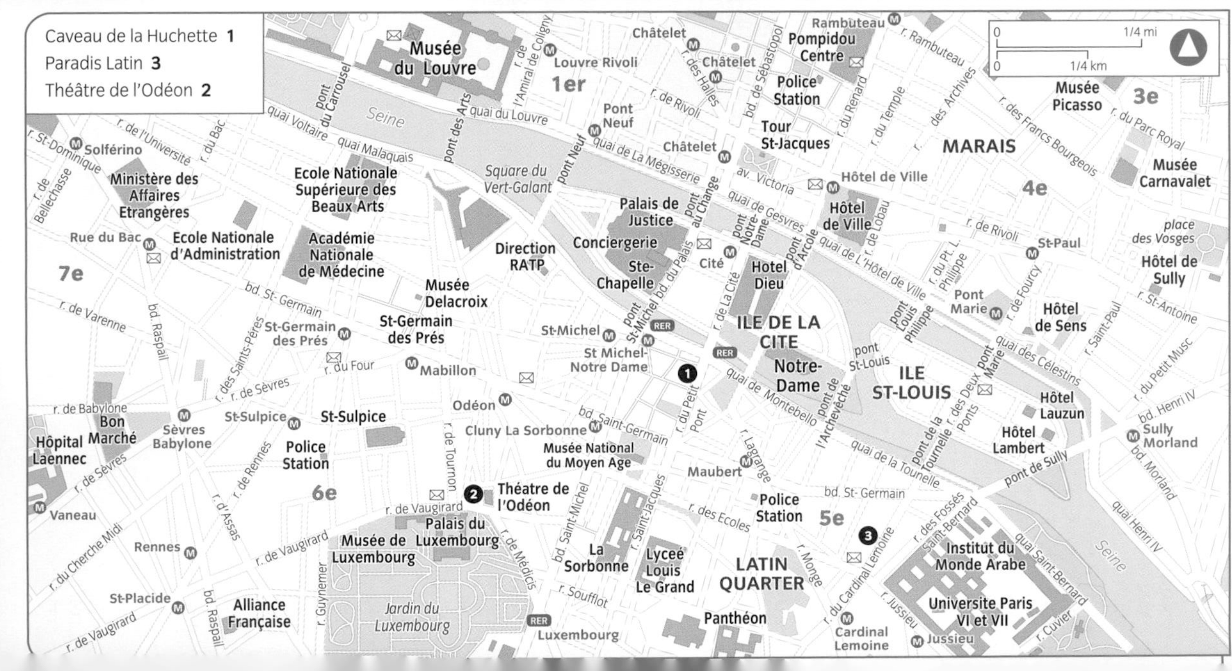

Arts & Entertainment A to Z

Theater & Musicals

★ **Comédie Française** PALAIS ROYAL Those with even a modest understanding of French will enjoy a sparkling production at this national theater, where the main goal is to keep the classics alive while promoting contemporary authors. *Place Colette, 1st. ☎ 08-25-10-16-80. www.comedie-francaise.fr. Tickets 20€–60€. Métro: Palais Royal–Musée du Louvre. Map p 128.*

★ **Théâtre de l'Odéon** ODEON More than just a theater, the Odéon hosts debates on literature, philosophy, and European politics—a Euro enthusiasm that is translated on stage with quality plays in different European languages, including English. *Place de l'Odéon, 6th. ☎ 01-44-85-40-40. www.theatre-odeon.fr. Tickets 10€–35€. Métro: Odéon. Map p 130.*

★★★ **Théâtre du Châtelet** CHÂTELET This Belle-Epoque masterpiece is the only place in Paris to perform Broadway standard musicals in English with full orchestras and parts sung by some of the world's best artists. Previous triumphs have included *Sweeney Todd* and the *Sound of Music;* and the program is completed with top-notch classical concerts, opera, and dance. *1 place du Châtelet, 1st. ☎ 01-40-28-28-40. www.chatelet-theatre.com. Tickets 20€–110€. Métro/RER: Châtelet. Map p 128.*

Opera, Dance & Classical

★ **Cité de la Musique** VILLETTE This multimillion-euro structure incorporates a network of concert halls, libraries, and a museum on musical instruments across the ages. It hosts a variety of concerts from Renaissance music to modern works. *221 av. Jean Jaurès, 19th. ☎ 01-44-84-44-84. www.cite-musique.fr. Tickets 8€–30€. Métro: Porte de Pantin. Map p 128.*

★★★ **La Salle Pleyel** TERNES Some say this modern, wooden concert hall has the best acoustics in Paris. It also has an eclectic program, ranging from Baroque quartets to symphonic orchestras, opera recitals, and jazz ensembles—all usually big names. The cheapest tickets are for the rows behind the orchestra, but your enjoyment won't be impeded. *252 rue du Faubourg St-Honoré, 8th. ☎ 01-42-56-13-13. www.sallepleyel.fr. Tickets 30€–190€. Métro: Ternes. Map p 127.*

★★★ **Opéra Bastille** BASTILLE This huge, contemporary building hosts outstanding opera performances, like Mozart's *Marriage of Figaro* and Tchaikovsky's *Queen of Spades,* in its three concert halls. Symphony and dance performances are held here occasionally as well. *2 place de la Bastille, 4th. ☎ 08-92-89-90-90. www.operadeparis.fr. Tickets opera 5€–120€; dance 20€–80€. Métro: Bastille. Map p 128.*

★★ **Opéra Comique** BOURSE Come to this charming venue, built in the 1880s, for light opera on a smaller scale than at the city's major opera houses. It's a lovely place to see *Carmen, Don Giovanni,* or *Tosca.* *5 rue Favart, 2nd. ☎ 08-25-01-01-23. www.opera-comique.com. Tickets 15€–100€. Métro: Richelieu-Drouot. Map p 128.*

Theatre Tip

Many theaters are closed over the summer, so check beforehand to

The windmill atop the Moulin Rouge is a landmark in Montmartre.

avoid disappointment. Also, where possible make advance reservations: Parisians are enthusiastic theatergoers and tickets can go like hotcakes.

★★★ Opéra Garnier OPERA The Phantom did his haunting here when it was a premier opera venue; now it's home to the city's ballet scene, although it still hosts opera from time to time. Charles Garnier's 1875 building is a rococo wonder with a centerpiece painted by Chagall. There are even beehives on the roof, which produce the Opéra honey for sale in the shop. *Place de l'Opéra, 9th. ☎ 08-92-89-90-90. www.operadeparis.fr. Tickets opera 20€–120€; dance 10€–70€. Métro: Opéra. Map p 128.*

Théâtre des Champs-Elysées CHAMPS ELYSEES National and international orchestras (such as the Vienna Philharmonic) fill this Art Deco theater with sound, to the delight of its well-dressed audiences. *15 av. Montaigne, 8th. ☎ 01-49-52-50-50. www.theatrechampselysees.fr. Tickets 10€–115€. Métro: Alma–Marceau. Map p 127.*

Cabarets

Cabaret Michou PIGALLE This eccentric place is run by a veteran impresario whose 20 cross-dressing belles lip-sync Whitney Houston and Mireille Mathieu while wearing bizarre costumes. If you don't have dinner, you must stand at the bar and pay a compulsory 31€ for your first drink. *80 rue des Martyrs, 18th. ☎ 01-46-06-16-04. www.michou.com. Cover including dinner (not drinks) & show 35€– 55€. Métro: Pigalle. Map p 127.*

★ Le Crazy Horse CHAMPS ELYSEES This sophisticated strip joint thrives on genuinely good choreography and the beauty of the girls, who dance dressed only in light. Not surprisingly, it's popular with businessmen, but women too will be surprised at how mesmerizing the show is. *12 av. George-V, 8th. ☎ 01-47-23-32-32. www.lecrazyhorseparis.com. Reservations recommended. Cover including ½ bottle champagne per person 70€–145€. Métro: George-V or Alma-Marceau. Map p 127.*

★★ Lido CHAMPS ELYSEES This glossy club puts on multimillion-euro performances in a dramatic reworking of the classic Parisian cabaret show, with special

Buying Tickets

The easiest way to get tickets nowadays is online, in advance from the venue's website. If you're staying in a first-class hotel, your concierge can probably arrange your tickets too. A service fee is added, but you won't waste precious sightseeing hours securing hard-to-get tickets.

Cheaper tickets, with discounts of up to 50%, can be found at the **Kiosque Théâtre,** 15 place de la Madeleine, 8th (no phone; Métro: Madeleine). They offer leftover tickets at about half-price on performance day. Tickets for evening shows are sold Tuesday to Friday from 12:30 to 8pm and Saturday from 2 to 8pm. Tickets for matinees are sold Saturday from 12:30 to 2pm and Sunday from 12:30 to 4pm. Students with ID can often get last-minute tickets by applying at the box office an hour before curtain time.

If you'd like to buy tickets before you go, check with **Keith Prowse** (www.keithprowse.com). The company will mail tickets to you, or leave tickets at the box office for pickup prior to the performance. There's a markup of about 25% over box-office prices on each ticket, which includes handling charges. Keith Prowse sells to customers all over the world, including the United States, Canada, the United Kingdom, Australia, and New Zealand.

Another good place to try is any branch of the FNAC media store (or www.fnac.com). They handle tickets for most museums, concerts, and shows across France. The Champs Elysées branch is open until midnight (p 88).

effects, including aerial and aquatic ballets—even an occasional ice rink. *116 bis av. des Champs-Elysées, 8th. ☎ 01-40-76-56-10. www.lido.fr. Show 70€–135€ (with ½ bottle champagne per person); dinner & show 150€–280€. Métro: George-V. Map p 127.*

★ **Paradis Latin** LATIN QUARTER Built by Gustave Eiffel, this club introduced vaudeville to Paris in the 19th century. Today its colorful performances, with singers, dancers, and special effects, hearken back to that time. Expect some toplessness and a French rather than a touristy crowd. Ticket prices include champagne. *28 rue Cardinal Lemoine, 5th. ☎ 01-43-25-28-28. www.paradis-latin.com. Show only 85€ (with ½ bottle champagne per person); dinner and show 123€–179€; lunch and show 100€; matinee show 65€–75€. Métro: Jussieu or Cardinal Lemoine. Map p 130.*

★ **Moulin Rouge** MONTMARTRE Toulouse-Lautrec immortalized this windmill-topped building and its scantily clad cancan dancers (this is where the risqué dance was invented). Today it's true to its original theme and very cheesy, but the dancing is perfectly synchronized and the girls are all beautiful. *Place Blanche, 18th. ☎ 01-53-09-82-82. www.moulinrouge.fr. Show only 90€; show and ½ bottle champagne 102€; dinner & show 150€–180€. Métro: Blanche. Map p 127.*

Jazz, Rock & More

Au Duc des Lombards CHATELET This thriving jazz club has hosted all the greats of Paris's jazz era. Today it features nightly performances that range in style from free jazz to hard bop. Tables can be reserved and meals are served (prepared with fair-trade produce only). ***42 rue des Lombards, 1st. ☎ 01-42-33-22-88. www.ducdeslombards.com. Cover varies. Métro: Châtelet. Map p 128.***

★ Caveau de la Huchette LATIN QUARTER This celebrated jazz cave draws a young crowd, mostly university students, who dance to the music of well-known jazz combos. Robespierre hung out here in his time, so you can tell everyone you're here for the history. ***5 rue de la Huchette, 5th. ☎ 01-43-26-65-05. www.caveaudelahuchette.fr. Cover 10€–14€. Métro: St-Michel. RER: St-Michel-Notre-Dame. Map p 130.***

★★ La Bellevilloise MENILMONTANT This multidisciplinary venue (set inside France's first cooperative building) has several bars, two restaurants, a nightclub, an exhibition space, and a concert hall where some of Paris's most exciting bands have been launched. It's a place in which to relax, soak up the atmosphere, and spend the whole evening. ***19 rue Boyer, 20th. ☎ 01-46-36-07-07. www.labellevilloise.com. Cover varies. Metro: Gambetta or Ménilmontant. Map p 128.***

La Boule Noire PIGALLE The Black Ball is one of those intimate, divey Parisian haunts that attract biggies such as the Dandy Warhols, Metallica, Cat Power, Franz Ferdinand, and Jamie Cullum. Despite the star-studded line up, prices tend to hover around the 20€ mark, making this one of the cheapest venues around. ***120 bd. Rochechouart, 75018. ☎ 01-49-25-81-75. www.laboule-noire.fr. Cover varies. Metro: Anvers or Pigalle. Map p 127.***

★★★ La Flêche d'Or PERE LACHAISE This funky rock, indie, and electro venue has highly credible acts (from both France and abroad), and the advantage of being set in a unique building—a former train station with a room that hangs over the tracks. This is a popular choice for trendy music buffs. ***102 bis rue de Bagnolet, 20th. ☎ 01-44-64-01-02. www.flechedor.fr. Cover***

Indy bands dominate the stage at La Flêche d'Or, in the 20th arrondissement.

Best Free Shows in Paris

As you stroll along the river, keep your eyes peeled for free entertainment by street performers. In the summer months, the area at the southeastern tip of Ile de la Cité, behind the Notre-Dame, becomes a stage of sorts when performance artists, musicians, jugglers, mimes, or magicians put on a show against the backdrop of the cathedral. The atmosphere is euphoric, the performances can be brilliant, and it makes for wonderful memories.

A later option is a stroll along the Seine after 10pm. From the pont de Sully, take a pathway down on the Left Bank (away from Notre-Dame) to the Square Tino Rossi—a free open-air sculpture museum. As you stroll, you'll pass musicians and other performers, and when the music is good, spontaneous tango parties often break out at the water's edge.

varies. Métro: Alexandre-Dumas. Map p 128.

★★ La Gaité Lyrique HAUT MARAIS This former opera house (where Offenbach once created the operetta genre) is a showcase for emerging digital art forms. After visiting the art installations, you can frequently attend an electronic pop/rock music concert in the Grand Salle, whose walls are giant speakers. International DJ Gilles Petersen and his musical discoveries are frequently programmed. ***3 bis rue Papin, 3rd. ☎ 01-53-01-51-51. www.gaite-lyrique.net. Cover varies. Métro: Réamur-Sébastopol. Map p 128.***

La Maroquinerie BELLEVILLE Up-and-coming rock acts take center stage at this hip concert venue, which doubles as a restaurant, bar, and literary cafe. You can easily spend the whole night here. ***23 rue Boyer, 20th. ☎ 01-40-33-35-05. www.lamaroquinerie.fr. Cover varies. Métro: Ménilmontant or Gambetta. Map p 128.***

L'International OBERKAMPF Arty types flock to this grungy bar for its winning formula of cheap beer and free live music concerts. A stream of on-the-up bands play here making it a great joint in which to spot the talent of the future and get to grips with Paris's electro-rock scene. ***5/7 rue Moret, 11th. ☎ 01-49-29-76-45. www.linternational.fr. Free entry. Métro: Menilmontant. Map p 128.***

Le Bataclan REPUBLIQUE Behind the brightly colored facade of this former music hall (established in 1864), the Bataclan is a flagship of Paris's music scene with top funk, rock, jazz, and hip-hop acts from across the globe. ***50 bd. Voltaire, 11th. ☎ 01-43-14-00-30. www.le-bataclan.com. Cover varies. Métro: Oberkampf. Map p 128.***

Le Sunset/Le Sunside CHÂTELET This staple of the Parisian jazz circuit is two bars in one, with separate jazz shows going on simultaneously. The look is minimalist, and artists are both European and U.S.-based. Le Sunside favors classic jazz, and Le Sunset goes for electric jazz and world music. Take your pick. ***60 rue des Lombards, 1st.***

La Bellevilloise is an entertainment emporium housing multiple venues.

☎ *01-40-26-21-25. www.sunset-sunside.com. Cover varies Métro: Châtelet. Map p 128.*

Les Trois Baudets PIGALLE Between 1947 and 1966 this small theater launched more musical careers than anywhere else (Gainsbourg, Brel, Hénri Salvador all started here). Nowadays it's Paris's main francophone music theater, with a jam-packed program of rock, electro, folk, *chanson,* and slam. ***64 bd. de Clichy, 18th.*** ☎ ***01-42-62-33-33.*** *www.lestroisbaudets.com. Cover varies. Metro: Pigalle. Map p 127.*

★ **New Morning** EASTERN PARIS Jazz fanatics pack this respected club to drink, talk, and dance—not to mention check each other out. Celebs like Spike Lee and Prince have been spotted here. The club is popular with African and European musicians. ***7–9 rue des Petites-Ecuries, 10th.*** ☎ ***01-45-23-51-41.*** *www.newmorning.com. Cover varies. Métro: Château d'Eau. Map p 128.*

OPA BASTILLE Join the young pretty things at industrial-chic OPA, which mixes live music with DJ nights (until 6am on weekends). Musicwise expect a large dose of rock, pop, and electro sound. ***9 rue Biscornet, 12th.*** ☎ ***01-46-28-12-90.*** *www.opa-paris.com. Metro: Bastille. Map p 128.* ●

9 The Best **Hotels**

Hotel Best Bets

Best **Balcony Views**
Hôtel Edouard 7 $ *39 av. de l'Opera, 2nd (p 146)*

Best **for Romantics**
★ Hôtel Duc de St-Simon $$$ *14 rue de St-Simon, 7th (p 146)*

Best **Fun Design**
The Five Hotel $$ *3 rue Flatters, 5th (p 144)*

Best **Boutique Hotel**
★ L'Hôtel $$$$ *13 rue des Beaux-Arts, 6th (p 150)*

Best **Kid-Friendly Hotel**
Hôtel Lion d'Or $$ *5 rue de la Sourdière, 1st (p 148)*

Best **Budget Sleep**
★ St Christopher's Inn $ *159 rue de Crimée, 19th (p 152)*

Best **Luxury Hotel**
★★★ Hôtel Shangri-Là $$$$$ *10 ave. d'Iéna, 16th (p 148)*

Best **21st-Century Luxury**
★★★ Hyatt Regency Paris Madeleine $$$$$ *24 bd Malesherbes, 8th (p 149)*

Best **Hip Hotel**
★★ Mama Shelter $$ *107 rue de Bagnolet, 20th (p 150)*

Best **Eco-Friendly Hotel**
Solar Hôtel $ *22 rue Boulard, 14th (p 152)*

Best **Family Run Hotel**
★★★ Aviatic Hotel $$$ *105 rue de Vaugirard, 6th (p 144)*

Best **for Literary Types**
★ Hotel Lenox $$ *9 rue de l'Université, 7th (p 147)*

Best **"Only in Paris" Hideaway**
★★ Pensions Les Marroniers $ *78 rue d'Assas, 6th (p 151)*

Best **Place to Detox**
★ Hotel Gabriel $$$ *25 rue du Grand Prieuré, 11th (p 146)*

Best **for Foodies**
Le Thoumieux $$$ *79 rue St Dominique, 7th (p 150)*

Best **Quirky Hotel**
Paris Yacht $$ *quai de la Tournelle, 5th (p 151)*

Previous Page: The Hôtel Chopin in the Passage Jouffroy.

Right Bank (8th & 16th–18th)

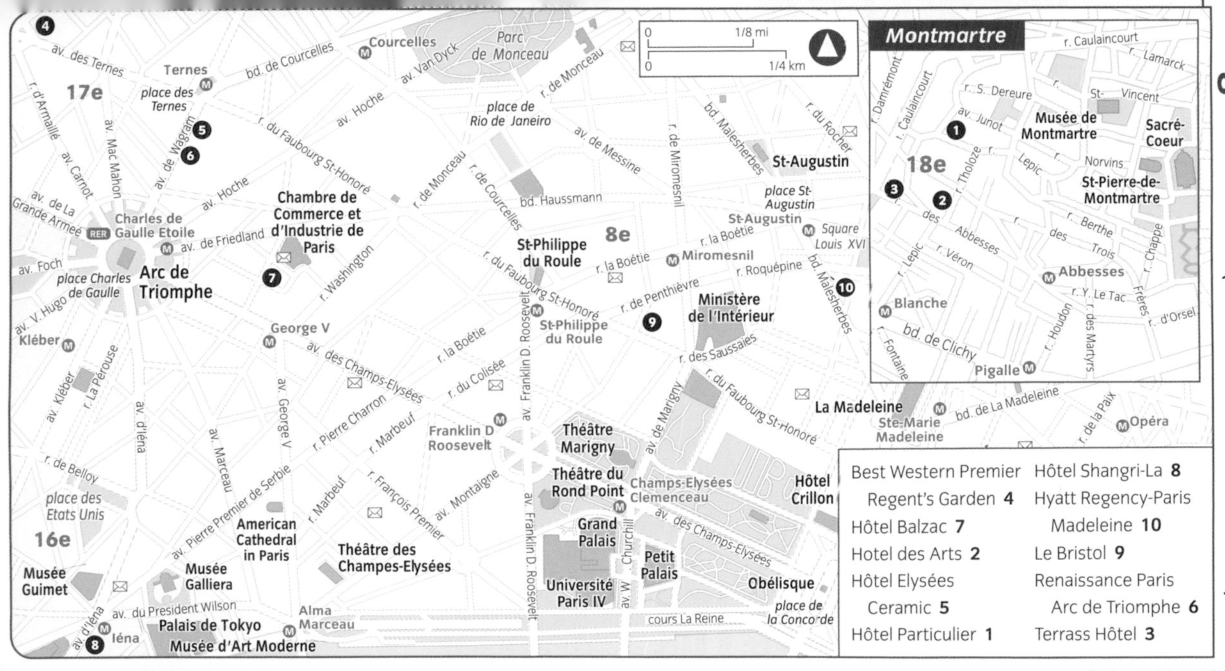

Right Bank (1st–4th & 9th–11th)

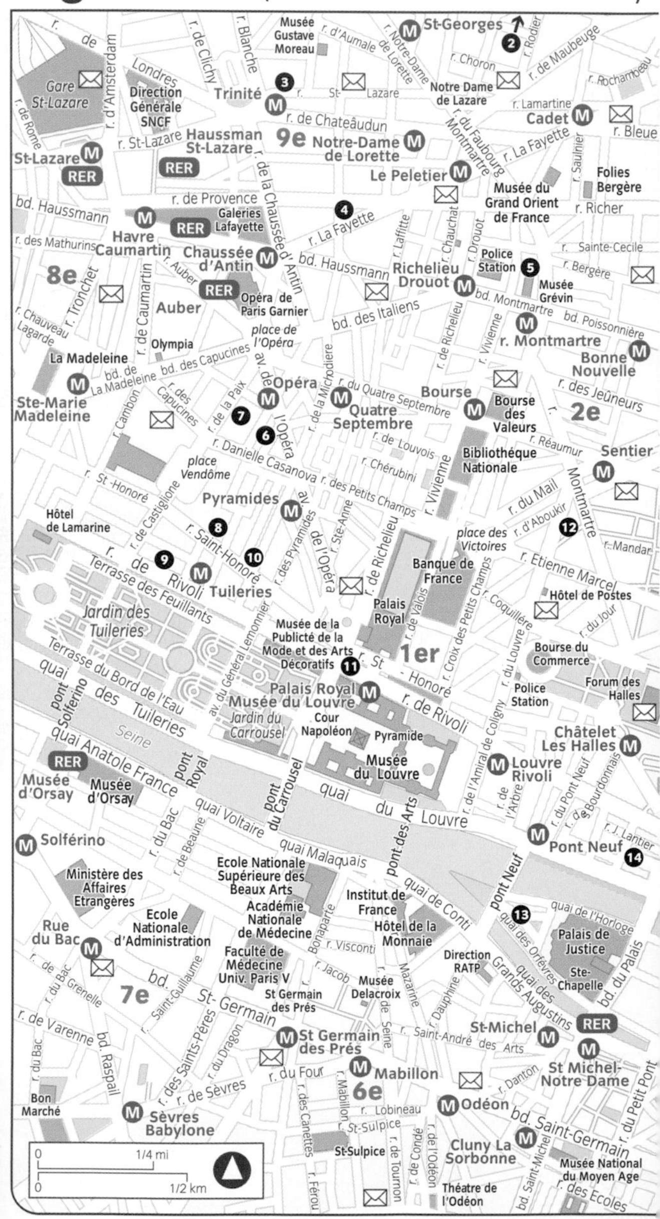

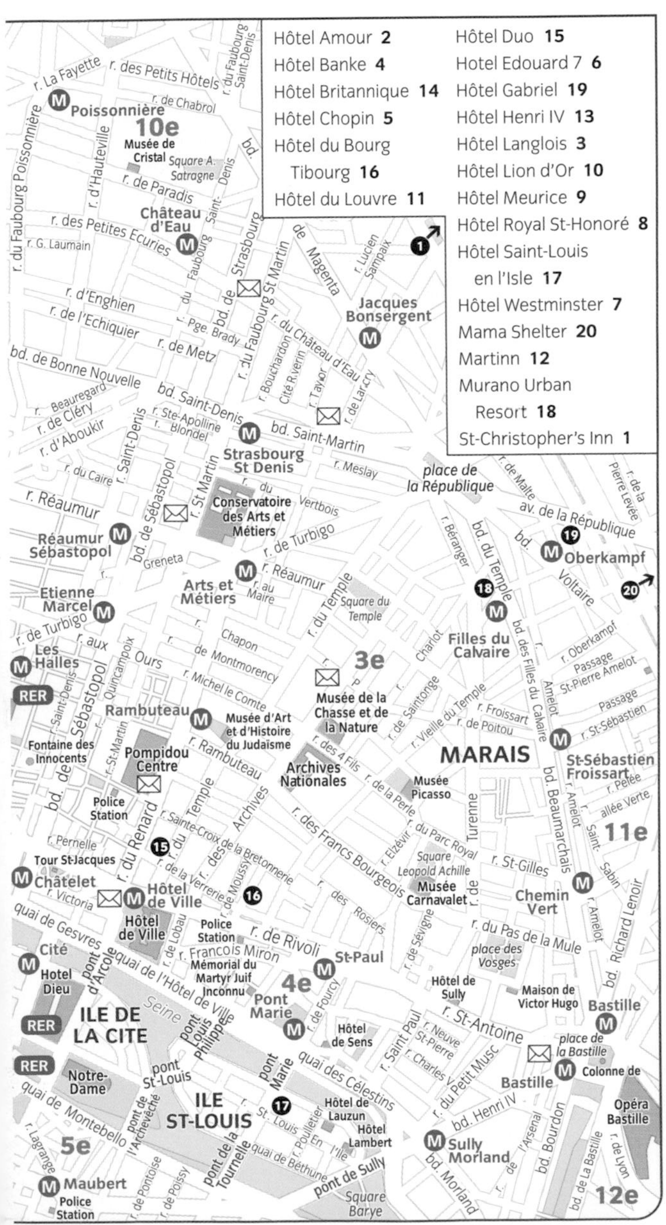
Hôtel Amour 2
Hôtel Banke 4
Hôtel Britannique 14
Hôtel Chopin 5
Hôtel du Bourg Tibourg 16
Hôtel du Louvre 11
Hôtel Duo 15
Hotel Edouard 7 6
Hôtel Gabriel 19
Hôtel Henri IV 13
Hôtel Langlois 3
Hôtel Lion d'Or 10
Hôtel Meurice 9
Hôtel Royal St-Honoré 8
Hôtel Saint-Louis en l'Isle 17
Hôtel Westminster 7
Mama Shelter 20
Martinn 12
Murano Urban Resort 18
St-Christopher's Inn 1
Poissonnière
10e
Musée de Cristal
Square A. Satragne
Château d'Eau
Jacques Bonsergent
Strasbourg St Denis
place de la République
Conservatoire des Arts et Métiers
Réaumur Sébastopol
Arts et Métiers
Oberkampf
Square du Temple
Filles du Calvaire
Etienne Marcel
Les Halles
RER
3e
Musée de la Chasse et de la Nature
Rambuteau
Musée d'Art et d'Histoire du Judaïsme
Fontaine des Innocents
Pompidou Centre
Archives Nationales
MARAIS
St-Sébastien Froissart
Musée Picasso
11e
Police Station
Tour St-Jacques
Square Leopold Achille
Musée Carnavalet
Châtelet
Hôtel de Ville
Chemin Vert
Cité
St-Paul
place des Vosges
Mémorial du Martyr Juif Inconnu
Hotel Dieu
4e
Hôtel de Sully
Maison de Victor Hugo
Bastille
Pont Marie
ILE DE LA CITE
Seine
Hôtel de Sens
place de la Bastille
Colonne de
Notre-Dame
ILE ST-LOUIS
Hôtel de Lauzun
Hôtel Lambert
Opéra Bastille
5e
Sully Morland
Maubert
Square Barye
12e

Left Bank (5th–6th)

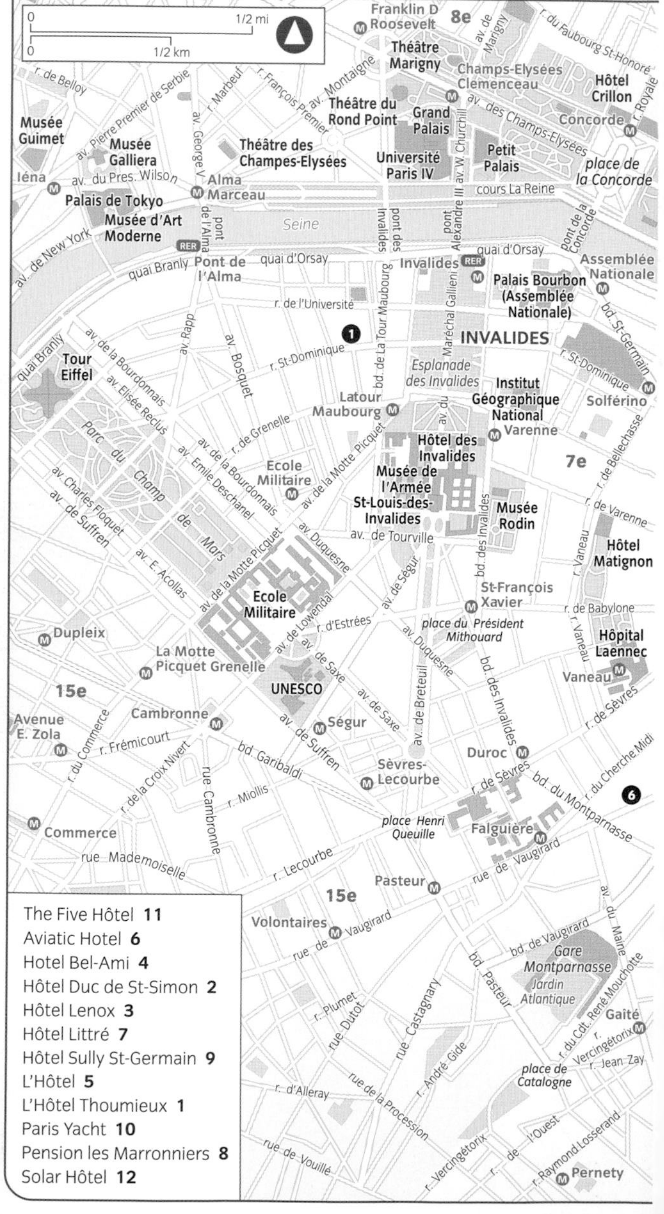

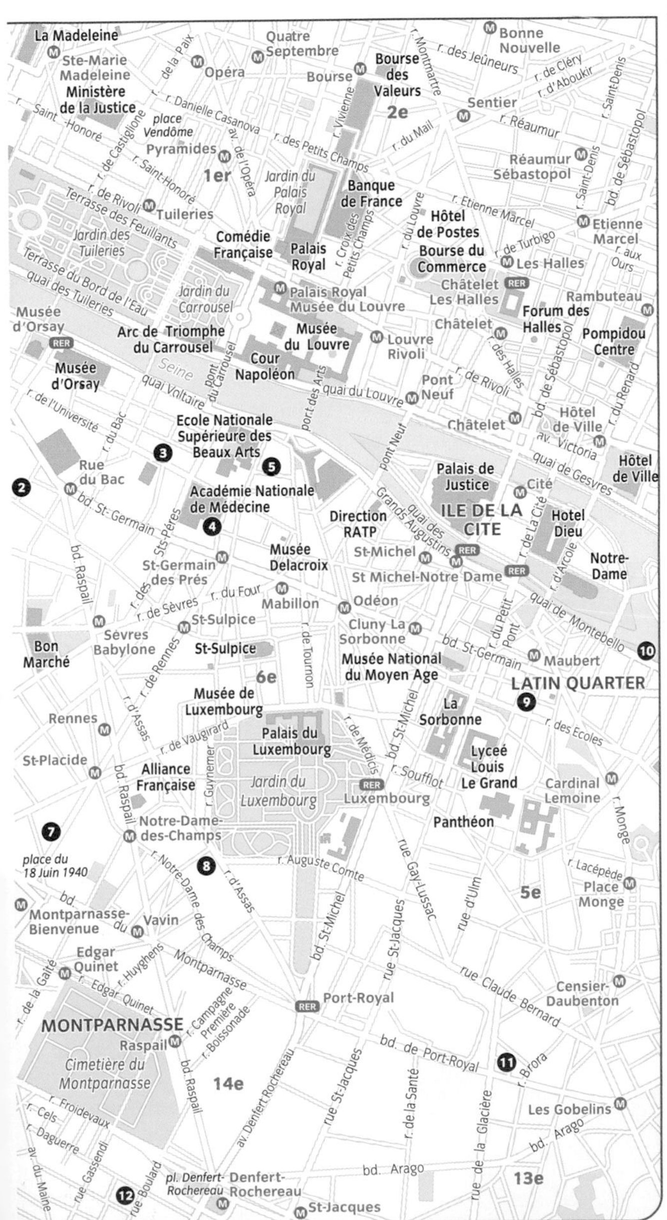
La Madeleine
Ste-Marie Madeleine
Ministère de la Justice
Opéra
Quatre Septembre
Bourse
Bourse des Valeurs
2e
Bonne Nouvelle
Sentier
Réaumur Sébastopol
Etienne Marcel
place Vendôme
Pyramides
1er
Jardin du Palais Royal
Banque de France
Hôtel de Postes
Bourse du Commerce
Les Halles
Châtelet Les Halles
Tuileries
Jardin des Tuileries
Comédie Française
Palais Royal
Palais Royal Musée du Louvre
Rambuteau
Forum des Halles
Pompidou Centre
Jardin du Carrousel
Musée d'Orsay
Arc de Triomphe du Carrousel
Musée du Louvre
Louvre Rivoli
Châtelet
Cour Napoléon
Musée d'Orsay
Seine
Pont Neuf
Châtelet
Hôtel de Ville
Ecole Nationale Supérieure des Beaux Arts
3
5
Rue du Bac
2
Palais de Justice
Hôtel de Ville
Cité
Académie Nationale de Médecine
4
Direction RATP
ILE DE LA CITE
Hotel Dieu
Musée Delacroix
St-Michel
St-Germain des Prés
St Michel-Notre Dame
Notre-Dame
Mabillon
Odéon
Sèvres Babylone
St-Sulpice
St-Sulpice
Cluny La Sorbonne
Bon Marché
Musée National du Moyen Age
Maubert
10
6e
LATIN QUARTER
Musée de Luxembourg
La Sorbonne
9
Rennes
Palais du Luxembourg
Lyceé Louis Le Grand
St-Placide
Alliance Française
Jardin du Luxembourg
Luxembourg
Cardinal Lemoine
Panthéon
Notre-Dame-des-Champs
7
place du 18 Juin 1940
8
5e
Place Monge
Montparnasse-Bienvenue
Vavin
Edgar Quinet
Censier-Daubenton
Port-Royal
MONTPARNASSE
Raspail
Cimetière du Montparnasse
14e
11
Les Gobelins
Denfert-Rochereau
pl. Denfert-Rochereau
12
St-Jacques
13e
bd. Arago
rue de la Glacière
r. de la Santé
rue St-Jacques
bd. de Port-Royal
rue Claude Bernard
rue Gay-Lussac
rue d'Ulm
bd. St-Michel
r. Auguste Comte
r. Soufflot
r. des Ecoles
bd. St-Germain
quai de Montebello
quai des Grands Augustins
quai du Louvre
quai Voltaire
r. de Rivoli
r. Saint-Honoré
bd. Raspail
r. de Rennes
r. d'Assas
r. de Vaugirard
bd. du Montparnasse
av. Denfert Rochereau
r. Froidevaux
av. du Maine
rue Gassendi
rue Boulard
r. Daguerre
r. Cels
r. de la Gaîté
r. Edgar Quinet
r. Huyghens
r. Campagne Première
r. Boissonade
r. Notre-Dame-des-Champs
r. Guynemer
r. de Médicis
r. de Tournon
r. du Four
r. de Sèvres
r. des Sts-Pères
r. du Bac
r. de l'Université
pont du Carrousel
pont des Arts
pont Neuf
r. du Petit Pont
r. de La Cité
r. d'Arcole
quai de Gesvres
av. Victoria
bd. de Sébastopol
r. des Halles
r. du Renard
r. aux Ours
r. de Turbigo
r. Etienne Marcel
r. du Louvre
r. Croix des Petits Champs
r. des Petits Champs
r. Vivienne
r. du Mail
r. Montmartre
r. des Jeûneurs
r. de Cléry
r. d'Aboukir
r. Saint-Denis
r. Réaumur
av. de l'Opéra
r. de Castiglione
r. de la Paix
r. Danielle Casanova
Terrasse des Feuillants
Terrasse du Bord de l'Eau
quai des Tuileries
r. Monge
r. Lacépède
bd. Arago
r. Broca

Paris Hotels **A to Z**

★★★ kids **Aviatic Hotel** MONTPARNASSE/ST-GERMAIN Rooms in this family-run hotel are lushly decorated in thick, patterned fabrics and parquet floors. The hearty breakfasts are served in a bistro-style room that feels like a Left Bank institution. Families are welcome here, but the atmosphere is nonetheless romantic too. *105 rue Vaugirard, 6th.* ☎ *01-53-63-25-50. www.aviatic hotel.com. 42 units. Doubles 95€–260€. AE, MC, V. Métro: Montparnasse or St-Placide. Map p 142.*

★★★ kids **Best Western Premier Regent's Garden** CHAMPS-ELYSEES A good, guilt-free night's sleep is guaranteed in this environmentally-friendly hotel, whose efforts to reduce carbon emissions have earned it the difficult-to-obtain European Ecolabel. Rooms are elegant, in bold stripes and patterns; there's a relaxing spa and a flower-filled courtyard—perfect for breakfast alfresco. *6 rue Pierre Demours, 8th.* ☎ *01-45-74-07-30. www.hotel-regents-paris.com. 40 units. Doubles 160€–320€. AE, MC, V. Métro: Ternes or Charles de Gaulle–Etoile. Map p 139.*

The Five Hôtel LATIN QUATER The ultra-modern rooms here are small but impressive, with Chinese lacquer, velvet fabrics, fiber-optic lighting that makes you feel as though you're sleeping under a starry sky, and your own room fragrance. In all, it's a fine design hotel and convenient base for exploring the Left Bank. *3 rue Flatters, 5th.* ☎ *01-43-31-74-21. www.thefive hotel.com. 24 units. Doubles 200€–350€. MC, V. Métro: Les Gobelins. RER: Port Royal. Map p 142.*

★ **Hôtel Amour** PIGALLE Rooms in this boutique hotel are individually decorated by progressive artists such as Sophie Calle, M&M, and Pierre Le Tan. The result in some is risqué (photos of bare bottoms), but if you mind, what are you doing in Pigalle? The brasserie-bar with a hidden garden is a hit with Paris's trendy crowd. *8 rue Navarin, 9th.* ☎ *01-48-78-31-80. www.hotel amourparis.fr. 20 units. Doubles 140€–275€. AE, MC, V. Métro: Pigalle or St Georges. Map p 140.*

★★ **Hôtel Balzac** CHAMPS-ELYSEES This Belle Epoque mansion

The Aviatic Hotel in St-Germain is family-friendly yet romantic.

The Hôtel Banke is lodged in, you guessed it—a former bank building.

with a pretty courtyard is luxuriously designed with ostentatious 19th-century touches and king-size beds. Its elegant restaurant is a hit with locals who come for its comparably low prices (45€ a head) and intimate atmosphere. ***6 rue Balzac, 8th. ☎ 01-44-35-18-00. www.hotelbalzac.com. 70 units. Doubles 330€–870€. AE, DC, MC, V. Métro: George-V. Map p 139.***

★ **Hôtel Banke** OPERA This smart hotel has a breathtaking neo–Belle Epoque lobby, left over from a time when the building was a bank (hence the name). Rooms are stylish in browns and reds, and beds have ultra-comfy mattresses. The restaurant serves a menu with a Spanish twist. ***20 rue Lafayette, 9th. ☎ 01-55-33-22-22. www.derbyhotels.com. 94 units. Doubles 200€–350€. AE, MC, V. Métro: Le Peletier. Map p 140.***

★ **Hotel Bel-Ami** LATIN QUARTER Recently restored, floor by floor, this sleek, arts-conscious hotel has a minimalist look with a clean design aesthetic. Earth-toned guest rooms have a Zen-like air. Check the website for deals. ***7–11 rue St-Benoit, 6th. ☎ 01-49-27-09-33. www.hotel-bel-ami.com. 115 units. Doubles 300€–400€. AE, DC, MC, V. Métro: St-Germain-des-Prés. Map p 142.***

★ **Hôtel Britannique** HOTEL DE VILLE Tastefully modern and plush, this place has cultivated a kind of English graciousness. Guest rooms are small but nicely appointed and soundproof. The location is so central you can walk almost anywhere. ***20 av. Victoria, 1st. ☎ 01-42-33-74-59. www.hotel-britannique.com. 39 units. Doubles 160€–200€. AE, DC, MC, V. Métro: Châtelet. Map p 140.***

★ **Hôtel Chopin** GRANDS BOULEVARDS This intimate, eccentric hotel is hidden inside a curious 19th-century covered passage. The Victorian lobby has elegant woodwork, rooms are comfortably furnished, and the staff is friendly. ***10 bd. Montmartre, 9th. ☎ 01-47-70-58-10. www.hotelchopin.fr. 36 units. Doubles 96€–110€. Métro: Grands Boulevards. Map p 140.***

Hôtel des Arts MONTMARTRE Rooms in this old-fashioned but utterly charming hotel are simple, but some look out over Montmartre's rooftops. You couldn't ask for a better spot for exploring La Butte, its galleries, and cobbled, hilly streets. ***5 rue Tholozé, 18th. ☎ 01-46-06-30-52. www.arts-hotel-paris.com. 50 units. Doubles 95€–165€. MC, V. Métro: Abbesses or Blanche. Map p 139.***

★ **Hôtel du Bourg Tibourg** MARAIS Hotels with far less style can cost twice as much as this well-located place. Rooms are small but comfortable, with romantic, modern decor and lush fabrics in everything from leopard print to stripes. ***19 rue du Bourg-Tibourg, 4th. ☎ 01-42-78-47-39. www.hoteldubourgtibourg.com. 30 units. Doubles 250€–270€. AE, MC, V. Métro: Hôtel-de-Ville. Map p 140.***

Camille Pissaro once lived in the palatial building that houses the Hôtel du Louvre.

★ Hôtel Duc de St-Simon
INVALIDES A sweet courtyard offers your first glimpse of this hopelessly romantic hotel that seduced the likes of Lauren Bacall. Rooms are filled with antiques, objets d'art, and lush fabrics. Some have terraces overlooking a garden. *14 rue de St-Simon, 7th. ☎ 01-44-39-20-20. www.hotelducdesaintsimon.com. 34 units. Doubles 265€–295€. AE, MC, V. Métro: Rue du Bac. Map p 142.*

★★ Hôtel du Louvre LOUVRE
This former home of painter Camille Pissarro is now a sort of Belle Epoque palace hotel, resplendent with marble, bronze, and gilt galore. Guest rooms are stuffed with antiques and heavy fabrics. *Place André Malraux, 1st. ☎ 01-44-58-38-38. www.hoteldulouvre.com. 177 units. Doubles 455€–590€. AE, DC, MC, V. Métro: Palais Royal or Louvre Rivoli. Map p 140.*

★★ Hôtel-Duo MARAIS One of the city's trendiest cutting-edge hotels, with a location right in the heart of the Marais. Decor has an old-world charm with a distinctly modern feel thanks to rooms all dressed up in cool browns, creams, and bold print wallpaper. *11 rue du Temple, 4th. ☎ 01-42-72-72-22. http://duo-paris.com. 45 units. Doubles 200€–380€. AE, DC, MC, V. Métro: Hôtel-de-Ville. Map p 140.*

★★ kids Hôtel Edouard 7
OPERA The Edouard 7's balcony views over the Opera Garnier are breathtaking. The hotel is also in a plum location for shopping at the Galeries Lafayette department store and visiting the Louvre. The large and airy rooms come in two designs: "Classical" with antique furniture and "Couture" in warm-toned velvets, rather like a boudoir. Kids get a gift when you check out. *39 ave de l'Opéra, 2nd. ☎ 01-42-61-56-90. www.edouard7hotel.com. 69 units. Doubles 250€–350€. AE, DC, MC, V. Métro: Opéra. RER Auber. Map p 140.*

★ Hôtel Elysées Ceramic
ETOILE An ornate ceramic facade helps make this celebrated Art Nouveau building easy to find. The clean, modern, attractive rooms are less over-the-top, and the shaded patio is a godsend in summer. *34 av. de Wagram, 8th. ☎ 01-42-27-20-30. www.elysees-ceramic.com. 57 units. Doubles 230€. AE, DC, MC, V. Métro: Charles-de-Gaulle-Etoile. Map p 138.*

★ Hôtel Gabriel REPUBLIQUE
Relaxing massages, healthy food, and Zen decor is what you get at Paris's first-ever detox hotel. Come here to wind down and escape the

city life outside. ***25 rue du Grand Prieuré, 11th.*** ☎ ***01-47-00-13-38. www.gabrielparismarais.com. 40 units. Doubles160€–280€. Métro: République. Map p 140.***

★★★ Hôtel Henri IV THE ISLANDS This is possibly Paris's best budget hotel, at the heart of the Ile de la Cité, near Notre-Dame and pont Neuf. Rooms are very basic but clean, and the top-floor rooms have balconies. Book way in advance. Only 11 rooms have en suite bathrooms. ***25 place Dauphine, 1st.*** ☎ ***01-43-54-44-53. www.henri4hotel.fr. 15 units. Doubles 45€–75€. MC, V. Métro: Pont Neuf. Map p 140.***

★ Hôtel Langlois GRANDS BOULEVARDS This charming hotel in a restored town house has such charming touches as a curving Parisian stairwell and an antique, wrought-iron elevator. Rooms are smallish but generally tasteful, some with fireplaces. ***63 rue St-Lazare, 9th.*** ☎ ***01-48-74-78-24. www.hotel-langlois.com. 27 units. Doubles 140€–150€. AE, DC, MC, V. Métro: Trinité. Map p 140.***

★ Hotel Lenox ST-GERMAIN-DES-PRES The staff will happily fill you in on the literary history of the hotel. (T.S. Eliot convinced James Joyce to stay here after Ezra Pound fell in love with the place.) The bar alone is

Hôtel Langlois features Belle Epoque architectural details and moderate rates.

worth a visit. The modern guest rooms, reached via a glass elevator, are decorated in creamy tones with rich blue accents and some antique reproductions. Some rooms have wondrous views. ***9 rue de l'Université, 7th.*** ☎ ***01-42-96-10-95. www.lenoxsaintgermain.com. 40 units. Doubles 190€–260€. AE, DC, MC, V. Métro: St-Germain-des-Prés. Map p 142.***

★★ kids Hôtel Lion d'Or TUILERIES The "Golden Lion" has bright, simple rooms plus fully furnished apartments that sleep up to five people. It's well located, too, right near the Louvre. ***5 rue de la***

Guests' health and well-being come first at the Hôtel Gabriel in the Republique.

Sourdière, 1st. ☎ 01-42-60-79-04. www.hotel-louvre-paris.com. 27 units. Doubles 120€–195€. Apartments: 280€–490€. MC, V. Métro: Tuileries. Map p 140.

★ **Hôtel Littré** MONTPARNASSE This family-run hotel, set inside a Victorian building of honey-colored stone, is a perfect example of understated refinement. Most rooms are large (for Paris) and have endearing (if not a little old fashioned) touches, such as balconies with views over the Eiffel Tower. *9 rue Littré, 6th. ☎ 01-53-63-07-07. www.hotellittre paris.com. 90 units. Doubles 164€–243€. AE, DC, MC, V. Métro: St-Placide or Montparnasse. Map p 142.*

★★ **Hôtel Meurice** CONCORDE Salvador Dalí once made this hotel his headquarters. It's gorgeous, with perfectly preserved mosaic floors, hand-carved moldings, and an Art Nouveau glass roof. Rooms are sumptuous and individually decorated, some with fluffy clouds and blue skies painted on the ceilings. *228 rue de Rivoli, 1st. ☎ 01-44-58-10-10. www.meurice hotel.com. 160 units. Doubles 620€–910€. AE, DC, MC, V. Métro: Tuileries or Concorde. Map p 140.*

★★★ **Hôtel Particulier** MONTMARTRE You'll be hard-pressed to find somewhere more romantic or stylish than this hidden gem, nestled down a leafy passage by a rock called Rocher de la Sorcière (Witch's Rock). Avant-garde artists have given each room a special touch. *23 av. Junot, 18th. ☎ 01-53-41-81-40. http://hotel-particulier-montmartre.com. 5 units. Doubles 290€–590€. MV, V. Métro: Lamarck-Caulincourt. Map p 138.*

★★ **Hôtel Royal St-Honoré** CONCORDE This oasis of charm attracts guests drawn by nearby shops like Chanel and Hermès. Contemporary styling contrasts nicely with antique furnishings. The bar is *très* chic. *221 rue St-Honoré, 1st. ☎ 01-42-60-32-79. www.hotel-royal-st-honore.com. 72 units. Doubles 230€–440€ w/breakfast. AE, DC, MC, V. Métro: Tuileries. Map p 140.*

★★★ **Hôtel Shangri-La** CHAILLOT Set inside the 19th-century palace Napoleon built for his great nephew Prince Roland Bonaparte, this hotel drips with fine furniture, chandeliers, and antiques. But there's a modern edge too, in the classy rooms, lounge, and two superlatively good eateries: **L'Abeille** for haute French cuisine (p 112) and **La Bauhinia** brasserie, which mixes Asian and French flavors. *10 ave. d'Iéna, 16th. ☎ 01-53-67-19-98. www.shangri-la.com. 81 units. Doubles 825€–900€. AE, DC, MC, V. Métro: Iéna. Map p 138.*

★ **Hôtel St-Louis en l'Isle** ILE ST LOUIS A charming family atmosphere reigns at this antiques-filled hotel in a 17th-century town house. Rooms are small but well decorated, there are lots of lovely touches, and the location is excellent. Great value for the price. *75 rue St-Louis-en-l'Ile,*

Contemporary artwork, sumptuous decor, and a secluded garden are the draws at the Hôtel Particulier.

Bed & Breakfasts in Paris

For a special, intimate Parisian experience, consider booking a B&B. Here are some reliable places to try: **Alcove & Agapes** (☎ 01-44-85-06-05; www.bed-and-breakfast-in-paris.com), with more than 100 regularly inspected addresses throughout central Paris; **Hôtes Qualité Paris** (www.hqp.fr), which has an excellent, trustworthy selection verified by City Hall; and **Alastair Sawday's** (www.sawdays.co.uk), which lists many special B&Bs and apartments to rent. For an eccentric stay in the heart of St-Ouen's flea markets, try **Le Loft** (www.chezbertrand.com)—a ground-floor apartment with a Citroën 2CV that snugly sleeps two lovers.

4th. ☎ 01-46-34-04-80. www.hotelsaintlouis.com. 19 units. Doubles 170€–240€. MC, V. Métro: Pont Marie or St-Michel-Notre-Dame. Map p 140.

★ **Hôtel Sully St-Germain** LATIN QUARTER With its neo-medieval-style decor and exquisite antiques, this is a good option for the money. Stylish guest rooms have brass beds and stone walls. ***31 rue des Ecoles, 5th. ☎ 01-43-26-56-02. www.hotel-paris-sully.com. 61 units. Doubles 165€–200€. AE, DC, MC, V. Métro: Maubert Mutualité. Map p 142.***

★★★ **Hôtel Westminster** OPERA This gorgeous hotel is favored by shoppers who prowl place Vendôme, rue du Faubourg St-Honoré, and the department stores around Opéra Garnier for chic attire. Decor is resolutely stylish: classic marbles, deep woods, and plush fabrics. The Michelin-starred restaurant is known for its fine contemporary French cuisine. ***13 rue de la Paix, 2nd. ☎ 01-42-61-57-46. http://warwickwestminsteropera.com. 102 units. Doubles 350€–650€. AE, MC, V. Métro: Opéra. RER: Auber. Map p 140.***

Hyatt Regency Paris-Madeleine MADELEINE This palace hotel is a citadel of luxurious 21st-century living. High ceilings and neo-Art-Déco touches make the hotel airy and dramatic. The sleek, modern fittings add to the luxury, as do the rich fabrics and precious wooden furniture. ***24 bd Malesherbes, 8th. ☎ 01-55-27-15-34. http://paris.madeleine.hyatt.com/hyatt/hotels. 86 units. Doubles 310€–700€. AE, DC, MC, V. Métro: St-Augustin. Map p 138.***

★★★ **Le Bristol** CHAMPS-ELYSEES Paris's most discreet palace hotel is a favorite with celebrities, politicians, and royalty. Guest rooms are lavish, large, and luxurious. The swimming pool has views over the whole city. The 2½ Michelin-starred restaurant sits inside a sumptuous oval dining area in winter and inside Paris's biggest palace garden (1,500 sq. m/16,146 sq. ft.) in the summer. This is one of the best places to stay in the city. If you can't afford a room, observe the glitterati over a cocktail in the bar. ***112 rue du Faubourg St-Honoré, 8th. ☎ 01-53-43-43-00. www.hotel-bristol.com. 170 units. Doubles 730€–2,200€. AE, DC, MC, V. Métro: Franklin-D.-Roosevelt. Map p 139.***

★ **L'Hôtel** ST-GERMAIN-DES-PRES The hotel where Oscar Wilde died is now one of the Left Bank's most distinctive boutique hotels. Each guest room is different, some with fireplaces, some with fabric-covered walls. There's a swimming pool in the cellar and the restaurant (p 111) is one of the best in town. *13 rue des Beaux-Arts, 6th. ☎ 01-44-41-99-00. www.l-hotel.com. 20 units. Doubles 285€–660€. AE, DC, MC, V. Métro: St-Germain-des-Prés. Map p 142.*

★★★ **L'Hôtel Thoumieux** INVALIDES Jean-François Piège is a celebrity chef in France, and this stylish, neo-70s style hotel is his new lair. The rooms (all in turquoises and animal prints) sit discreetly above his restaurants—the *gastronomique* **Le Restaurant de Jean-François Piège** (p 111), and the **Thoumieux Brasserie** (p 111)—which means you only have to stumble upstairs after dinner. The problem is that both are so good, and the rooms so cozy, you might never go anywhere else in Paris. *79 rue St-Dominique, 7th. ☎ 01-47-05-79-00. www.thoumieux.fr. 15 units. Doubles 250€ –450€. AE, MC, V. Métro: La Tour Maubourg. Map p 142.*

The young and stylish flock to Mama Shelter In the 20th arrondissement.

The palatial yet discreet hotel Le Bristol.

★★ **Mama Shelter** PERE-LACHAISE Rooms in this starkly modern designer hotel, set in a converted car park, are simple with fun touches, such as superhero-mask light shades and working Apple computers on the walls. Downstairs, a bar, pizza parlor, and restaurant draw a stylized crowd of international trendies. It's the place to see and be seen. *107 rue de Bagnolet, 20th. ☎ 01-43-48-48-48. www.mamashelter.com. 170 units. Doubles 89€–400€. MC, V. Métro: Alexandre Dumas or Porte de Bagnolet. Map p 140.*

★★ **Martinn** SENTIER This self-catering, one-bedroom apartment is the sort of place you wished you owned: Heavy doors open onto a lovely taffeta-clad bedroom, an airy living area, and a kitchen that cries out to be cooked in. Cooking classes and wine tastings are available on request. *62 rue d'Argout, 2nd. ☎ 06-23-55-34-82. www.key2paris.com. 1 unit. 680€ per week. MC, V. Métro: Sentier. Map p 140.*

★ **Murano Urban Resort** MARAIS This oddity with fur-lined elevators is a trend-setting, minimalist hotel whose wild and angular interior decor is not everyone's cup of tea. Those into cutting-edge design will find it fun, well thought

Murano Urban Resort promises to deliver "when sleeping is not enough."

through, and possibly the most memorable place they've stayed in. The restaurant on the ground floor serves excellent cuisine appreciated by locals. *13 bd. du Temple, 3rd. ☎ 01-42-71-20-00. www.murano resort.com. Doubles 400€–600€. AE, MC, V. Métro: Filles du Calvaire or Temple. Map p 140.*

★★★ Paris Yacht THE ISLANDS Fancy your very own houseboat at the foot of Notre-Dame? This 1930s barge, which sleeps up to four guests, has to be one of the most original places you can stay in the city—as long as you don't suffer from seasickness. In fine weather, the upper deck provides a panoramic, Seine-side setting for a drink or dinner. *Quai de la Tournelle, 5th. ☎ 06-88-70-26-36. www.paris-yacht.com. From 300€ night. No credit cards. Métro: Maubert-Mutualité. Map p 142.*

★★★ Pension les Marronniers LUXEMBOURG This is one of the city's very last *pensions de famille* (boarding houses)—perfect for nostalgic travelers looking for a slice of Paris in days gone by. It has been in the owner's family since the 1930s and offers great views over the Luxembourg Gardens. Rooms are cluttered—just as they should be. Half-board is available. *78 rue d'Assas, 6th. ☎ 01-43-26-37-71. www.pension-marronniers.com. 7 units. Doubles 40€–70€. No credit cards. Weekly and monthly rentals. Métro: Vavin. Map p 142.*

Dine and sleep on the Seine in a 1930s barge, Paris Yacht.

The Renaissance Paris Arc de Triomphe offers views of the Eiffel Tower and Indonesian cuisine.

★★ Renaissance Paris Arc de Triomphe CHAMPS-ELYSEES Order a Paris Sky View Room and watch the Eiffel Tower twinkle from your balcony in this trendy 5-star hotel. It has elegantly modern architecture, and the Macassar restaurant serves scrumptious Indonesian-inspired cuisine like *ikan dabu dabu* (marinated, roasted swordfish, with basmati rice and sauce vierge). ***39 ave de Wagram, 17th. ☎ 01-55-37-55-37. www.marriott.co.uk. 118 units. Doubles from 289€–599€. MC, V. Métro: Ternes. Map p 139.***

★★★ Solar Hôtel DENFERT-ROCHEREAU Paris's first low-budget, environmentally friendly hotel has a fabulous concept: Modern rooms without frills but with A/C, TV, and phones; a pretty garden where you can picnic and hire bikes; static prices year-round; and a genuine low-carbon charter. ***22 rue Boulard, 14th. ☎ 01-43-21-08-20. www.solarhotel.fr. 34 units. Doubles 59€. MC, V. Métro/RER: Denfert-Rochereau. Map p 142.***

Named for the patron saint of travelers, St-Christopher's Inn shelters an endless stream of backpackers.

St-Christopher's Inn STALINGRAD This English youth hostel chain, set inside an old boat hangar, has funky decor and unbeatable prices. Private rooms and dormers are marine-themed. Dorms are single-sex and mixed, so check when you book. ***159 rue de Crimée, 19th. ☎ 01-40-34-34-40. www.st-christophers.co.uk. 350 beds. Dorm 12€ (occasional special offers)–28€. Doubles 38€–50€. Métro: Crimée. Map p 140.***

★ Terrass Hôtel MONTMARTRE This hotel is a find, with a marble-floored lobby, blond-oak paneling, antiques, and paintings. Guest rooms have high ceilings and sophisticated decor. ***12 rue Joseph de Maistre, 18th. ☎ 01-46-06-72-85. www.terrass-hotel.com. 100 units. Doubles 285€–395€. Métro: Place de Clichy or Blanche. Map p 139.*** ●

10 The Best Day Trips & Excursions

Decadent Versailles

1. Palace of Versailles
2. Gardens of Versailles
3. Apollo Fountain
4. Grand Canal
5. Grand Trianon
6. Marie Antoinette's Estate
7. Le Chapeau Gris
8. Grande Ecurie
9. Potager du Roi

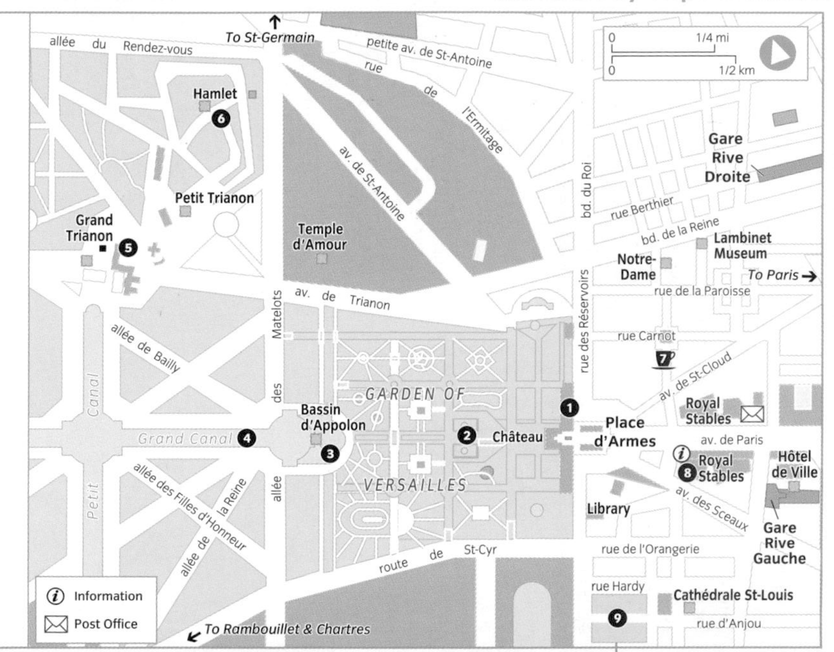

Previous page: The Sun King's Hall of Mirrors reflects natural light back into the garden at Versailles.

Yes, it's touristy, and yes, it will be crowded in the summer, but come anyway. This extraordinary palace must be seen to be believed, and it is well worth the 35-minute journey to the Parisian suburbs. It took 40,000 workers 50 years to convert Louis XIII's hunting lodge into this extravagant palace. Work started in 1661, and before it was finished, entire forests had been moved to make way for its extensive gardens. It was here that French royalty lived a life so decadent in a time of widespread poverty that their excesses spurred a revolution.

❶ ★★★ Palace of Versailles. This vast palace of 2,300 rooms is actually dwarfed by the grounds, which stretch for miles. Inside the palace, it's all over the top, all the time. Not a corner was left unpainted. Every cherub? Gilded. The king and his family lived in the Petits Appartements much of the time, where the king's apartment and the queen's bedchamber are exquisitely overdone. One room, the cabinet of the Meridian, was where Marie-Antoinette finally gave birth to an heir in 1781. The King's Grand Apartement is actually an enfilade of seven exquisitely decorated rooms—showpieces for visitors to the court. The largest is the Hercules Salon, where the ceiling is painted with the *Apotheosis of Hercules*. The elaborate Mercury Salon is where the body of Louis XIV lay in state after his death. But the apartments pale in comparison to the 71m-long (233-ft.) Hall of Mirrors designed by Mansart to reflect sunlight back into the garden and remind people that the "Sun King" lived here. On June 28th, 1919, the treaty ending World War I was signed in this hall. Elsewhere in the palace there's an impressive library and a Clock Room with a gilded bronze astronomical clock designed to keep perfect time until 9999. ⌚ *2 hr.*

❷ ★★★ Gardens of Versailles. These vast, varied, vainglorious gardens were created by the landscape artist Le Nôtre, who used lakes, canals, geometric flower beds, long avenues, fountains, and statuary to create a French Eden. The creation of the gardens required masses of work. Tons of soil, trees, and rock had to be moved to make way for flowerbeds, the fountains, and the Canal. Thousands of men from across the country were employed to do it; and the result—even hundreds of years on—is simply breathtaking. ⌚ *2 hr.*

The courtyard of Versailles.

The gardens of Versailles nearly outdo the palace itself.

3 Apollo Fountain. At one time, hundreds of fountains splashed and burbled around the grounds. The most famous surviving fountain is the Apollo fountain (created in gilded lead by Tuby after a drawing by Le Brun, between 1668 and 1670), which depicts Apollo's chariot being pulled from the water by four horses surrounded by Tritons.

4 Grand Canal. The 1.6km (1-mile) canal is surrounded by lush planted forests crossed by straight paths. So precise was Le Nôtre's design that on St. Louis Day (Aug 25) the sun sets in perfect alignment with the Grand Canal. The works took 11 years to complete, from 1668 to 1679, and Louis kept a fleet of gondolas for parties on the water. In winter, when the canal froze, the royal family and courtiers swapped the boats for ice-skates.

5 ★★ Grand Trianon. The elegant Grand Trianon was designed in 1687 by Jules Hardouin Mansart, who called it "A little pink marble and porphyry palace with delightful gardens." The Sun King sometimes occupied the Grand Trianon, but it was usually used for family visitors. It was later the home of Napoleon and his family. Then in 1963, President Charles de Gaulle had it turned into a guesthouse for French Presidents. The northern wing, the Trianon-sous-Bois is still used today for presidential functions. *30 min.*

6 Marie Antoinette's Estate. Louis XVI's young wife is famed for her desire to flee the pomp of the Versailles court. Her retreat was this estate—made up of the Petit Trianon (where Louis XV held "meetings" with Madame de Pompadour), the Queen's Gardens, and the ***Hameau de la Reine*** (a lovely, thatch-roofed hamlet of fanciful faux farmhouses). Nobody could visit her here without her permission. *30 min.*

Travel Tip

Both the Grand Trianon and Marie Antoinette's estate can be reached by the "Petit Train" from the Parterre Nord (☎ 01-39-54-22-00; www.train-versailles.com; 6.70€). The round trip is commentated and takes 50 minutes, but you can hop on and hop off at each site.

7 Le Chapeau Gris. Stop for a bite of French country cuisine in Versailles' oldest restaurant whose building (with paneled walls and beamed ceilings) dates back to the

Versailles: Practical Matters

Versailles (☎ 01-30-83-78-00; www.chateauversailles.fr) is open Tuesday through Sunday from 9am to 5:30pm (until 6:30pm Apr–Oct). The gardens are open daily year round from 8am to 6pm (til 8:30pm Apr–Oct). Admission to the chateau is 13€ to 15€. Admission to the Grand Trianon and Marie Antoinette's estate is 6€ to 10€. Admission to the gardens is free (except during the Grandes Eaux, 8€). However, the best and easiest way to visit Versailles is to buy a *Passeport Versailles* (18€–25€; children 17 and under, and 25 and under from the E.U. free all year, except for the Grandes Eaux and Jardins Musicaux events), which allows quick access to main Château, the Grand Trianon, and Marie Antoinette's estate. Buy tickets online or at a FNAC (p 88). If you already have your ticket when you arrive, head straight to door A. To buy your ticket head to the Information/ticket point in the south wing. For tickets to the Grand Trianon and Marie Antoinette's estate, head straight to that entrance in the gardens.

There are two stations in Versailles—Rive Gauche (the nearest one to the chateau) and Rive Droite. To get to the nearest one take RER C5 from central Paris to Versailles-Rive Gauche; or take a normal train from Gare St-Lazare to Versailles–Rive Droite, then walk 10 minutes. By car, take the D-10 or the A-13 from Paris to the Versailles–Château exit. The trip to Versailles takes about 30 to 40 minutes by car or train.

construction of the chateau. The prix fixe menus, at 22€ and 30€, are excellent values. *7 rue Hoche.* ☎ *01-39-50-10-81. www.auchapeaugris.com. $$.*

8 Grande Ecurie. The famous Versailles horses are kept in high style here, and trained in a variety of equine performance arts (at the Académie du Spectacle equestre). You can watch the horse trainers at work on Saturday, Sunday, and some Thursday mornings, or take in a performance on weekend afternoons or evenings (and some Thursdays). For times check the website or call in advance 🕘 *1 hr 15 min. Near the palace entrance on av. Rockefeller.* ☎ *01-41-57-32-19. www.acadequestre.fr. Admission 12€; performances 25€.*

9 Potager du Roi. This enclosure, made up of 5,000 fruit trees tapered into extravagant shapes, is where the Sun King's fruit and vegetable plot stood. In true Versailles style, it was laid out to impress the king as he strolled about his gardens. The garden is now separate from the chateau and well worth visiting whether your fingers are green or not. 🕘 *30 min. Access via rue du Maréchal Joffr (left main entrance).* ☎ *01-39-24-62-62. www.potager-du-roi.fr. Admission 3€, free for children 12 and under. Apr–Oct Tues, Thurs & Sat 10am–6pm; Nov–Mar Tue, Thurs 10am-6pm, some Sat 10am–1pm.*

Disneyland Paris

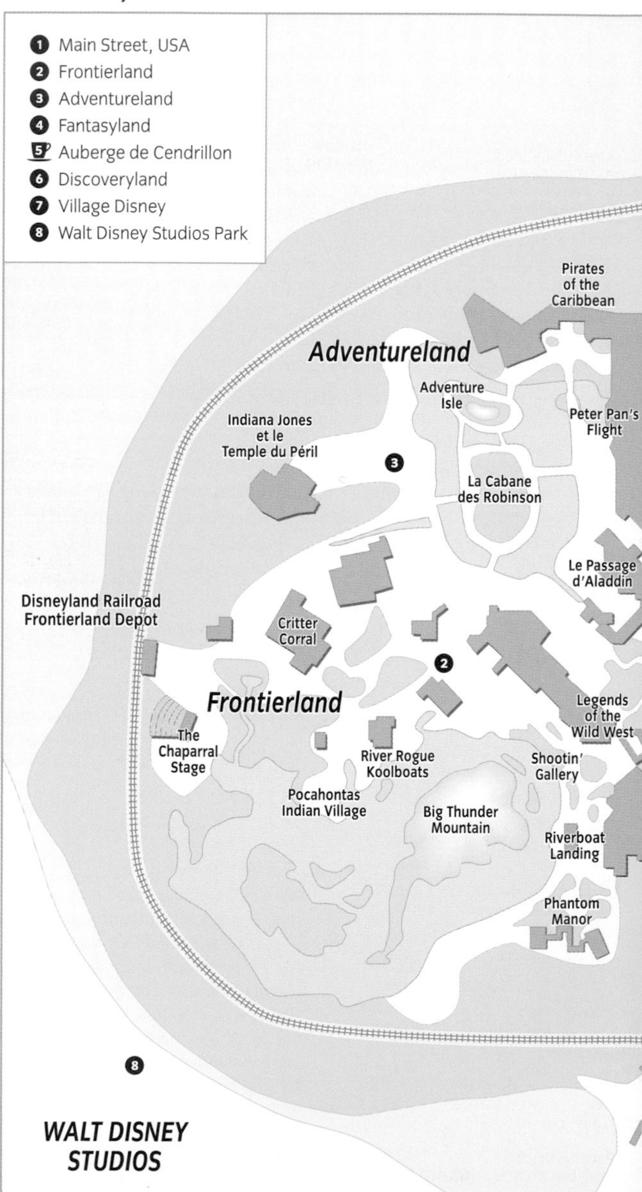
1 Main Street, USA
2 Frontierland
3 Adventureland
4 Fantasyland
5 Auberge de Cendrillon
6 Discoveryland
7 Village Disney
8 Walt Disney Studios Park
Pirates of the Caribbean
Adventureland
Adventure Isle
Peter Pan's Flight
Indiana Jones et le Temple du Péril
La Cabane des Robinson
Le Passage d'Aladdin
Disneyland Railroad Frontierland Depot
Critter Corral
Legends of the Wild West
Frontierland
The Chaparral Stage
River Rogue Koolboats
Shootin' Gallery
Pocahontas Indian Village
Big Thunder Mountain
Riverboat Landing
Phantom Manor
WALT DISNEY STUDIOS

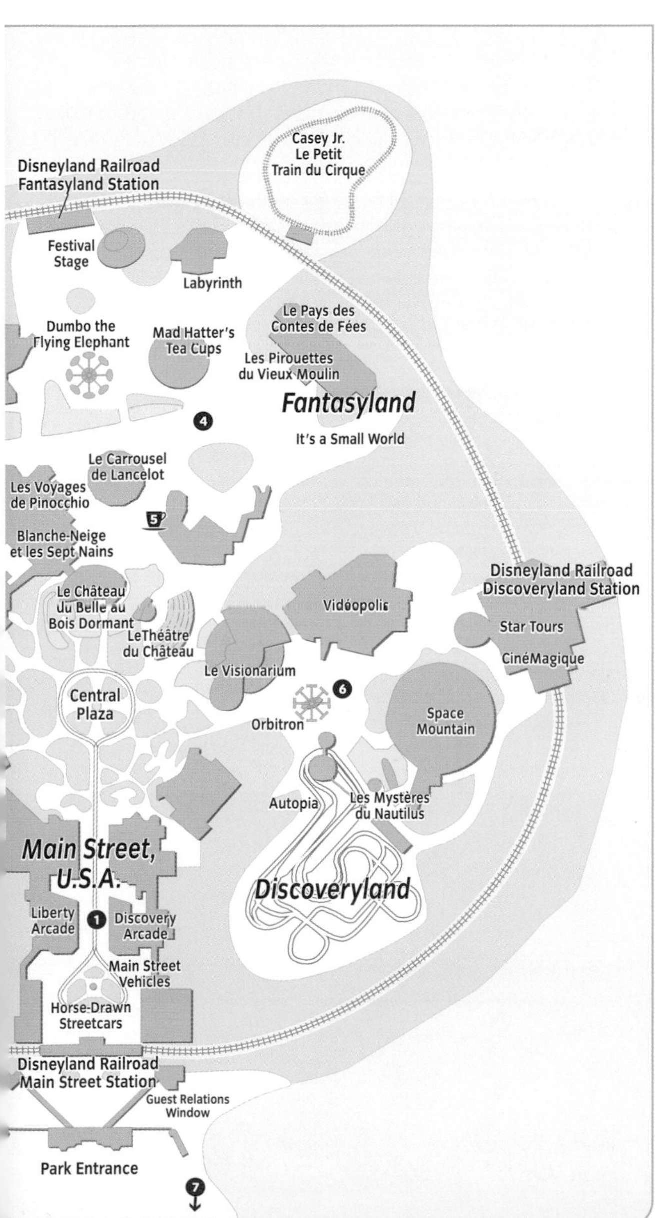
Casey Jr.
Le Petit
Train du Cirque
Disneyland Railroad
Fantasyland Station
Festival
Stage
Labyrinth
Le Pays des
Contes de Fées
Dumbo the
Flying Elephant
Mad Hatter's
Tea Cups
Les Pirouettes
du Vieux Moulin
Fantasyland
4
It's a Small World
Le Carrousel
de Lancelot
Les Voyages
de Pinocchio
5
Blanche-Neige
et les Sept Nains
Disneyland Railroad
Discoveryland Station
Le Château
du Belle au
Bois Dormant
Vidéopolis
Star Tours
LeThéâtre
du Château
CinéMagique
Le Visionarium
6
Central
Plaza
Orbitron
Space
Mountain
Autopia
Les Mystères
du Nautilus
Main Street,
U.S.A.
Discoveryland
Liberty
Arcade
1
Discovery
Arcade
Main Street
Vehicles
Horse-Drawn
Streetcars
Disneyland Railroad
Main Street Station
Guest Relations
Window
Park Entrance
7

Disneyland Paris is a blessing for travelers with kids who have wearied of the museums and churches and just want to go on the rides for 1 day, pleaseplease*please!* Overall, there's little difference between this amusement park and those in Florida and California, except here the cheeseburgers comes with *pommes frîtes* instead of fries. There are two main parks: Disneyland Park with its five lands and Walt Disney Studio Park, split into lots.

❶ **Main Street, USA.** Immediately after entering the park, you'll find yourself in an idealized American town, complete with horse-drawn carriages and street-corner barbershop quartets. If you're here after dark, you can take in the surprisingly lovely Electric Parade (nightly July–Aug), when all the Disney characters pass by along with brightly illuminated floats.

❷ **Frontierland.** In this "pretend America" it's a conveniently short hop to the West, particularly if you board one of the steam-powered trains that takes you through a Grand Canyon diorama to Frontierland. Pocahontas's Indian village is a fine spot to get young kids away from the crowds. If it gets too hot, you and the kids can ride the nearby paddle-wheel steamship.

❸ **Adventureland.** The trains will take you on to Adventureland, where swashbuckling pirates battle near the Swiss Family Robinson's treehouse. If that's too tame, head for the Indiana Jones and the Temple of Peril ride. It travels backward at breakneck speed, the only Disneyland roller coaster in the world to do so.

❹ **Fantasyland.** Young children will be charmed by Sleeping Beauty's Castle (*Le Château de la Belle au Bois Dormant*) and its idealized interpretation of a French château, complete with the obligatory fire-breathing dragon in its dungeon. From here, a visit with Dumbo the Flying Elephant may be necessary, and perhaps a whirl on the giant teacup ride.

Cruise along a fake lake at Disneyland Paris.

The parade never ends at Disneyland.

5 Auberge de Cendrillon. If you're looking for a nice sit-down lunch, try this restaurant for traditional French dining in Cinderella's country inn. (Reservations are recommended.) Otherwise, take your pick from any of the dozens of dining options scattered throughout the park—although don't expect high standards or healthy options. ***Fantasyland.* ☎ *01-64-74-24-02. $$$.***

6 Discoveryland. Explore the visions of the future displayed here, with designs drawn from the works of Leonardo da Vinci, Jules Verne, and H. G. Wells, as well as from more modern fictional creations like *Star Wars*. This is the park's most popular area, with its own version of Space Mountain, which emulates Jules Verne's version of what a trip from Earth to the moon would be like.

7 Village Disney. This haven for adults features endless entertainment options—dance clubs, snack bars, restaurants, shops, and bars. There's also a massive 3D Imax cinema, where you can see all the latest blockbusters.

8 Walt Disney Studios Park. Split into four lots (Toon Studio, Backlot, Front Lot, and Production Courtyard), the emphasis in this second park is on film production and special effects. Feel the flames as you play an extra in the Armageddon disaster movie, plunge 13 floors down an elevator shaft in the brand-new Twilight Tower of Terror, or get your kids to talk live with the mischievous alien Stitch in his interactive stage show.

Disneyland Paris: Practical Matters

Drive 32km (20 miles) along the A4 east from Paris to exit 14. Or take the RER A to the Marne-la-Vallée–Chessy stop (about 40 min.) Marne-la-Vallée, Paris. ☎ 08-25-30-02-22. www.disneylandparis.com. Parking 15€ per day. Admission 1-day (one park) 53€ adults, 45€ ages 3–11, free for children 2 and under; 1-day hopper (both parks) 67€ adults, 57€ ages 3–11. Disneyland Park: Sept to mid-July Mon–Fri 10am–8pm, Sat–Sun 10am–9pm; mid-July to Aug daily 10am–11pm. Walt Disney Studios Park: winter daily 10am–6pm; summer daily 10am–7pm.

The resort was designed as a total vacation destination, so within the enormous compound there are not only the two parks, but also six hotels, campgrounds, the Village Disney entertainment center, a 27-hole golf course, and dozens of restaurants and shops.

The Cathedral at Chartres

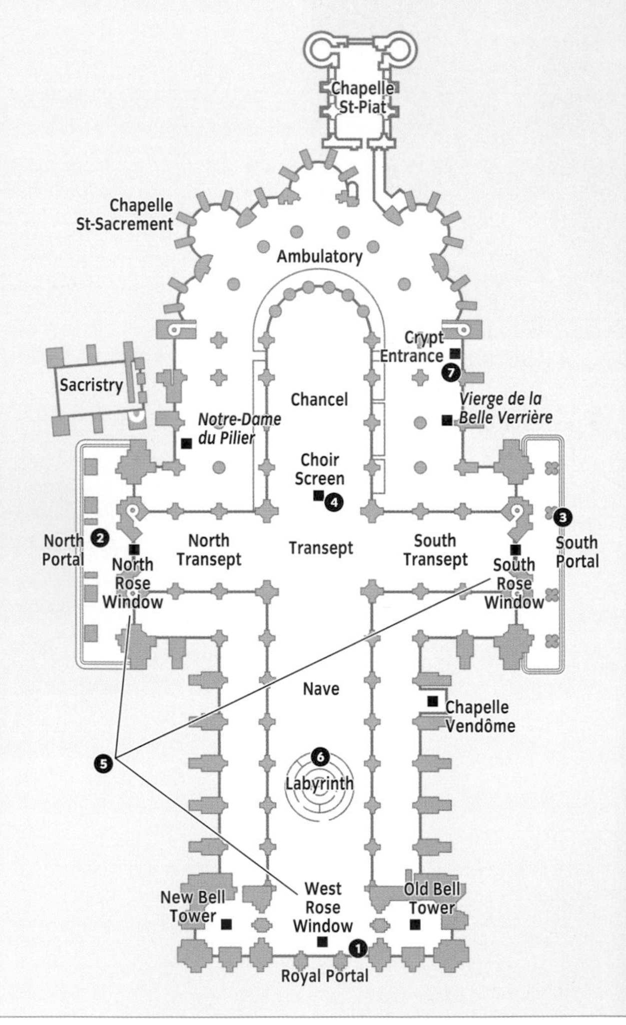

1 Royal Portal
2 North Portal
3 South Portal
4 Choir Screen
5 Rose Windows
6 Floor Labyrinth
7 Crypts

An hour from Paris, standing at the gateway to the Loire Valley, Chartres represents the highest architectural and theological aspirations of the Middle Ages in France. The cathedral was much the same in medieval times as it is now, which should give you a sense of how impressive it must have been in 1260, when it was completed. Rodin described it as the French Acropolis, and once you've seen it you'll be hard pressed to disagree with him.

One of the cathedral's magnificent rose windows.

❶ **Royal Portal.** The sculpted bodies around it are elongated and garbed in long, flowing robes, but their faces are almost disturbingly lifelike—frowning, winking, and smiling. Christ is shown at the Second Coming—his descent to Earth on the right, his ascent back to Heaven on the left.

❷ & ❸ **North and South Portals.** Both the North Portal and the South Portals are carved with Biblical images, including the expulsion of Adam and Eve from the Garden of Eden.

❹ **Choir Screen.** This celebrated screen dates to the 16th century. It has 40 niches holding statues of Biblical figures. Don't be so dazzled by all the stained glass (see next stop) that you overlook its intricate carvings.

❺ ★★★ **Rose Windows.** No cathedral in the world can match Chartres for its 12th-century glass (saved from damage during World War I and World War II by parishioners who removed it piece by piece and stored the pieces safely). It gave the world a new color—Chartres

A Special Place to Stay near Chartres

With its moat, forest walks, and 60 hectares (148 acres) of gardens, the Renaissance ★★ **Château d'Esclimont** is a fairy-tale place in which to stay and dine, between Chârtres and Paris, at St-Symphorien Le Château (☎ 02-37-31-15-15; www.grandesetapes.fr; doubles from 185€; 3 courses 90€; lunch menu from 38€). The gourmet restaurant (think French classics like beef tournedos and lobster) overlooks the gardens. In good weather, you can even eat in a hot-air balloon while sailing over the forested countryside (from 1,200€ for in-flight dinner). Rooms are stately, with marble bathrooms and thick drapes.

Chartres: Practical Matters

From Paris's Gare Montparnasse, trains run direct to Chartres (1 hr.). By car, take A-10/A-11 southwest from the Périphérique and follow signs to Le Mans and Chartres (about 1½ hr.). The cathedral is open May through October daily from 8am to 8pm, and November through April daily from 8am to 7:15pm. Admission is free. Guided tours of the cathedral are available in English much of the year Monday through Saturday at noon and 2:45pm; meet at the gift shop. Call ☎ 02-37-21-72-02 for more information.

Any trip to the cathedral should include a visit to the cobbled, medieval streets of **Chartres's Vieux Quartier (Old Quarter),** which stretches from the cathedral down to the Eure River. **Rue Chantault,** where the 800-year-old houses have wonderfully colorful facades, is particularly lovely. Also, stop in at the **Musée des Beaux Arts de Chartres,** right next to the cathedral, at 29 Cloître Notre-Dame (☎ 02-37-90-45-80; admission 3.50€). It has an excellent collection covering the 16th through the 20th centuries. You'll find a vibrant food market Saturdays and Wednesdays mornings in the market hall located at Place Billard, near the cathedral. There's also a flower market on Tuesdays, Thursdays, and Saturdays at Place du Cygne. For lunch, try **Le Saint-Hilaire,** 11 rue Pont Saint-Hilaire (☎ 02-37-30-97-57), a traditional French restaurant that specializes in Chartres pâté.

blue—and it is absolutely exceptional. All of its windows are glorious, but the three rose windows may be the best.

❻ **Floor Labyrinth.** Many Gothic cathedrals once had labyrinths like the one on the floor of the nave, but virtually all were destroyed over time, so this one, which dates from around 1200 is very rare. It is thought that such labyrinths represented the passage of the soul to heaven. Its 261.5 meter path was either walked, in prayer, as a symbolic pilgrimage to Jerusalem, or as path of repentance, upon which case the sinner would cover the distance on his knees.

❼ **Crypts.** Those who would like to visit the underground crypts can usually only do so as part of a guided tour. An English language one is held twice a day (and covers the whole cathedral) most of the year by lecturer Malcolm Miller at noon and 2:45pm Monday through Saturday. *Admission 10€. For tour information, inquire in the gift shop or call Miller at ☎ 02-37-28-15-58.* ●

The Savvy Traveler

Before You Go

Government Tourist Offices

In the US: Information line only (☎ 514/288-1904; info.us@franceguide.com; http://us.franceguide.com). **In Canada:** Maison de la France, 1800 Ave. McGill College, Suite 1010, Montreal H3A 3J6 (☎ 514/288-2026). **In the UK:** Maison de la France, Lincoln House 300 High Holborn, London WC1V 7JH (☎ 09068/244-123). **In Ireland:** Information line only (☎ 15-60-235-235, 0.95€/min.; info.ie@franceguide.com; http://ie.franceguide.com). **In Australia:** French Tourist Bureau, 25 Bligh St., Sydney, NSW 2000 (☎ 02/9231-5244); info.au@franceguide.com; http://au.franceguide.com.

The Best Times to Go

Paris is less crowded in **August,** when the locals traditionally take their annual holiday. This is also a time for some of Paris's best outdoor festivals. However, cheaper hotels tend to fill up with students and budget travelers, and many (but by no means all) of the smaller shops, restaurants, and galleries close for 2 weeks at the beginning of the month. You may want to avoid **late September/early October,** when the annual auto show attracts thousands of enthusiasts. Spring in Paris is still a good time to come, but so too is December when many hotels have special offers on the run up to Christmas—although you might not get any sunshine.

The Weather

Generally speaking, summers are warm and pleasant, with only a few oppressively hot days. Although more and more hotels are adding air-conditioning to the rooms, many cheaper accommodations still get hot and stuffy. Rain is common throughout the year, especially in winter.

Previous Page: One of Hector Guimard's iconic Art Nouvea Métro stations.

Useful Websites

- www.parisinfo.com and www.nouveau-paris-ile-de-france.fr: Comprehensive information about traveling to Paris and Île de France, including hotels, sightseeing, and notices of special events.
- www.mappy.fr and www.viamichelin.com: Online maps and journey planner. Covers Paris and the whole of France.
- www.pagesjaunes.fr: Online phone directory for businesses and services.
- www.culture.fr: Extensive listings of upcoming cultural events.
- www.parissi.com: Guide to the Parisian music scene, with an emphasis on nightclubs.
- www.paris.fr: The City Hall's guide to Paris, with museum and exhibition listings.

Cellphones (Mobile Phones)

If your phone has GSM (Global System for Mobiles) capability, and you have a world-compatible phone, you should be able to make and receive calls to and from France. Only certain phones have this capability, though, and you should check with your service operator first. Call charges can be high. Alternatively, you can rent a phone through **Roadpost** (www.roadpost.com), **In Touch Global** (www.intouchglobal.com), **Cellhire** (www.cellhire.com; www.cellhire.co.uk; www.cellhire.com.au). After a simple online registration, they will ship a phone (usually with a U.K. number) to your

PARIS'S AVERAGE DAILY TEMPERATURE & RAINFALL

	JAN	FEB	MAR	APR	MAY	JUNE
Temp. (°F)	38	39	46	51	58	64
Temp. (°C)	3	4	8	11	14	18
Rainfall (in.)	3.2	2.9	2.4	2.7	3.2	3.5
	JULY	AUG	SEPT	OCT	NOV	DEC
Temp. (°F)	66	66	61	53	45	40
Temp. (°C)	19	19	16	12	7	4
Rainfall (in.)	3.3	3.7	3.3	3.0	3.5	3.1

home or office. Usage charges can be astronomical, so read the fine print.

U.K. mobiles work in France; call your service provider before departing your home country to ensure that the international call bar has been switched off and to check call charges, which can be extremely high. Also remember that you are charged for calls you *receive* on a U.K. mobile used abroad.

Car Rentals

There's very little need to rent a car in Paris, but if you're determined to do so, it's usually cheapest to book a car online before you leave your home country. Try **Hertz** (www.hertz.com), **Avis** (www.avis.com), or **Budget** (www.budget.com). If you're in the USA, you should also consider **AutoEurope** (www.autoeurope.com), which sends you a prepaid voucher, locking in the exchange rate.

Getting **There**

By Plane

Paris has two international airports—**Orly** (☎ 39-50) and **Charles de Gaulle** (☎ 39-50). At Charles de Gaulle, Air France flights arrive at Terminal 2, while all other flights come into Terminals 1 and 3. At Orly, international flights arrive at Orly Sud (South) and domestic flights at Orly Ouest (West). Free shuttle buses operate between the airports.

From Charles de Gaulle: RER trains leave every 15 minutes (5am–approximately midnight), serving several of the major downtown Métro stations (trip time: 35 min.). Air France also operates two shuttle-bus services into Paris: one departing every 12 minutes (5:35am–11pm) for place d'Etoile and porte Maillot, and the other every 30 minutes (7am–9:30pm) for Gare Montparnasse and Gare de Lyon. A taxi to the city costs about 55€; the fare is higher at night (8pm–7am). The trip takes 40 to 50 minutes by bus or taxi.

From Orly: There are no direct trains to central Paris, but the airport is served by **monorail** (Orly Val) that takes you to the RER station Anthony where you can catch line B into the city (trip time about 30 min.). Air France buses leave from Orly Ouest and Orly Sud every 12 minutes (5:45am–11pm) for the Gare des Invalides, where you can catch a taxi or the Métro. A taxi from the airport into Paris costs about 45€ (more at night). It takes 25 minutes to an hour to get to

Paris by bus or taxi, depending on traffic.

By Car

The main highways into Paris are the A-1 from the north (Great Britain and Benelux); A-13 from Rouen, Normandy, and northwest France; A-10 from Bordeaux, the Pyrenees, southwest France, and Spain; A-6 from Lyon, the French Alps, the Riviera, and Italy; and A-4 and A-5 from eastern France.

By Train

North Americans can buy a **Eurailpass** or individual tickets from most travel agencies, or at any office of **Rail Europe** (☎ 800/622-8600 in the U.S., 800/361-RAIL in Canada; www.raileurope.com). For details on the rail passes available in the United Kingdom, visit or call the **National Rail Inquiries,** Victoria Station, London SW1V 1JZ (☎ 08705/848-848; www.nationalrail.co.uk). From the U.K., you can travel to Paris under the English Channel via the Eurostar (trip time about 2½ hr.). Buy tickets directly from **Eurostar** (☎ 08705-186-186 from the U.K., ☎ 44-1233-617-575 from outside the U.K., ☎ 08-92-35-35-39 in France; www.eurostar.com).

By Bus

Bus travel to Paris is available from London and several other cities on the Continent. The arrival and departure point for Europe's largest bus operator, **Eurolines France** (www.eurolines.fr), is a 15 to 25 minute Métro ride from central Paris, at the terminus of Métro line 3 (Galleini). Because Eurolines doesn't have sales agents outside Europe, most non-European travelers wait until they reach the Continent to buy their tickets. Any European travel agent can arrange this for you, or you can book online at www.eurolines.co.uk. (☎ 08/717 81-8181, from the U.K.). Before you travel between London and Paris by bus, check the Eurostar website for offers as train tickets sometimes dip to as little as 66€ return, about 30€ more than a bus ticket—you may find spending the extra cash worthwhile for the upgrade in comfort and speed.

Getting **Around**

By Public Transportation

The **Métro** network is vast, reliable, and cheap, and within Paris you can transfer between the subway and the **RER** (Réseau Express Régional) regional trains at no extra cost. The Métro runs from 5:30am to 12:30am Sunday to Thursday (til 1:15am Fri–Sat). Detailed information is at www.ratp.fr.

The Métro is reasonably safe at any hour, but use your common sense, and be on your guard for pickpockets. Châtelet-les-Halles RER is best avoided at night as troublemakers tend to loiter here. For ticket advice see below.

Buses are slower than the Métro but reliable, and offer sightseeing opportunities. Most buses run from 7am to 8:30pm, after which a nighttime service covers key areas until 5:30am. Services are limited on Sunday and public holidays. At certain stops, signs list the destinations and numbers of the buses serving that point. Bus and Métro fares are the same (although each require a separate ticket), and you can use the same carnets on both.

Buying Tickets

Single journey tickets, or packs of ten tickets (un carnet, pronounced car-*nay*) can be bought from a machine in the subway station (with cash or a credit card) or from a ticket window. Individual tickets cost 1.80€ and a package of ten is 12€ (prices as of press time; they may be higher once you get there). If you plan to ride the Métro a lot, the Paris Visite pass (☎ 08-92-69-32-46; www.ratp.info/touristes; available from all RATP desks in the Métro and from tourist offices) may be worthwhile. You get unlimited rides for 1, 2, 3, or 5 days for access to zones 1 to 3, which includes central Paris and its nearby suburbs, or zones 1 to 6, which includes Disneyland (zone 5), Versailles (zone 4), and the Charles de Gaulle (zone 5) and Orly (zone 4) airports. Prices range from 9.30€ to 51.20€ depending on the zone covered and the number of days.

Carte allows unlimited travel on bus, subway, and RER lines during a 1-day period for 6.10€ to 17.30€, depending on the zone. Ask for it at any Métro station. You will also need a passport photo for each family member.

By Taxi

You can hail a taxi when its sign reads LIBRE. The flag drops at 5.10€, and from 7am to 7pm you pay 1€ per kilometer (or 1.20€ the rest of the time). Cabs are scarce during rush hour and when the Métro closes. Avoid unlicensed cabs (which are usually just a person with a car). You could find yourself the victim of a robbery—or worse. If you need to call a cab, try **Les Taxis Bleus** (☎ 36-09; www.taxis-bleus.com) or **Taxi G7** (☎ 36-07; www.taxisg7.fr).

By Car

Driving in Paris is not recommended. Parking is difficult, traffic is dense, and networks of one-way streets make navigation, even with the best of maps, a problem.

By Foot

The best way to take in the city is to walk. The center is very pedestrian-friendly, and so long as you follow all the usual rules of thumb—buy a good map (or carry this guide with you), and stick to busy, well-lit places at night—you're bound to make a few unexpected discoveries along the way.

By Bike

Paris does have cycle paths, even if you have to compete with heavy traffic, and it's a fine way to sightsee.

The best deal for short journeys is the Vélib, Paris' excellent self-service bike scheme, available 7 days a week; for just 1€, you can take a bike from any stand (there are over 20,000 across the city), use it, replace it, and take a new one over a 24-hour period. The first 30 minutes are free of charge; after that, return it to any bike stand. If a rack is full, check the map on the service point for the nearest stand. Tickets can be bought with your credit card at any service point. You'll have to authorize a 150€ deposit, which will be taken from your card only if the bike is not returned, and type in a pin number of your choice. The machine will give you a card, with a code that you can use to unlock the bikes.

Over 20,000 bikes are available. After the first free 30 minutes, every extra 30 minutes costs 1€ extra (i.e., if you keep the bike for 6 hours, you'll pay 11€; if you return it to a stand every 30min however, and wait 5-min before taking out a new one, it's free).

Fast **Facts**

APARTMENT RENTALS A California-based company promoting upmarket B&B accommodations in Paris is **European B&B,** 437 J St., Ste. 210, San Diego, CA 92101 (☎ 800/872-2632; www.parisbandb.com). In Paris, contact their affiliate, **Alcôve & Agapes,** (☎ 01-44-85-06-05; www.bed-and-breakfast-in-paris.com). **Good Morning Paris** (☎ 01-47-07-28-29; www.goodmorningparis.fr) also has over 100 rooms in the city, plus apartments for two to four people (99€–125€); or try the excellent **Hôtes Qualité Paris** (www.hqp.fr) with apartments approved by the City of Paris. **Alastair Sawdays** (www.sawdays.co.uk) also offers an excellent collection of charming B&Bs and tourist apartments in Paris. **New York Habitat** (☎ 212/255-8018; fax 212/627-1416; www.nyhabitat.com) rents furnished apartments and vacation accommodations in Paris and the south of France.

ATMS/CASHPOINTS Most banks charge a fee for international withdrawals—check with your bank before you leave home.

BABYSITTERS Most expensive and some moderately priced hotels offer babysitting services, usually subcontracted to local agencies and requiring at least 24 hours notice. You usually pay the sitter directly and rates average 10€ to 13€ per hour. One good agency is **Baby Sitting Services** (1 place Paul Verlaine, 92100 Boulogne Billancourt; ☎ 01-46-21-33-16; www.babysittingservices.com). Also, try the American Church's basement bulletin board where English-speaking (often American) students post notices offering babysitting services. The church is located at 65 quai d'Orsay, 7th (☎ 01-45-62-05-00; www.acparis.org; Métro: Invalides).

BANKS Most banks are open Monday to Friday from 9am to 4:30pm. A few are open Saturday mornings. Shops and most hotels will cash traveler's checks, but most banks and foreign exchanges will give you a better rate.

BUSINESS HOURS Shops tend to be open from 9:30am to 7pm, some traditional shops open at 8am and close at 8 or 9pm, but the lunch break can last up to 3 hours, starting at 1pm. Most museums close 1 day a week (Mon or Tues) and on some national holidays.

CONSULATES & EMBASSIES **United States Embassy,** 2 av. Gabriel, 8e (☎ 01-43-12-22-22); **United States Consulate,** 2 rue St-Florentin (☎ 01-43-12-22-22); **Canadian Embassy,** 35 av. Montaigne, 8e (☎ 01-44-43-29-00); **United Kingdom Embassy,** 35 rue Faubourg St-Honoré, 8e (☎ 01-44-51-31-00); **United Kingdom Consulate,** 18 bis rue d'Anjou, 8e (☎ 01-44-51-31-02); **Irish Embassy,** 12 av. Foch, 16e (☎ 01-44-17-67-00); **Australian Embassy,** 4 rue Jean-Ray, 15e (☎ 01-40-59-33-00); **New Zealand Embassy,** 7 ter rue Lêonard-de-Vinci, 16e (☎ 01-45-01-43-43).

CREDIT CARDS See Money (p 173).

CURRENCY EXCHANGE Exchange your money for euros at banks or foreign exchange offices, not at shops or hotels. Most post offices change traveler's checks or convert money as well. Currency exchanges are also found at Paris airports and train stations, and along most of the major boulevards.

CUSTOMS Customs restrictions for visitors entering France differ for citizens of the European Union and for citizens of non-E.U. countries.

For U.S. Citizens For specifics on what you can bring back from your trip to France, download the invaluable free pamphlet *Know Before You Go* online at www.cbp.gov.

For Canadian Citizens For a clear summary of Canadian rules, call for the booklet *I Declare,* issued by the Canada Customs and Revenue Agency (☎ 800/461-9999 in Canada, or 204/983-3500 from outside Canada; www.cbsa-asfc.gc.ca).

For U.K. Citizens For more information, contact **HM Revenue & Customs** at ☎ 0845/010-9000, or +44 (0)2920/501-261 from outside the U.K., or consult the website www.hmrc.gov.uk.

For Australian Citizens A helpful brochure available from Australian consulates or Customs offices is *Know Before You Go.* For more information, call the **Australian Customs Service** at ☎ 1300/363-263, (+61 2 6275-6666 from outside Australia) or log on to www.customs.gov.au.

For New Zealand Citizens Request the free pamphlet *New Zealand Customs Guide for Travelers,* Notice no. 4, from New Zealand Customs Service, The Customhouse, 17–21 Whitmore St., Box 2218, Wellington (☎ 0800/428-786 or +64 9 300-5399 from overseas: www.customs.govt.nz).

DENTISTS See "Emergencies," below.

DOCTORS See "Emergencies," below.

DRUGSTORES After regular hours, ask at your hotel where the nearest 24-hour pharmacy is. You'll also find the address posted on the doors or windows of other drugstores in the neighborhood. One all-night drugstore is **Pharmacie Les Champs,** 84 av. des Champs-Elysées, 8e (☎ 01-45-62-02-41).

EMERGENCIES For the police, call ☎ 17. To report a fire, call ☎ 18. For an ambulance, call the fire department at ☎ 18 or the S.A.M.U., a private ambulance company, at ☎ 15. From anywhere in Europe including France, the general emergency number is ☎ 112. If you need nonurgent medical attention, practitioners in most fields can be found at the Centre Médical Europe, 44 rue d'Amsterdam, 9e (☎ 01-42-81-93-33; http://www.centre-medical-europe.com). For emergency dental service, call S.O.S. Dentaire, ☎ 01-43-36-36-00. Hospitals with English-speaking staff are Hopital Americain, 63 bd. Victor Hugo, Neuilly-sur-Seine (92) (☎ 01-46- 41-25-25) and Hopital Franco Britannique, 3 rue Barbes, Levallois Perret (92) (☎ 01-46-39-22-22).

U.K. nationals will need a European Health Insurance Card (EHIC; www.ehic.org.uk) to receive free or reduced-cost health benefits during a visit to a European Economic Area (EEA) country (European Union countries plus Iceland, Liechtenstein, and Norway) or Switzerland.

The quickest way to apply for one in the U.K. is online (www.ehic.org.uk), or call ☎ 0845/606-2030 (+44 191 218 1999 from abroad) or get a form from the post office. You still pay upfront for treatment and related expenses; the doctor will give you a form to reclaim most of the money (about 70% of doctor's fees and 35%–65% of medicines/prescription charges), which you should send off while still in France (see the EHIC website for details, or see www.dh.gov.uk/travellers). Non-E.U. nationals—with the exception of Canadians, who have the same rights as E.U. citizens to medical treatment in France—need comprehensive travel insurance that covers medical treatment overseas. Even then, you pay bills upfront and apply for a refund.

EVENT LISTINGS ***Pariscope*** and the ***Officiel du Spectacle*** (sold in newspaper kiosks) provide listings of everything that's going on in the city. ***Le Figaro*** carries a special listings supplement every Wednesday.

FAMILY TRAVEL The official website of the French Tourist Board, France Guide (www.franceguide.com), has sections on family travel. Other useful websites include:

- Family Travel (www.familytravel.com)
- www.france4families.com
- www.totstofrance.co.uk

GAY & LESBIAN TRAVELERS Gay Paree is a hospitable city for gay and lesbian travelers. **La Maison des Femmes** (☎ 01-43-43-41-13; http://maisondesfemmes.free.fr) offers information about Paris for lesbians. Paris's largest gay bookstore is **Les Mots à la Bouche,** 6 rue Ste.-Croix-de-la-Bretonnerie, 4th (☎ 01-42-78-88-30; www.motsbouche.com).

HOLIDAYS Public holidays include: New Year's Day (Jan 1), Easter Monday (Mar or Apr), Labor Day (May 1), Victory Day 1945 (May 8), Ascension Day (40 days after Easter), Whit Monday (11 days after Ascension Day), National Day/Bastille Day (July 14), Assumption Day (Aug 15), All Saints' Day (Nov 1), Armistice Day 1918 (Nov 11), and Christmas Day (Dec 25).

INSURANCE North Americans with homeowner's or renter's insurance are probably covered for lost luggage. If not, inquire with **Travel Assistance International** (☎ 800/821-2828; www.travelassistance.com) or **Travelex** (☎ 800/228-9792; www.travelex.com). These insurers can also provide trip-cancellation, medical, and emergency evacuation coverage abroad. The website www.moneysupermarket.com compares prices across a wide range of providers for single- and multitrip policies. **For U.K. citizens,** insurance is always advisable, even if you have an EHIC form. (See "Emergencies," above.)

INTERNET ACCESS Most hotels offer Internet access (usually at a price) and many are equipped with both Wi-Fi and a computer; alternatively, many cafes offer Wi-Fi. There are also over 400 free Wi-Fi spots dotted around the city (check www.paris.fr for details). To surf the Net or check your e-mail, try **Milk;** one of several locations is 31 be de Sébastopol, 1e (☎ 08-20-00-10-00; www.milklub.com).

LIQUOR LAWS Supermarkets, grocery stores, and cafes sell alcoholic beverages. The legal drinking age is 16, but children under that age can be served alcohol in a bar or restaurant if accompanied by a parent or legal guardian. Hours of cafes vary; some even stay open 24 hours. It's illegal to drive while drunk. If convicted, motorists face a stiff fine and a possible prison term.

LOST PROPERTY If your luggage is lost, immediately file a lost-luggage claim at the airport, detailing the luggage contents. For most airlines, you must report delayed, damaged, or lost baggage within 4 hours of arrival. If you loose any belongings in Paris, try the **Service des Objets Trouvés** (Lost-Property Bureau)**,** 36 rue des Morillons, 15th (☎ 08-21-00-25-25), which collects everything that is found in the city. You might be lucky.

MAIL/POST OFFICES Most post offices in Paris are open Monday through Friday from 8am to 7pm and Saturday from 8am to noon. However, the **main post office (PTT),** at 52 rue du Louvre (☎ 08-99-23-24-64), is open 24 hours a day for stamps, phone calls, and sending faxes and telegrams. Stamps can usually be purchased from your hotel reception desk and at cafes with red TABAC signs.

MONEY The currency of France is the euro, which can be used in most other E.U. countries. The exchange rate varies, but at press time, 1 euro was equal to US$1.80. The best way to get cash in Paris is at ATMs or Cashpoints (see above). Credit cards are accepted at almost all shops, restaurants, and hotels, but you should always have some cash on hand for incidentals and sightseeing admissions.

NEWSPAPERS & MAGAZINES English-language newspapers are available from most kiosks, including the *International Herald Tribune* and *USA Today,* and British papers such as the *Times,* the *Guardian* and the *Independent.* The leading French-language domestic papers are *Le Monde, Le Figaro,* and *Libération.*

PASSPORTS If your passport is lost or stolen, contact your country's embassy or consulate immediately. (See "Consulates & Embassies," above.) Before you travel, you should copy the critical pages and keep them in a separate place.

POLICE Call ☎ **17** for emergencies. The principal *Préfecture* (police station) is at 9 bd. du Palais, 4e (☎ 08-91-01-22-22); Métro: Cité.

SAFETY The center of Paris is relatively safe. Look out for pick-pockets—especially child pickpockets. Their method is to get very close to a target, ask for a handout, and deftly help themselves to your money or passport. Robbery at gun or knife point is rare, but not unknown. For more information, consult the U.S. State Department's website at www.travel.state.gov; in the U.K., consult the Foreign Office's website, www.fco.gov.uk; and in Australia, consult the government travel advisory service at www.smartraveller.gov.au.

SENIOR TRAVELERS As in most cities, people over the age of 60 qualify for reduced admission to theaters, museums, and other attractions, as well as discounted fares on public transportation.

SMOKING Smoking is now illegal in public places (including restaurants, bars, theaters, and on public transportation), but is tolerated outside and on cafe terraces. Some hotels still provide smokers bedrooms (so ask when making reservations) otherwise they may fine you for smoking in a nonsmoking room.

TAXES Value Added Tax, or VAT (TVA in French) is 19.6%, but non-E.U. visitors can get a refund if you spend 182€ or more in any store that participates in the VAT refund program. The shops will give you a form, which you must get stamped at Customs. (Allow extra time.) Mark the paperwork to request a credit card refund; otherwise you'll be stuck with a check in euros. An option is to ask for a **Global Refund form** (☎ 800/566-9828; www.globalrefund.com; ☎ 01-41-61-51-51 in France) when you make your purchase, and take it to a Global Refund counter at the airport. Your money is refunded on the spot, minus a commission.

TELEPHONES Public phones are found in cafes, some Métro stations, and post offices, and on the street. Coin-operated telephones are rare. Most phones take ***télécartes,*** prepaid calling cards available at kiosks and post offices. Their cost ranges from about 8€ to 16€ depending on how many units you buy. To make a **direct international call,** first dial 00, then dial the country code, the area code (minus the first zero), and the local number. The country code for the **U.S. and Canada** is 1; **Great Britain,** 44; **Ireland,** 353; **Australia,** 61; and **New Zealand,** 64. You can also call the U.S.,

Canada, the U.K., Ireland, Australia, or New Zealand using **USA Direct/ AT&T World Connect,** which allows you to avoid hotel surcharges. From within France, dial ☎ **0800/99-00-11-10-11,** then follow the prompts.

TICKETS There are many theater ticket agencies in Paris, but buying tickets directly from the box office or at a discount agency can be up to 50% cheaper. Try **Kiosque Théâtre,** 15 place de la Madeleine (no phone). Tickets for many shows, events, and tours can also be purchased in advance in your home country through your travel agent or through **Keith Prowse** (☎ 800/669-8687 from the U.S. or ☎ 0870-848-6666 from the U.K.; www.keithprowse.com).

TIPPING In cafes and restaurants, waiter service is included, though you can round the bill up or leave some small change, if you like. The same goes for taxi drivers. In more expensive hotels a tip of 1€ to 2€ for porters.

TOILETS If you use a toilet at a cafe or brasserie, it's customary to make some small purchase. In the street, the domed self-cleaning lavatories are an option if you have small change. Some Métro stations have public toilets, but the degree of cleanliness varies. Be prepared—in some places, the facilities on offer may be nothing more than a porcelain hole in the floor.

TOURIST OFFICES For tourist information, try **Office du Tourisme,** 25 rue des Pyramides, 1st (www.parisinfo.com.).

TRAVELERS WITH DISABILITIES Nearly all modern hotels in France now have rooms designed for people with disabilities, but many older hotels do not so check when booking. Most high-speed trains within France have wheelchair access, and guide dogs ride free. Paris's Métro and RER system does have some life access, but it is very difficult to use if you're in a wheelchair. **Paris Info** (www.parisinfo.com) has resources for travelers with disabilities, including a list of accessible hotels. The **Association des Paralysés de France** (☎ 01-40-78-69-00; www.apf.asso.fr) provides help for individuals who use wheelchairs. **Access-Able Travel Source** (www.access-able.com) offers a comprehensive database on travel agents from around the world with experience in accessible travel; destination-specific access information; and links to such resources as service animals, equipment rentals, and access guides. British travelers should contact **Holiday Care** (☎ 0845-124-9971 in the U.K. only; www.holidaycare.org.uk) to access a wide range of travel information and resources for elderly people and those with disabilities. **AirAmbulanceCard.com** (☎ 877/424-7633) is now partnered with SATH and allows you to preselect top-notch hospitals in case of an emergency. For more on organizations that offer resources to travelers with disabilities, go to Frommers.com or consult the following organizations:

- **MossRehab** (☎ 800/CALL-MOSS [225-5667]; www.mossresourcenet.org)
- **American Foundation for the Blind** (AFB; ☎ 800/232-5463; www.afb.org)
- **Society for Accessible Travel & Hospitality** (SATH; ☎ 212/447-7284; www.sath.org)
- **Flying with Disability** (www.flying-with-disability.org)
- **Mobility-Advisor.com** (www.mobility-advisor.com)

Paris: **A Brief History**

2000 B.C. The Parisii tribe founded the settlement of Lutétia alongside the Seine.

52 B.C. Julius Caesar conquers Lutétia during the Gallic wars.

300 Lutétia is renamed Paris. Roman power begins to weaken in France.

1422 England invades Paris during the Hundred Years' War.

1429 Joan of Arc tries to regain Paris for the French; she is later burned at the stake by the English in Rouen.

1572 The wars of religion reach their climax with the St. Bartholomew's Day massacre of Protestants.

1598 Henri IV endorses the Edict of Nantes, granting tolerance to Protestants.

1643 Louis XIV moves his court to the newly built Versailles.

1789 The French Revolution begins.

1793 Louis XVI and his queen, Marie Antoinette, are publicly guillotined.

1799 A coup d'état installs Napoleon Bonaparte as head of government.

1804 Napoleon declares France an empire and is crowned emperor at Notre-Dame.

1804–1815 The Napoleonic wars are fought.

1814 Paris is briefly occupied by a coalition, including Britain and Russia. The Bourbon monarchy is restored.

1848 Revolutions occur across Europe. King Louis-Philippe is deposed by the autocratic Napoleon III.

1860S The Impressionist style of painting emerges.

1870–71 The Franco-Prussian War ends in the siege of Paris. The Third Republic is established, while much of the city is controlled by the revolutionary Paris Commune.

1914–18 World War I rips apart Europe. Millions are killed in the trenches of northeast France.

1940 German troops occupy France during World War II. The French Resistance under Gen. Charles de Gaulle maintains symbolic headquarters in London.

1944 U.S. troops liberate Paris; de Gaulle returns in triumph.

1958 France's Fourth Republic collapses. General de Gaulle is called out of retirement to head the Fifth Republic.

1968 Parisian students and factory workers engage in a general revolt; the government is overhauled in the aftermath.

1994 François Mitterrand and Queen Elizabeth II open the Channel Tunnel.

1995 Jacques Chirac is elected president over François Mitterrand. Paris is crippled by a general strike.

2002 The euro replaces the franc as France's national currency.

2003–04 French opposition to the war in Iraq causes the largest diplomatic rift with America in decades.

2007 Nicolas Sarkozy replaces Jacques Chirac as president of France.

2012 General elections.

French **Architecture**

This section serves as a guide to some of the architectural styles you'll see in Paris. However, it's worth pointing out that very few buildings (especially churches) were built in one particular style. These massive, expensive structures often took centuries to complete, during which time tastes changed and plans were altered.

Romanesque (800–1100)

Taking their inspiration from ancient Rome, the Romanesque architects concentrated on building large churches with wide aisles. Few examples of the Romanesque style remain in Paris, but the church of **St-Germain-des-Prés** (oldest part, 6th century A.D.) is a good example. The overall building is Romanesque, but by the time builders got to creating the choir, the early Gothic was on—note the pointy arches.

Gothic (1100–1500)

By the 12th century, engineering developments freed church architecture from the heavy, thick walls of Romanesque structures.

Instead of dark, somber, relatively unadorned Romanesque interiors that forced the eyes of the faithful toward the altar, the Gothic interior enticed the churchgoers' gaze upward to high ceilings filled with light. The squat, brooding Romanesque exteriors were replaced by graceful buttresses and spires. Arguably the finest example of Gothic church architecture anywhere in the world is **Notre-Dame** (1163–1250).

Renaissance (1500–1630)

In architecture, as in painting, the Renaissance came from Italy and took some time to coalesce. And, as in painting, its rules stressed proportion, order, classical inspiration, and precision, resulting in unified, balanced structures. The 1544 **Hôtel Carnavalet** (23 rue de Sévigné), a Renaissance mansion, is the only 16th-century hotel left in Paris. It contains the **Musée Carnavalet** (p 62), a museum devoted to the history of Paris and the French Revolution.

Classicism and Rococo (1630–1800)

From the mid–17th century, France took the fundamentals of Renaissance classicism even further, finding inspiration in the classic era. During the reign of Louis XIV, art and architecture were subservient to political ends. Buildings were grandiose and severely ordered on the Versailles model. Opulence was saved for interior decoration, which increasingly became an excessively detailed and self-indulgent rococo (*rocaille* in French). Rococo tastes didn't last long, though, and soon a neoclassical movement was raising structures such as Paris's **Panthéon** (1758), based even more strictly on ancient models than the earlier classicism was.

The 19th Century

Architectural styles in 19th-century Paris were eclectic, beginning in a severe classical mode and ending with something of an identity crisis—torn between Industrial Age technology and Art Nouveau organic. During the reign of Emperor Napoleon III (1852–1870), classicism was reinterpreted in an ornate, dramatic mode. Urban planning was the architectural rage, and Paris became a city of wide boulevards courtesy of **Baron Georges-Eugène Haussmann** (1809–91), commissioned by Napoleon III in 1852 to redesign the city. Paris owes much of its remarkably unified look to Haussmann.

Expositions in 1878, 1889, and 1900 were the catalysts for constructing huge glass-and-steel structures that showed off modern techniques. This produced such Parisian monuments as the **Tour Eiffel** and **Sacré-Coeur.** However, the subsequent emergence of the Art Nouveau movement was, in many ways, a rebellion against such late-19th-century industrial zeal. Peaking around the turn of the century, it celebrated the unique nature of asymmetrical, curvaceous designs, often based on plants and flowers. It was during this short period that the famous Art Nouveau **Métro station entrances** were designed by **Hector Guimard** (1867–1942). A recently renovated entrance is at the **porte Dauphine** station on the No. 2 line. The best example of Art Nouveau architecture is the fine, intricately decorated apartment block at 29 av. de Rapp in the 7th.

The 20th Century

The ravages of war stalled the progress of French architecture for a number of decades, but the latter half of the 20th century was to see some the most audacious architectural projects in French history—and certainly some of the most controversial. It has taken decades for structures such as the **Centre Pompidou** or the **Louvre**'s glass pyramids to become accepted by most Parisians, but now they are a well-loved part of the skyline.

The 21st Century

The face of Paris is ever changing. The new era has already seen the arrival of the **Musée du Quai Branly** (2006) an impressive, angular struc ture designed by Jean Nouvel, whose bright colors and clever use of vegetation are a flagship for 21st-century architecture within the city center. The sleek **Passerelle Simone de Beauvoir** bridge (2006) is another new addition linking the Bercy district to the François Mitterand library's towers. West of Paris in the **La Defense business district,** the fight is on to build Paris's tallest skyscraper, and back in the center, architect David Mangin's designs for a brand-new **Les Halles** district (including a park and underground shopping mall) should begin in 2008 or 2009.

Useful Phrases & Menu Terms

It's amazing how often a word or two of halting French will change your host's disposition. At the very least, try to learn basic greetings, and—above all—the life-raft phrase, *Parlez-vous anglais?* ("Do you speak English?")

Useful Words and Phrases

English	French	Pronunciation
Yes/No	Oui/Non	wee/noh
Okay	D'accord	dah-core
Please	S'il vous plaît	seel voo play
English	French	Pronunciation
Thank you	Merci	mair-see
You're welcome	De rien	duh ree-ehn
Hello (during daylight)	Bonjour	bohn-jhoor

English	French	Pronunciation
Good evening	Bonsoir	bohn-swahr
Good bye	Au revoir	o ruh-vwahr
What's your name?	Comment vous appellez-vous?	kuh-mahn voo za-pell-ay-voo?
My name is	Je m'appelle	jhuh ma-pell
How are you?	Comment allez-vous?	kuh-mahn tahl-ay-voo?
So-so	Comme ci, comme ça	kum-see, kum-sah
I'm sorry/Excuse me	Pardon	pahr-dohn
Do you speak English?	Parlez-vous anglais?	par-lay-voo zahn-glay?
I don't speak French	Je ne parle pas français	jhuh ne parl pah frahn-say
I don't understand	Je ne comprends pas	jhuh ne kohm-prahn pas
Where is . . . ?	Où est . . . ?	ooh eh . . . ?
Why?	Pourquoi?	poor-kwah?
here/there	ici/là	ee-see/lah
left/right	à gauche/à droite	a goash/a drwaht
straight ahead	tout droit	too drwah

Food, Menu & Cooking Terms

English	French	Pronunciation
I would like	Je voudrais	jhe voo-dray
to eat	manger	mahn-jhay
Please give me	Donnez-moi, s'il vous plaît	doe-nay-mwah, seel voo play
a bottle of	une bouteille de	ewn boo-tay duh
a cup of	une tasse de	ewn tass duh
a glass of	un verre de	uh vair duh
a cocktail	un apéritif	uh ah-pay-ree-teef
the check/bill	l'addition/la note	la-dee-see-ohn/la noat
a knife	un couteau	uh koo-toe
a napkin	une serviette	ewn sair-vee-et
a spoon	une cuillère	ewn kwee-air
a fork	une fourchette	ewn four-shet
fixed-price menu	un menu	uh may-new
Is the tip/service included?	Est-ce que le service est compris?	ess-ke luh ser-vees eh com-pree?
Waiter!/Waitress!	Monsieur!/Mademoiselle!	mun-syuh/mad-mwa-zel
wine list	une carte des vins	ewn cart day van
appetizer	une entrée	ewn en-tray
main course	un plat principal	uh plah pran-see-pahl
tip included	service compris	sehr-vees cohm-pree
tasting/chef's menu	menu dégustation	may-new day-gus-ta-see-on

Index

See also Accommodations and Restaurant indexes, below.

Accommodations

Photo **Credits**

p vii: © Nicholas MacInnes; p 3: © Nicholas MacInnes; p 4: © Markel Redondo; p 5: © Markel Redondo; p 7: © Markel Redondo; p 8, left: © Markel Redondo; p 8, right: © Markel Redondo; p 9: © Markel Redondo; p 10: © Nicholas MacInnes; p 13: © Markel Redondo; p 14: © Markel Redondo; p 15: © Markel Redondo; p 16: © Alden Gewirtz; p 17: © Markel Redondo; p 22: © Markel Redondo; p 23: © Markel Redondo; p 24: © ELISABETH BLANCHET; p 25: © Markel Redondo; p 28, top: © ALDEN GEWIRTZ; p 28, bottom: © Elisabeth Blanchet; p 29: © ALDEN GEWIRTZ; p 32: © Markel Redondo; p 33: © Markel Redondo; p 34: © Markel Redondo; p 35: © Markel Redondo; p 37: © Markel Redondo; p 38: © Markel Redondo; p 39, top:© Markel Redondo; p 39, bottom: © Elisabeth Blanchet; p 42, top: © Markel Redondo; p 42, bottom: © Markel Redondo; p 43, top: © Elisabeth Blanchet; p 43, bottom: © Elisabeth Blanchet; p 45: © Markel Redondo; p 46: © ALDEN GEWIRTZ; p 47: © Markel Redondo; p 49: © Jon Arnold Images Ltd/Alamy; p 50, top: © Markel Redondo; p 50, bottom: © Markel Redondo; p 51: © Markel Redondo; p 53: © Markel Redondo; p 54, top: © ALDEN GEWIRTZ; p 54, bottom: © NICHOLAS MACINNES; p 55: © Markel Redondo; p 57: © Markel Redondo; p 58: © Markel Redondo; p 59: © Paul Maguire/Alamy; p 61, bottom: © Georgios Makkas; p 61, top: © Markel Redondo; p 62: © Elisabeth Blanchet; p 63, top: © Markel Redondo; p 63, bottom: © Nicholas MacInnes; p 65: © Markel Redondo; p 66, top: © Markel Redondo; p 66, bottom: © Markel Redondo; p 67: © Markel Redondo; p 69: © Markel Redondo; p 70: © Georgios Makkas; p 71, top: © Markel Redondo; p 71, bottom: © Markel Redondo; p 73, top: © Axel Drosta/age fotostock; p 73, bottom: © Fritz Langmann/age fotostock; p 74: © Markel Redondo; p 75: © Markel Redondo; p 76: © Markel Redondo; p 82: © Markel Redondo; p 83: © Markel Redondo; p 84, top: © Markel Redondo; p 84, bottom: © Markel Redondo; p 85: © Markel Redondo; p 86: © Markel Redondo; p 87: © Markel Redondo; p 88: © Alden Gewirtz; p 89: © Smitty615 / Frommers.com ; p 91: © Nicholas MacInnes; p 94: © Elisabeth Blanchet; p 95: © Elisabeth Blanchet; p 97: © Markel Redondo; p 99: © Georgios Makkas; p 100: © Markel Redondo; p 106, top: © Markel Redondo; p 106, bottom: © Markel Redondo; p 107, top: © Nicholas MacInnes; p 107, bottom: © Markel Redondo; p 108: © Georgios Makkas; p 109: © Markel Redondo; p 110: © Markel Redondo; p 111: © Georgios Makkas; p 113: © Georgios Makkas; p 114: © Markel Redondo; p 115: © Markel Redondo; p 116: © Markel Redondo; p 117: © Elisabeth Blanchet; p 125: © Markel Redondo; p 127: © IndexStock / SuperStock ; p 132: © Georgios Makkas; p 134: © Markel Redondo; p 136: © Markel Redondo; p 137: © Markel Redondo; p 144: © Courtesy Hotel Aviatic; p 145: © Courtesy Hotel Banke; p 146: © Courtesy Hotel du Louvre; p 147, bottom: © Courtesy Hotel Gabriel; p 147, top: © Courtesy Hotel Langlois; p 148: © Courtesy Hotel Particulier; p 150, top: © Courtesy Le Bristol; p 150, bottom: © Markel Redondo; p 151, top: © Hemis / Alamy; p 151, bottom: © Yacht de Paris; p 152, top: © Courtesy Renaissance Paris Arc de Triomphe; p 152, bottom: © Courtesy St Christopher's Inn; p 153: © Markel Redondo; p 155: © Markel Redondo; p 156: © Markel Redondo; p 160: © Liv Carlé Mortensen/age fotostock; p 161: © Mohammed Ansar/age fotostock; p 163: © Markel Redondo; p 165: © Markel Redondo